Rethinking Social Issues in Education for the 21st Century:

UK Perspectives on International Concerns

Rethinking Social Issues in Education for the 21st Century:

UK Perspectives on International Concerns

Edited by

Wendy Sims-Schouten and Sylvia Horton

Cambridge
Scholars
Publishing

Rethinking Social Issues in Education for the 21st Century:
UK Perspectives on International Concerns

Edited by Wendy Sims-Schouten and Sylvia Horton

This book first published 2016

Cambridge Scholars Publishing

Lady Stephenson Library, Newcastle upon Tyne, NE6 2PA, UK

British Library Cataloguing in Publication Data
A catalogue record for this book is available from the British Library

ISBN (10): 1-4438-9942-9
ISBN (13): 978-1-4438-9942-0

Contents

LIST OF TABLES AND FIGURES

Tables

Figures

Acknowledgements

We would like to express our thanks to the contributors to this book for their support throughout the time it has taken to make it happen.

Our thanks are also due to Cambridge Scholars Publishing for agreeing to publish the book and particularly to Victoria Carruthers who assisted us in the final stages with advice on the preparation and submission of the manuscript.

Finally, a big thankyou to Amanda Jones and Hannah Squire for their assistance with the production of this manuscript. Without their help we would not have met our submission deadline.

Wendy Sims-Schouten and Sylvia Horton
Portsmouth 2016

PREFACE

This book is based on papers presented at annual symposia organised by the School of Education and Childhood Studies of the University of Portsmouth. The content relates to the programmes taught in the School which range from full time undergraduate degrees in Early Childhood Studies, Childhood and Youth Studies and combined degrees in Childhood and Youth Studies and Early Years Childhood Studies with Psychology; Master's Degrees in Education Leadership and Management, Teaching and Learning and Education Studies; and PGCE courses in Secondary Education. Staffs within the School are research active and these papers reflect some of their work and that of research collaborators.

There are many social issues currently on the political and governmental agendas in the UK and other countries. Some of those issues relate to children and young people and are of concern to those working and researching in education. The boundaries between the academic disciplines of politics, sociology, economics, psychology and education are porous. Multi-disciplinary approaches to social issues reflect that fact. This collection of chapters illustrates how common interests and collaboration can assist in our understanding of complex social issues; the evaluation of current governmental responses; and the promotion of ideas about the way forward into the 21st century.

The book is divided into three parts corresponding to different levels within the education system: PART ONE consists of chapters on Early Years and Primary Schooling; PART TWO relates generally to Secondary Education and youth while PART THREE combines chapters on Tertiary Education.

Chapter 1 addresses issues to do with safeguarding children. The Laming Report of 2003 responded to the circumstances surrounding the death of nine year old Victoria Climbié. It was highly critical of the Child Protection System, pinpointing a dearth of communication between professionals and a lack of commonality across agencies in their approach to child protection. As a result, protecting children in the UK took on a new identity of "Safeguarding", with the concept of integrated practice running through its core. The workforce was tasked with ensuring effective intervention at the earliest possible stage involving all the relevant professions such as early years professionals, health visitors and teachers. Collaboration amongst the professions of health, social work and police was not a new concept at the time, but there was a lack of consensus as to what collaboration actually means.

The chapter focuses on the practice experience of early intervention in safeguarding. It considers the scope of the intended change within the sector and questions the extent to which the practice reflects the policy intentions of the government. Establishing "universal" practitioners as professionals with the skill set to safeguard children, and a common understanding of levels of need, underpins the ability and willingness of the sector to respond to the call for early intervention. The key roles of health visitors, early years practitioners and school teachers are explored via a case study and barriers to communication, including bureaucracies and organisational cultures, are identified .The chapter concludes on a positive note with the development of Multi Agency Strategic Hubs (MASH) pointing the way.

Chapter 2 examines issues to do with childhood obesity and healthy eating. Childhood obesity has reached epidemic proportions in the UK according to both the government and the media, and calls have been made for strategies to reverse this "unhealthy" trend. Research suggests that this is due to a complex interplay of demographic, social and family variables and to deal with the "obesity crisis" early intervention is necessary. Government "health" policies and practices are becoming radically interventionist, ranging from adaptations to school health and physical education, to the threat of "obese children" being removed from their families and placed into social care.

The chapter explores how talk and discourses around health circulate both relationally and affectively within school contexts. Schools and pre-school settings subject children to an increasing range of surveillance techniques, in an attempt to monitor and regulate diets, healthy eating and children's' weight. This involves controlling children's lifestyles, inside and outside of school, by influencing their food choices and more directly by collecting information on their bodies with a view to monitoring and addressing the issue of weight. This is fuelled by the construction of obesity as a "moral" crisis. Here, however, mixed messages are sent out, suggesting that "fat" is "bad" while encouraging children to "eat well", and have a "good appetite" to be healthy.

The chapter shows that the discourses of health, which circulate in schools and pre-school settings, impact significantly on children's embodied consciousness. The authors highlight the relationship between obesity, the media and other eating disorders and the links between unhealthy eating behaviours and bullying, particularly "body-bullying", as weight-related criticism is associated with pre-adolescent children's body self-perceptions and associated conditions such as bulimia and anorexia.

The literature on health education and prevention programmes, demonstrates that dominant approaches and discourses are currently following neo-liberal principles in placing responsibility and accountability for health with the individual and the family. The "blame" for childhood obesity is located within the family. An association is also made between weight and socio-economic status. The chapter traces the development of government policies and practices in the UK with their focus on controlling and regulating children's bodies because they are the most amenable to change. It concludes that government intervention is a blunt instrument but may lead the way to changing people's eating habits as well as reducing the costs on the NHS.

Chapter 3 examines children's underachievement in reading at school with special reference to race and ethnicity. Reading is a foundation skill and remains central to success both in school and the labour market. Literacy also has the potential for empowerment and can open doors to social mobility and success in life. It facilitates learning, the acquisition of knowledge and the ability to influence decisions. There are many children who struggle with reading and as a consequence underachieve in the school curriculum. This has consequences for the schools that have targets to reach, for the children who lose out on learning opportunities, and for society as these children often drop out of school, become unemployed or involved in crime. It is therefore a social issue.

The author examines a brief history of reading policy and the origins of the "poor reader". Before mapping out the debates around race, reading and attainment at school, she exposes the ways in which this is part of wider debates within left wing and neo-liberal discourses and demolishes the claim that race is no longer an issue in education, even though the evidence is that "black boys" and other ethnic minorities feature significantly in under-achievement in reading. A backwards glance at education policy on reading reveals traditional differences between Conservative and Labour governments although a convergence to neo-liberal discourses occurred in the 1990s.

Race did not appear as a feature of "poor readers" until the immigration of large numbers of people from the commonwealth countries of India, Africa and the Caribbean in the 1960s. These immigrants were referred to as "black" and so race became identified with "Blackness". "Poor readers" now appeared to be rooted in race rather than class. Immigrant communities tended to be concentrated in London and other metropolitan areas and Local Education Authorities such as the Inner

London Education Authority (ILEA) produced books and materials reflecting the racial compositions of their communities, and pursued integration policies. The radical education reforms of the 1980s however transformed the system of decentralised administration and teacher control of the curriculum. The introduction of a national curriculum; the creation of local management of schools; and increased centralisation, monitoring and regulation of schools through inspection by OFSTED took their place. Governments set down reading programmes and teaching methods to be used.

Racial discrimination has been dealt with by law since the 1966 Race Relations Act which established the right not to be discriminated against on the grounds of race. Further legislation has extended that right to gender, ethnicity, religion, disability, age and sexual orientation. However, institutional racism is still endemic in schools and other major institutions. Research studies highlight a combination of factors which support racism. These include the low expectations of "black" children, especially "black boys"; the"white" based cultures of schools and the inappropriateness of the metrics which govern testing of reading for "black" and ethnic minority children. This is compounded by the dominance of a neo-liberal ideology which lays responsibility for poor reading on the individual and the family and not the school system.

The chapter ends with a discussion of data collected by the author when researching "pupil" and "teacher" voices. The narratives provide a different lens through which to view the issues of race, reading and achievement pointing the way to revisiting the social issue of "race" in schools.

Chapter 4 addresses the issue of cyberbullying which is a matter of concern to both the public and governments. Over the last 25 years a growing body of research has investigated both bullying and cyberbullying in schools. Much of this research has interpreted bullying based on a definition rooted in a power imbalance behaviour framework and conceptual understanding of language. The author reflects on that research and associated policy interventions placing them alongside his own research findings, which illuminate the socialising practices and language codes of young people in both physical and digital networking sites. The chapter theorises that the students' language codes used on digital networks and other working sites are not in flux and self-referential as others suggest but rather located in a reality constructed outside the digital sites. The language codes and behaviours of young people identified in physical sites are being re-presented and re-constructed on digital sites. These behaviours support the building and maintaining of young people's narratives but are identified as in juxtaposition to "legitimised" interpretations of behaviour and may result in perceived bullying within schools and on digital social networks.

At a practical level, the chapter discusses the implications of current education policy which favours academic (particularly cognitive) skills development over social and emotional aspects of learning and restricts the students' socialising practices in physical school sites and the classroom. This policy, alongside restrictions on students' opportunities to gather in public spaces, requires them to manage the self-project substantially through digital networking sites. The discussion identifies the recent trend towards networking using media, which have a limited range of characters available to convey language codes and behaviours used in physical socialising sites. This raises concerns that communication between students will become increasingly problematic and will lead to further difficulties in interpreting students' behaviours. The chapter challenges educators to re-think cyber-bullying and digital social-networking issues and urges the need for further research into how social relationships are managed on digital networking sites.

Chapter 5 examines absence from school. With the introduction of compulsory schooling, the concept of absence from school, or "non-attendance" arose. The extent to which the state intervenes in family life through the provision of a service that must be used, with legal sanctions for not using it, provides the backdrop to the chapter. Compulsory schooling raises broader issues about the role of schools, social control and the resistance of children, young people and some parents to the attempt by the state to exercise control over where children spend their time and who should be held accountable. The chapter draws on comparative research on persistent and serious absence from school in England and the Netherlands.

These two countries illustrate different perspectives on the application of legal sanctions. In England the focus of sanctions is on the parents, but in the Netherlands, it is on the young person. Sanctions include fines and imprisonment (in both countries) and community service in the Netherlands. These contrasting responses to the issue are located within a review of the wider research. Absence from school is a complex phenomenon that takes a number of forms and is referred to by several different terms, which relate both to the degree of control or choice exercised by the child/young person/parent(s)/carer(s), as well as the extent to which absence from school relates to problems at home or in school, and finally to the severity of these problems.

The term 'truancy' is generally used to refer to the decision not to attend school being in the control of the child/young person. Children who do not attend school for whole days are called "blanket truants". "Post-registration truancy" refers to children who do attend school but miss particular lessons. The latter form of truancy is harder to register and monitor and is likely to be under-reported in attendance data. Other concepts including, "school phobia", "separation anxiety" and "school refusal" are also discussed. "Persistent absence" from school is a more serious problem, because this is likely to be connected to a range of vulnerabilities, and sometimes offending and anti-social behaviour. It also has consequences for the future employment, life style and integration of young people into society and is thus a social issue.

The chapter offers a critical review of the role of the state in relation to enforcing school attendance in the context of the often contradictory responses to home education and exclusion from school. It also provides some wider international data confirming this issue is not confined to the case study countries.

Chapter 6 addresses issues to do with educational standards, teaching methods and the UK's relatively low position in the world of comparative education. In the 2015 Programme for International Student Assessment (PISA) tests, carried out by the Organisation for Economic Co-operation and Development (OECD) and involving students from all 34 OECD member countries and 31 partner countries, the UK came 23rd in Reading and 26th in Maths. This was well below countries in the Far East including Korea, China and Singapore. The PISA testing cycle covers Science, Reading and a particular focus on Mathematics. The results provoked concern in the UK from academics, teachers, their professional associations, the national media and politicians who perceived this as a threat to the nation's economic future.

This chapter explores ideas about education, teaching, learning and assessment that are currently endorsed by English government ministers responsible for education and their policy advisers. In the PISA test countries the high scores are often attributed to intensive and excessive student workloads, a focus on testing and rote learning. The Chinese education system is acknowledged as "excellent" in preparing outstanding test takers, like other education systems within the Confucian cultural circle: including Singapore, Korea, Japan and Hong Kong. Vietnam, an OECD partner country, also out-performs the UK in Science, Mathematics and Reading. The Vietnamese secondary education system has been influenced by the education models of the former Soviet Union, the French elitist system, as well as Confucian traditions from the Chinese.

But there is now a growing recognition of the need to renovate the existing curriculum and explore new teaching methods to move away from rote learning.

The authors report on a small scale action-orientated study carried out in a selective high school in Vietnam that educates "gifted and talented" young people aged from 16 to18 years. Although it is a requirement of the Vietnamese national curriculum, the study of literature is not popular amongst gifted and talented science and mathematics students who prefer to study the subjects they specialise and excel in. Parents often share this view. This led to posing the research question: 'How can we improve the teaching and learning for students who are gifted in the natural sciences and mathematics in the study of literature to develop alternative skills?

The research project is contextualised, identifying the key characteristics of Vietnamese education, teaching, learning and assessment, explaining the continuing influence of Confucian philosophy. Details of the research site, the sample of students, who are gifted in mathematics, physics and informatics, and a full account of the two stage research process, are provided. Findings are presented with data based on student and staff responses. Tentative conclusions are drawn from the research and issues are identified which may be of interest to teachers and other educational professionals in the UK, given current concerns arising from the PISA outcomes and the most recent government policies.

Chapter 7 explores the subject of dyslexia. Despite the raft of approaches to supporting learning needs, and policies of inclusion, which have proliferated since the Warnock Report in 1978, the identification and effective support of those with dyslexia remains a problem. There is evidence that failing to adopt a systematic approach to identifying and remediating the learning challenges experienced by children with dyslexia and other literacy difficulties, has long term social and economic implications. The social impact of dyslexia includes low self-esteem, a sense of failure and frustration, leading to behaviour problems, school exclusion, inability to find jobs, apply for benefits or pass theory driving tests, spiralling sometimes into petty offences, a life of crime, prison and serial re-offending.

The author demonstrates that while dyslexia is a complex and confounding learning difference, more is now known about how it impacts on learning and the role that neurological differences have to play. However, no single cognitive or neurological model seems to fit all of the data and this opens the way for "sitting on the fence", not identifying dyslexia, and consequently not addressing the learning needs of one in 10 of the population whilst they are in school and when intervention is easier and most appropriate. Whilst highlighting the many difficulties faced in diagnosing and responding to the needs of children with dyslexia the author highlights that when mixed with the Government's agenda on raising standards in schools, it is clear why addressing the needs of such learners remains so challenging.

The chapter draws on neurological research and the nature of literacy development. Contrary to the belief that the aetiology of dyslexia stems from brain differences, which exist at birth, the author conjectures that these brain differences are created by a "disordered reading experience". Understanding dyslexia is just the first step in appropriate intervention and support but it remains a key piece of the jigsaw. Following an overview of the social and emotional costs of dyslexia and the effect of limited literacy skills in the personal and societal contexts the author cites the disproportionate number of prisoners in the UK who are dyslexic. Research has shown that giving prisoners literacy support can have a significant social impact in reducing recidivism.

The chapter concludes by discussing the findings of the Rose Review on the teaching of children with dyslexia. Its far-reaching recommendations, including the training of 4000 specialist dyslexia teachers, demonstrated a will to recognise and address the waste of human resources created by failing to address the issue but there is still scant evidence that this has made a real difference so far!

Chapter 8 is written by a sports scientist with an interest in mental health. Childhood is a critical time in which physical, social, emotional and cognitive development takes place. A mental health problem that emerges in childhood can be profoundly disruptive and may affect the way that individuals think, feel, be productive, relate to others and function socially. It is perceived that mental health problems amongst children in developed economies are rising and are estimated to affect as many as 20 per cent of the population in some areas. Identifying and treating mental health problems early is therefore essential to avoid impairment of children's cognitive, social and emotional development. This chapter examines a wide range of international research into the effects of mental health interventions in schools to promote mental health literacy, detect mental health problems and address stigmatization.

The author reviews 47 studies selected on the basis of clear criteria. The majority of studies took place in the United States, Canada, Australia and the UK but eight other countries were involved. Most investigations were based in secondary schools and consisted of mainly female participants between the ages of 8 and 18 years old. Many different research methods were used and the interventions were delivered by teachers, health care professionals and individuals living with mental health problems themselves.

The findings are discussed in three sections. The first relates to mental health knowledge where it is evident that the knowledge of the children was significantly improved about a wide range of mental illnesses including depression, anxiety and bi-polar disorder amongst others. They were able to show awareness of symptoms of different conditions. However, some research revealed that mental health knowledge decreased over time. The second section reports on the attempts to change attitudes towards mental health and stereotyping. Again, the results were positive with improvement in attitudes, understanding and compassion and a willingness to interact with individuals living with mental illness.

The third section of the chapter is focused on health seeking behaviour. Here, the results are more mixed, with some evidence that post intervention individuals were more willing to seek help, but not all research projects found such positive results in spite of improvement in attitudes towards mental illness. These general findings are examined more closely in the seven studies based in the UK where the author examines in detail the research methods used, the numbers of respondents involved and the specific findings

A discussion follows on the value of the heterogeneous interventions identified and what research is currently underway. The latest research is helping to provide evidence to support new curricula, resourcing requirements and delivery of programmes. The author recommends the use of the Medical Health Council (MRC) Framework to conduct a wide scale project in the UK on mental health literacy programmes for children in schools. The chapter concludes with a thought provoking list of what we do know and what we need to know about mental health education in schools.

Part 3 of the book consists of four chapters about issues in higher education. Chapter 9 explores bullying and discrimination in universities. Over the past 25 years, a substantial body of research has investigated bullying (and more recently cyberbullying) among school children on the one hand and among adults in the workplace on the other. However, only a very small number of studies address aspects of bullying in higher education, despite the fact that the National Union of Students (NUS) annual Student Experience Report highlights the problem, with disturbing case study accounts of long-term damage to self-esteem, academic achievement and emotional well-being experienced by some students.

The author describes the literature on bullying/cyberbullying amongst university students, with particular emphasis on gender issues and on discrimination on the grounds of ethnicity and sexual orientation. She then explores some of the reasons why bullying amongst young people in this age-group (18-30) may have been overlooked by educators and researchers. At a practical level, the chapter discusses implications, which include the role of student unions, the role of the university health and counselling services, and the need for stronger anti-bullying and anti-harassment policies. At a more theoretical level, the chapter explores two explanatory models including the Social Identity model of De-individuation Effects (SIDE) and Participant Role Theory. A discussion follows of social aspects to the under-researching of cyberbullying amongst university students, for example, the extent to which students are considered by the authorities and by themselves as independent adults rather than young people in need of support. The study of cyberbullying amongst university students has the potential to illuminate our understanding of social relationships during the transition from adolescence to adulthood and from higher education to the workplace. Finally, in harmony with the aim of the book to explore current social issues, there is a discussion of equality and inclusion in the context of higher education.

Chapter 10 also addresses the issue of diversity within a higher education context with specific reference to black and minority ethnic students. Using the acronyms BME (Black and Minority Ethnic) and BAME (Black, Asian and Minority Ethnic) the authors differentiate those people who are of non-white descent but permanently resident in the UK from international students who have come to the UK to study but will return to their own country when their studies are completed.

The chapter explores the respective needs of these two groups and the extent to which higher education institutions acknowledge and accommodate these needs.

Governments have been committed to increasing participation of BME students in higher education and to ensuring that the educational profession itself reflects the wider society. These objectives have been challenging and the record of recruitment, retention and achievement of BME students in higher education and in teacher recruitment falls far short of the government's stated aims. This chapter investigates the reasons for this and provides a case study of how one university sought to increase recruitment, retention and achievement of BME trainee teachers on a PGCE (Post graduate Certificate in Education) programme.

The authors first explore "race" as an ideology and whether that ideology plays any part in outcomes for BEM students. They see race as multi-layered and argue it has evolved into a more subtle form of prejudice based on ethnicity and the distinction of "insiders" and "outsiders" and "otherness". The literature review provides evidence of assumptions made about particular ethnic groups and particularly teachers' prejudgements and lower expectations of such groups. They refer to this as a hidden form of racism along with the statement that people are "colour blind" as this is a denial of their different cultural backgrounds. The same issue arises if domestic and international BME are grouped together ignoring their different backgrounds and identities.

The case study describes how one institution sought to increase recruitment of BME students to a post graduate teacher training programme and developed strategies to meet their needs and overcome the problems they faced. The study involved the use of surveys and interviews over a period of time and included evaluations by OFSTED of the course's success in promoting equality and diversity. The findings demonstrate that increased recruitment was achieved due to reframing the content of the programme, highlighting cultural diversity and the inclusivity of the institutional setting itself. Advertisements were placed in specialist journals which targeted BME. The course was also promoted in a number of community settings and help was given to potential applicants in preparing application forms and advice on interviewing.

Retention was also a major focus as there is evidence that the placement periods in schools are often bad experiences for BME trainee teachers. A series of interventions including additional English language classes, the training of school mentors in sensitivity to BME students' needs; the appointment of a BME support tutor, herself with an ethnic minority heritage and English as her second language. The role of this tutor is multifaceted and key to many of the developments which have resulted in the course being found "outstanding" in the last two OFSTED ratings.

The authors conclude that although the UK has moved forward in integrating BME students and increasing diversity there is much still to be done. Prejudice, covert forms of racism, and ignorance of diverse cultural heritages need to be removed as we move forward into the 21st century.

Chapter 11 fits nicely with the previous chapters in PART 3 as it focuses on higher education and issues of inclusion, gender and equality using the work of the social theorist Pierre Bourdieu. Under-representation of students from less privileged social backgrounds in UK higher education institutions is an enduring problem. While there are examples of productive participation, the pattern of collective trajectories of this group differs sharply from that of traditional entrants. The onus falls largely on individual students to adapt to established practices, which remain strongly oriented towards traditional white middle-class populations. The chapter draws on research exploring the educational experiences of students from non-traditional academic backgrounds and illustrates the ways in which social provenance influences students' transitions into university; their experiences within it; the successes they achieve; and the resources they accrue as a result.

Following a review of changes in the higher education landscape, especially those associated with the widening participation agenda, readers are introduced to a case study of a university programme related to occupational therapy (OT). The national intake consists of mainly mature women students and both ethnic minorities and men are under-represented. A substantial number of students have prior experience of working in the health and social care sectors but many enter with 'non-traditional' academic backgrounds. Using regression analysis the progression routes of 239 OT students are examined, highlighting that less privileged socio-economic backgrounds were a significant predictor of poorer outcomes. To establish a deeper understanding of some of the challenges underpinning these quantitative findings, the author considers in more detail the findings of the qualitative arm of the research. Bourdieu's work provides the theoretical framework within which the research findings are further examined. Key forms of capital, including academic, linguistic, social and professional, were found to be central to students' development and successful engagement with the logic of practice in the higher education field. The influence of these capitals on the experiences and trajectories of participants are highlighted and their relevance to other disciplines and implications for academic practice and social inclusion in higher education are discussed.

Chapter 12 explores reflective practice in teacher training and education. Firstly, the author introduces Finlay's reflective practice continuum of reflection, critical reflection and reflexivity, and Schon's and Ghaye's types of technical reflection, before examining their role in the training of student teachers. A literature review confirms that reflective practice is a well-established feature of the teaching profession in developing professionalism among graduate teachers and that it is a "process of learning through and from experience towards greater insights of self or practice" (Finlay, 2008, p.1). This 'process of learning' is the basis for all interpretations of the term, but contention amongst researchers and educators occurs when discussing what it is that student should be learning when engaging in that reflective practice.

Based on a case study of six trainee teachers on a university PGCE programme, the author provides further evidence of the practice of each form of reflection but challenges the view that they are experienced sequentially as Finlay's continuum implies. Using the data and narratives collected from semi-structured interviews and a study of the students' reflective practice sheets, the author demonstrates that critical refection and reflexivity are often fused and experienced simultaneously by student teachers, and again may be found while students are involved in the more technical forms of reflection. She explains why this is the case and what triggers each form of reflection, while making the point that the student teachers are not just gaining 'greater insights of "self"', they are redeveloping and questioning their identity and their social environment. The students are recreating their own practice almost daily by changing and improving that practice, and their teaching identity is also constantly changing. From her study a more accurate definition of reflective practice in ITE, is posited, as "the questioning of practice, purpose, identity and the social context due to an increase in knowledge and experience".

Finally, the chapter traces the changes currently taking place in teacher education in England with the move towards locating it entirely in schools rather than in universities. This raises concerns about the effects this could have in limiting teacher student's exposure to different school or college environments, their institutional identities, and internal power structures. The conclusion reached is that all forms of reflective practice are important in the development of professionalism amongst teachers .They are also important in empowering teachers to be continually learning and developing but with an awareness of the power structures and ideology within which they function.

We recommend these chapters to you with the hope that they will stir your interest and participation in finding solutions to these and other issues in the field of education in the 21st century.

Sylvia Horton and Wendy Sims-Schouten, August 2016.

CONTRIBUTORS

Professor Helen Cowie, Emeritus Professor in the Health and Social Care Division, Faculty of Health and Social Sciences, University of Surrey

Dr Simon Edwards, Senior Lecturer, School of Education and Childhood Studies, University of Portsmouth

Dr Caroline Emery, Health Visitor Practitioner, Lecturer, School of Education and Childhood Studies, University of Portsmouth

Dr Paul Gorczynski, Lecturer, Department of Sports and Exercise Sciences, University of Portsmouth

Sukhbinder Hamilton, Senior Lecturer, School of Education and Childhood Studies, University of Portsmouth

Dr David Holloway, Principal Lecturer, School of Education and Childhood Studies, University of Portsmouth

Dr Sylvia Horton, Honorary Principal Lecturer, School of Education and Childhood Studies, University of Portsmouth

Professor Carol Hayden, Professor in Applied Social Research, Institute of Criminal Justice Studies, University of Portsmouth

Emma Maynard, Senior Lecturer, School of Education and Childhood Studies, University of Portsmouth

Charlotte Meierdirk, Senior lecturer, PGCE Initial Teacher Training Business Studies, School of Education and Childhood Studies, University of Portsmouth

Chris Neanon, Principal Lecturer, School of Education and Childhood Studies, University of Portsmouth

Cung Mi Thi Ngyen, Teacher , Le Quy Don High School for Gifted Students, Da Nang City, Vietnam

Tanya Riordan, Senior Lecturer, PGCE Initial Teacher Training, Modern Foreign Languages, School of Education and Childhood Studies, University of Portsmouth

Dr Alexandra Scherer, Senior Lecturer, School of Education and Childhood Studies, University of Portsmouth

Dr Wendy Sims-Schouten, Senior Lecturer, School of Education and Childhood Studies, University of Portsmouth

Helga Stittrich-Lyons, Early Years Practitioner, Senior Lecturer, School of Education and Childhood Studies, University of Portsmouth

Myrte Van Veldhuizen, PhD candidate, Institute of Criminal Justice Studies, University of Portsmouth

Dr Jo Watson, Associate Head of Department of Professional Practice and Health Studies, University of Southampton

PART 1

CHAPTER ONE

"YOU SHARE COFFEE, YOU SHARE CASES": THE PROFESSIONAL EXPERIENCE OF SAFEGUARDING IN UNIVERSAL PRAXIS

EMMA MAYNARD, HELGA STITTRICH-LYONS AND CAROLINE EMERY

Introduction to the Issue

Public policy in the UK and Channel Islands has established Safeguarding as a matter for professionals, supported by the Children Act 2004 and the Local Safeguarding Children Boards (Webber, McCree and Angeli, 2013). *Every Child Matters* (DfES, 2004) sets out a classification of Universal, Targeted and Specialist Support services for children. Of these, Universal Services included those professionals with whom all children are in contact on a regular basis. These are practitioners within schools, nurseries, and primary care, from whom the majority of the 11 million children in the UK will have professional input (Parton, 2011). Sharing information is part and parcel of the work of Universal Services professionals, acting as the primary assessors and, to some extent, gatekeepers to more targeted and specialist services. Given the mandate for safeguarding children across the whole children's workforce (DfE, 2011; DfE, 2014; Siraj-Blatchford, Clarke and Needham, 2007), it is important to consider the experiences of professionals working at the Universal stage in the Safeguarding agenda. This is especially significant at the early help stage, which is about:

> "providing support as soon as a problem emerges, at any point in a child's life, from the foundation years through to the teenage years. [...] it [is also] provided as part of a support plan where a child has returned home to their family from care" (DfE, 2015, p.12)

Prior to 2014, statutory authorities had a legal position within a family, but the DfE (2014) signposted that the "Early Help" assessment should be undertaken by a "lead professional" (p. 5), which could be anyone from a Teacher, Special Education Needs Coordinator (SENCO), General Practitioner (GP), Family Worker or a Health Visitor. At this problem point assessment and intervention rest at an informal level dependent on the willingness of both the agencies and families to engage in the consent-based, voluntary nature of the assessment process. It also represents an assumption and expectation that all such professionals will accept responsibility for intervention, rather than referring on to social services at times of apparent risk (DfE, 2011; Ofsted, 2015). The significance of raising the profile of multi-agency responsibility gives rise to questions of status, power, scarcity of resources, values, language and entrenched ways of working, as traditional groups of professionals are challenged to work differently and be accountable to one another in a new way (Powell and Uppal, 2012). Though highlighted more than 10 years ago, in the green paper *Every Child Matters* (DfES, 2003), this remains a challenging area of practice. Agreement as to what is considered suitable for a Common Assessment Framework (CAF) remains hotly contested (Ofsted, 2015). Furthermore, the onus on Universal Service practitioners to "hold the baton" (McCulloch, 2007, p. 37), rather than leave child protection to social workers, is central to the discourse of safeguarding. Mukherji and Albon (2010) talk about the fact that "truth varies according to perspectives" (p. 10) and with professionals holding the baton in Safeguarding it is important, to find out what they really experience. For teachers, early years professionals and health visitors, amongst others, the shift to safeguarding and the onus on early intervention has represented a significant shift in their role and, as stated above, given rise to issues of status, power, values, language and entrenched ways of working (Powell and Uppal, 2012). Despite some progress, these issues remain difficult to negotiate (Ofsted, 2015).

Our considerations, in this chapter, are informed by our own professional involvement as Health visitor, Early Years Practitioner and an Assessment and Intervention Team Manager (Early Intervention). Using a semi-structured interview approach, we conducted interviews with five practitioners, which focused on:

i) their understanding of and responsibility in safeguarding;
ii) the ethical standards they took into consideration;
iii) the range of their professional experiences, and the adopted praxis in working within the safeguarding agenda;
iv) their perceived successes and the shortcomings of the system.

This chapter sets out to investigate the complexities, successes and pitfalls of effective integrated working of those professionals involved in safeguarding children.

Literature Review and Context to Safeguarding

In order to give context to our discussion we draw on two models which explain the structures of the Children's Workforce (Figure 1.1), and indicate levels of intervention (Figure 1.2). These models have permeated the sector and have remained central concepts for the system throughout policy changes of the intervening years.

Establishing ownership of safeguarding amongst the Children's Workforce is viewed as critical to the effective availability of early help to families (DfE, 2011). High profile "Serious Case Reviews", such as that of Victoria Climbié and Baby Peter Conelly (Akister, 2011), have given rise to widespread criticism of practice in the UK, questioning what makes multi-agency collaboration effective. Horwarth (2009) identifies a lack of consensus amongst the children's workforce as to what safeguarding actually means, pinpointing the variability in activity and outcome. The shared vision and purpose of a true team approach is something quite different to a linear sharing of information that is complicated by different employers and priorities. This is debated by Stafford, Smith and Vincent (2011) who consider the child protection system at different levels (macro, meso and micro). Figures 1.1 and 1.2 illustrate the children's workforce and are a means of identifying levels of intervention (Figure 1.1), and positioning children on a spectrum of need (Figure 1.2).

Figure 1.1 The Categorisation of the Children's Workforce.

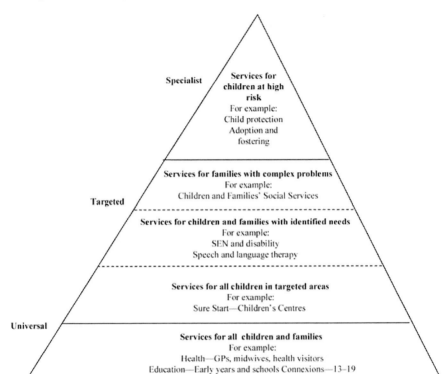

Source: *Every Child Matters,* DfES, 2003, p. 21.

Figure 1.2 CAF (Common Assessment Framework) Continuum of Need

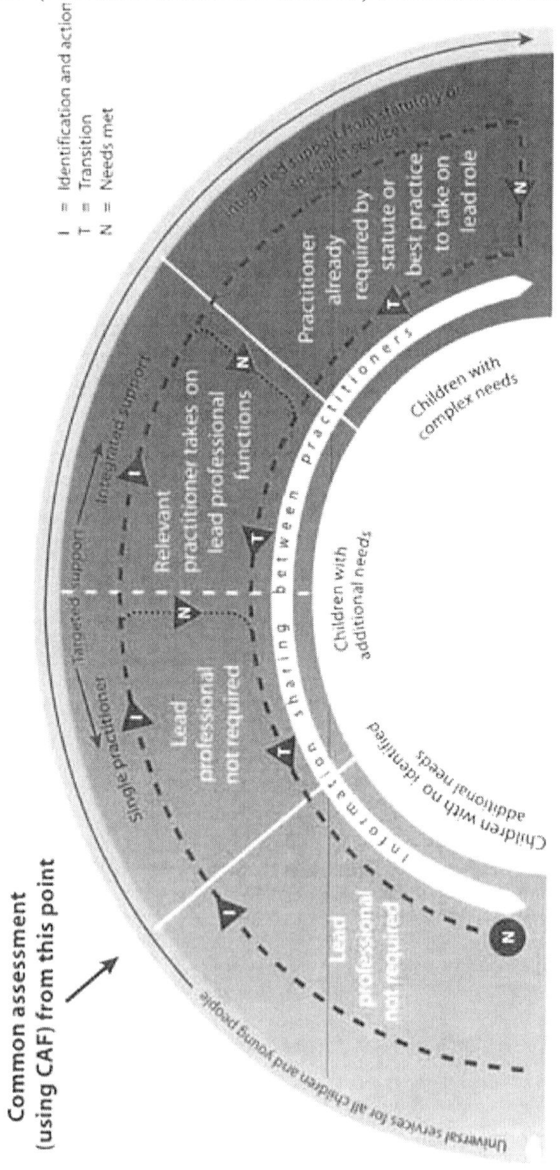

Source: CWDC, 2009, p. 31.

See centrefold for this image in colour

Early warning Signs of Childhood Need or Neglect

Everyone has a responsibility for Safeguarding children (DfE, 2014), but recognising signs and symptoms of childhood need and neglect can be challenging. All early years professionals need to understand what these terms mean, in order to effectively identify concerns and then offer support and help. Reports published by the Royal College of Paediatrics and Child Health (2014), and the Care Quality Commission (2014), detail extensive requirements of GPs and other health care providers in regard to multi-agency safeguarding practice including early intervention, thus placing them at the heart of recognising child neglect and physical, emotional and sexual abuse. *Keeping Children Safe in Education* (DfE, 2014) is the latest statutory guidance, for professionals working with young children to ensure education settings safeguard and promote children's welfare. This replaces the previous policy; *Safeguarding Children and Safer Recruitment in Education* (DfES, 2003). The new guidance sets out that those working with children in educational settings need to know that safeguarding children and promoting welfare means:

> "protecting children from maltreatment; preventing impairment of children's health or development; ensuring that children grow up in circumstances consistent with the provision of safe and effective care; and taking action to enable all children to have the best outcomes" (DfE, 2014, p. 3).

Parton (2011) also sets this in a political context, arguing that New Labour sought to work with the direction of social change towards increased individualisation. Strengthening stability and secure attachments for children have become the focus of policy and practice, rather than attempting to reinforce family values, once seen as the bedrock of continuity of care (Laming, 2003). This is reflected in safeguarding policy such as *Every Child Matters* (DfES, 2003), *The Assessment Framework* (Department of Health, 2000) and the *Common Assessment Framework*, (CWDC, 2009) and the shift in language from "child protection" to "safeguarding". Parton (2011) identifies this as representing a shift "from dangerousness to risk" (p. 860); from an acute focus on a risk of immediate danger to a child, to a broader concept of risk and vulnerability. The move enabled assessment and intervention at an earlier stage through understanding family and community influences.

Richardson and Asthana (2006) also raise the political backdrop of this agenda, given the apparent fixation of social welfare policy on collaborative practices, which are constantly thrown into the public spotlight by high profile tragedies. Identifying the legal position of appropriate information sharing and collaboration under the *Children Act* (2004), the authors highlight the intention to provide a seamless service for families via professionals working for different agencies but within the same legal framework. The bundle of legislative obligations placed willing collaboration into a complex arena. The compulsion to share information beyond issues of consent as per the Children Act (1989) raised critical questions for practitioners regarding roles, responsibilities, and shared concepts of risk, resilience and intervention.

Within this discourse, perspectives on what constitutes "early intervention", and understanding levels of need, have become hotly contested (Powell and Uppal, 2012). Amidst the increase in referrals in the wake of the Baby P (Peter Conelly) case and the repositioning of social work to high end child protection (Baginsky, 2008; Parton, 2011), has come the realisation that responsibility for "early help" has landed on the shoulders of a range of Universal Services professionals (DfE, 2015). However, at the heart of this lies a lack of consensus (Baginsky, 2008) as to the identification and understanding of risk factors for children, and the ability of key professionals to make adequate representation as to their concerns but also to be taken seriously, once a concern about a child has been raised.

This lack of consensus in regard to what constitutes "abuse" also considers the expectations of Winnicott's (1988) "good enough parenting" and the unclear expectations of professional collaboration itself. Winnicott (1988) identified the relative ease with which practitioners identify "good" *or* "poor" parenting, but made clear the immense complexity of identifying that which is "good enough" (Taylor et al., 2009). McCulloch (2007) argues that the establishment of universal practitioners, as professionals with the skill set to safeguard children, is at the crux of the sector's capacity to respond to the call. However, both the literature and practice experience suggest this goes further than a training need.

Stafford, Smith and Vincent (2011) discuss the significant influence of the media on safeguarding practice and public judgement of it, owing to high profile news headlines and emotive subtexts that:

> "not only do the media have the power to transform the private into the public, it also has the power – at the same time – to undermine trust, reputation and legitimacy in the process" (p. 30).

Similarly, Warner (2015) argues that the press actively sought to stir public anger towards social workers in the aftermath of the Baby P case and cites David Cameron's own emotive response to the professional agencies involved. In contrast Munro (DfE, 2011), herself a social worker, argues that to suggest risk to children can be eradicated is to set the system up to fail. The popular misconception is that social workers are to blame or held morally responsible for child deaths, in a bid to quench the public's need for someone to blame (Burke, 2013). Nelson (2009) also commented on media criticism of medics in the aftermath of Baby P. The wrong judgement quickly becomes one of moral wrong-doing. Fook (2006) identifies the tension around this point in the system, that it is only by achieving the right outcome that we can acknowledge our judgement was right.

The relationship between the media coverage of safeguarding has led to increased scrutiny and correction of apparent professional failings. This has contributed to a de-professionalization of child protection practices (Ayre 2001). Ayre comments that the "news" media has been a key instigator of a fear and blame culture; through over-representation of predatory risk to children, and media spin in headlines blaming professional practices for the deeds of child abusers. Furthermore, he comments that this leads professional practice to focus on failings within a code of compliance, focused on activity and process, rather than their reflexive praxis and direct work with children. This is echoed in Munro's (DfE, 2011) recommendation to remove assessment timescales from social work practice, so that the focus remains on the child and family rather than a ticking clock.

Within this context lies a 10.8% increase in social services referrals in 2013-14 (Ofsted, 2015). This reflects perhaps a professional consciousness heightened by media representation of failings. The question is what impact the media and public portrayal of safeguarding may have had on integrated practice; a system which seems to restrict creativity in a bid to deliver to a strict process. Ayre (2001) argues this culture of fear and blame also echoes throughout education via Ofsted judgements, attainment targets and league tables. He suggests that this is highly problematic for a system, which advocates a creative response to children's needs and that professionals, mindful of getting it wrong, are less likely to be innovative and move beyond restrictive thinking.

Amongst the media furore surrounding Victoria Climbié, Baby P, Daniel Pelka and others, it was noted that these children were often held at a non-statutory, informal position in the system. Baby P had been regarded as high risk and subject to a CP (Child Protection) Plan, but due to his mother's interview performance there were thought to be improvements in the family and therefore it was deemed to be less "risky" (Laming, 2009; Haringey Local Safeguarding Children Board [LSCB], 2009). The emergent thinking from the Laming report was the need for ownership at an early stage, from universal professionals (primary care, schools and early years). Specific concerns for a child's safety are supported now by LSCB arrangements and named officers in schools and health settings. Responding to early signs of vulnerability is widely discussed in the literature and is also reflected in policy (Lord Laming, 2009; Parton, 2011).

The Ofsted Report (2015) *Early Help; Whose Responsibility?* makes worrying reading. The report indicates a lack of co-ordination and ownership at the "early help" stage, and pinpoints the issue of thresholds as a critical weakness in the system. Ofsted claims social services thresholds are set too high, and that multi-agency professionals appear to refer cases deemed unsuitable. Furthermore, they state that following a social services decision not to assess the family, there is then a lack of outcome focused, co-ordinated planning around the child. Despite the call to offer early help (DfE, 2011), too frequently referrals, which are not taken up by the local authority social services, do not receive additional input from universal services. Munro's (DfE, 2011) recommendation that local authorities should be obliged to offer early help was rejected by the government of the time, who opted to use the Children Act 2004 as the only directive required. However, Ofsted (2015) reaffirmed that more was needed:

> "The evidence on this inspection indicated that current statutory powers do not provide a sufficient focus for any one agency or partners collectively to give early help the priority that it requires" (Ofsted, 2015, p. 24).

Furthermore, the report adds that because there is no duty to enforce the obligation to co-operate on "early help" cases, little has changed for many children at this level. Cronin and Smith (2010) commented that *Every Child Matters* (DfES, 2003) did not go far enough in tackling issues for families early on, and questioned whether the then anticipated Laming's recommendations (Laming and Herbert, 2009) after Baby P's death in 2007 would make any difference. From the 2015 Ofsted report it appears not.

The Tribes of Practice

Further to the concerns raised by Ofsted (2015) it is evident from the literature that issues of role confusion and professional hierarchy surround effective safeguarding (Tucker and Trotman, 2010; Watson, 2010). Watson (2010) argues that while the sharing of responsibilities and commonality of skills can enable positive collaboration, it also elicits potential for ambiguity and tension through increased demands and lack of clarity in the boundaries of professionals' roles. Watson points out that the notion of hierarchy is inflated, citing Reder (1993) who notes that it acts as a barrier to some practitioners who feel they are lower down the chain. Leese (2011) discusses Foucault's work on subjugated knowledge applied to multi-agency practice, where some ideas receive less value than others. Leese (2011) comments, "an example of this could be where medical knowledge is given more weight than the views of the nursery worker within an inter-agency team meeting" (p. 146). Indeed, as Gardner, Fook and White (2006), and Siraj-Blatchford, Clarke and Needham (2007) note, power is a central dynamic within all professional relationships. The practitioner has power over the client, but is beneath the power of their superiors. The inter-professional dynamics are impacted by power, and therefore there is a need for professionals to find the common ground in multi-agency safeguarding (Leese, 2011). Further, Watson (2010) identifies that some groups within practice may become polarised, holding a sense of mistrust about one another.

Thus, it can be argued that at the heart of the multitude of issues surrounding risk and responsibility for children, lays professional culture. Richardson and Asthana (2006) refer to "tribal variations" (p. 662) in professional practice. This is a view corroborated by Brandon et al (2011) who suggest that language and culture pivot around specific disciplines of health, social care and education, and are distinctively different in ways which involve language, hierarchy and practice. We would also add here, both "education" and "early years" are complimentary, yet distinct disciplines with their own inherent culture and ethos (Leese, 2011). Furthermore, Floyd and Morrison (2014) identify relationships between agencies, their cultures and identities, as central to inter-professional working, acknowledging the tension surrounding role and identity formation as professional profiles morph within multi-agency contexts (Moran et al., 2007). Leese (2011) identifies the concept of "professional habitus" (Bourdieu) and points to the fact that training and practice establish particular ways of thinking and doing.

Fundamental differences in the way these cultures view the treatment of a "problem", influences the collaboration with parents, parameters of confidentiality, and the wider context of the work (Leese, 2011; Tucker and Trotman, 2010). There is a need to recognise the distinctions in professional contact with families. Within healthcare children are usually seen in clinical settings with their parents, when their parents choose to present them as a result of illness or concern. However, health visitors may also see children in their home environment and on a more routine basis in the first few months of life, depending on parental engagement, and the presenting need. Teachers and practitioners in schools and early years settings see children every day, and are the few professionals who see children without their parents, yet have little remit to see children in their home environment. Therefore, each professional group sees children in a different context; with and without parents, at home or in external settings (Kendrick et al., 2000).

Each of these contexts provides a different opportunity to *be curious*, identified by those in the field as pivotal to our understanding of the needs of children (Brandon et al., 2011). Indeed Brandon et al. (2011) relate this need for curiosity to the distinct skills and knowledge base of different professional groups. Their discussion identifies that, while social workers should have a "good working knowledge" (p. 22) of child development, so as to understand where children are failing to thrive, reports have identified this as an area of professional weakness in some cases. Brandon et al. (2011) argue that case histories, collated by health visitors, should inherently consider developmental milestones for children, including dynamics between parent and child, and the parents' own understanding of the child's developmental and personal needs. In education, including early years, Brandon et al. (2011) identified similar developmental features in the given context, with any learning difficulty and behaviour being of key relevance to safeguarding. Thus, it is clearly identified that expertise in the sector should be shared, but is variable across professional groups. Roles are both distinct and complementary in forming a holistic picture of a child's wellbeing.

Cleaver and Cawson (2009) discuss complexities of cases where concerns for children emerge over time. These cases are less clear than those where abuse is disclosed directly, or where possible signs of abuse are immediately apparent. They indicate the importance of empowering staff, who may have little knowledge of a child, to "be worried and take action" (p. 152) who might otherwise lack confidence. The narrative from interviews we undertook (see below), combined with learning from serious case reviews, suggest that even when staff have a detailed knowledge of children, they can struggle to make their concerns felt in a way which promotes statutory action. Brandon et al. (2011) make the point that those children who lost their lives through abuse, neglect and professional failings, were known in the system by both, universal and specialist agencies. Perhaps, therefore, it is not a lack of willingness that impacts the effectiveness of multi-agency practice, but rather the finer points of professional terminology and shared understanding of risk that impedes our ability to do so.

It is also linked to communication. Richardson and Asthana (2006) identify complexities in this area, laying out four models of information sharing. The first of these is termed *Ideal*, whereby information is both shared and withheld with good cause, indicating a robust assessment and decision making process. In the *Over-Open model* information can be shared without good cause and practitioners risk a breach of confidentiality; however, in this case the risk of neglecting collaboration is low. An *Over-Cautious* model sees a greater degree of withholding information – caution being skewed towards confidentiality. Lastly the *Chaotic* model involves both over-sharing and under-sharing of information without due cause, which speaks of a high level of anxiety meeting a low level of confidence in a context which falls short of supporting effective safeguarding practice.

Case Study - Interviews with Professionals

We set out to capture the experiences of universal services professionals by interviewing a small sample of one Health Visitor, two Early Years Practitioners and two Primary School Senior Management staff. A qualitative methodology, namely thematic analysis (Braun and Clarke, 2006), was chosen as the focus was on the messages, words, and meanings, given by our respondents. Whilst the data findings will not be representative of the whole workforce, the narratives reflect on the themes working with other professionals, interpersonal relationships, communication, commitment and ownership, emerging from the literature discussed above.

The focus was on the following 3 questions;

1) What do you understand to be your responsibility for safeguarding when:
    a) immediate child protection issues occur?
    b) in early intervention; do you have an ongoing concern about a child?
2) What do you think about the expectations on you/your team for safeguarding issues?
3) What is your experience of working with key partner agencies at both these levels?

It was clear from the interviews that all professionals emphasise the importance of working with other professionals. A Safeguarding officer of one preschool emphasised the importance of working with others, including individual professionals' with their distinct expertise and pointed towards a health visitor as a good port of call, as she was deemed likely to respond.

> "The Health Visitors are a good port of call as well with whom we have a very good link. We phone the HV when we have a concern and the HV can call the parents and arrange for their pre-school check-up which gives them access into the home. I think that working with outside agencies is really important; we regard it as very important. I find a lot of outside agencies don't regard Early Years as professional as school teachers for example. It's like the children can go up to school and all of a sudden everybody can get involved and information sharing gets on between agencies and as an Early Years setting, we have been forgotten about." (Safeguarding Officer, pre-school setting).

A head teacher of a primary school, however, pointed to one of the problems as staff turnover:

> "If you're talking about working together we can only do that properly if we have built relationships with people, or at least with the service, so we know what the expectations are and how the service works, and their expectations of us. The difficulty with social care comes because they have so many staff changes that getting the consistency can be extremely difficult." (Head teacher, Primary School).

This was echoed by the SENCO of the pre-school:

> "It's like the young lady we have got at the moment. She arrived with one Social Worker, who we are in contact with, who has now left and another Social Worker has taken over [...] only that we were not told, and we did not know. And it is the same within the Local Council. They all have a shuffle and they don't tell you and you try to contact someone. It is a chasing game. I am not scared of phoning up and asking for advice. I had this young boy and I knew instantly that something was not quite right. I was emailing and phoning, it was not our Local Authority but a neighbouring one and it can be quite difficult when children come from different authorities." (SENCO Pre-school).

The above practitioner explained that she feels information is not always communicated effectively to key partners, and that as a result she has become more determined to ensure she shares information herself, but she does not assume others will do the same, despite professional directives to do so. Richardson and Asthana (2006) emphasised that shared ways of working do over time create a culture of collaboration and effective relationships. This point was identified as pivotal by a head teacher; speculating that where she and her school are known by other agencies, they trust her judgement:

> *"It makes a big difference if you know who you are speaking to directly – sometimes when you've got a concern and you're not certain it's CP (Child Protection) - if you know who you are speaking to on the other end of the phone you know the sort of answers they will give you – it's the trust you build up with them. The frustration comes when it's a social worker you don't know and they don't seem to take it seriously".* (Primary School Head Teacher).

Similarly a pre-school SENCO reported she could verbally agree concerns about a child with a paediatrician, but found the systems between health, education and the local authority delayed assessment and also intervention.

These comments also indicate issues of confidentially and the timely sharing of information, identified in the Laming Inquiry (2009) as being of optimum importance. The comments of the head teacher suggest that locally the model of information sharing rests on the ease of interpersonal relationships. This could lend itself to any of the four communication models detailed above, and even skew it towards a chaotic system with information being passed on, with varying degrees of clarity and openness depending on the relationships which surround it.

The professional experiences of the authors confirm the exhortation: *"We told social services; they did nothing"*; reflecting those professionals who, as identified by Cleaver and Cawson (2009), were motivated to worry about children, sought help, but then were left holding the baton themselves. The bulk of CAF work and its local applications are undertaken within education and health services; i.e. universal practitioners who raise the alarm but find themselves still case-holding. Baginsky (2008) identifies the frustration of schools in finding disparity between their idea of a realistic threshold, and that of social services' colleagues. Though disillusioned, both parties continue to negotiate this difficult ground although it cannot deliver the best outcome for children. This is reinforced here by several interviewees, who identify the safeguarding expectations of their role as a significant issue;

> *"We had one case where we had to exclude one of the children in Local Authority care and Social Services were useless. I just wanted someone even to say there is nothing we can do – phone the police, but they suggested we should tell the child it was dangerous to (be on the shed roof) – its' like "yes, we did that.." […] they don't always seem to realise the*

lengths we've already gone to when we make that call." (Primary School SENCO).

This comment indicates a gap in professional understanding. The SENCO was articulating that rather than social services referrals being a knee jerk reaction to any concern, they are well thought through and often seen as a last resort. However, it is not the intention here to disenfranchise integrated practice by criticising the role of social workers. Likewise, the professionals we spoke to, while voicing a reality check of frustrations and concerns, also spoke of the times that collaboration works well.

To exemplify this point, an interview with a Primary head teacher signifies the importance of professional relationships and trust:

> *"We have done some really good work so it's not all negative [...] it's frustrating [...] staff keep changing and you don't know them, you invite them to meetings and they don't come because nobody told them, or they accuse you of not sharing information that you have already shared. What's good is when you have stability of workers – you know how they work and we have communication over the small as well as the big issues. With some Social Workers we have daily contact"* (Head Teacher Primary School).

> *"The strength of the safeguarding support is very good. There's a big Child Protection team I can ring as soon as there is an issue."* (Head Teacher Junior School).

The gap in professional understanding is exemplified further in the following comment given by the SENCO and Pre-School practitioner:

> *"When going back to the Laming Report and all the issues raised about multi-agency communication, I still think we make a lot of the contact and don't get the same back. We are very pro-active and where we had safeguarding concerns and contacted outside agencies, we found that there had been outside agencies involved but that we were not informed. Because we have a good relationship with the schools, the Health Visitor, the Educational Psychologist, the Paediatrician. I know who to go to. But [*she refers to the local authority and local council here] *when there is this continual shuffle, with staff leaving.it is then, when they don't tell us about changes, that is a problem"* (SENCO Pre-school).

When asked about the role they play regarding safeguarding, professional responses indicated both commitment and ownership of their protective role:

> *"Because they don't have the resources they used to, it's now; can you as a school do that? – can you make contact and knock on the door [...]. You*

could say not, but actually who else is going to do it? And if our children need it, they need it. You get into that cycle, because if the school will, no one else needs to." (Head teacher Primary School).

The interviews undertaken with the health visitor echoed the challenges and issues faced by primary school SENCOs, head teachers, and preschool practitioners. One health visitor reflected on the valuable links and good communication with preschool settings around safeguarding suggesting:

"Nursery and preschool settings are very good at sharing their concerns about a child with safeguarding issues with us, and as health professionals we really value their opinions, we have early year practitioners working in our team. However our Social Work colleagues need to also value their knowledge and role and ensure their views are heard at core group and case conferences. Often they are not even invited." (Health Visitor).

Another issue raised by a health visitor, echoing the point made by Primary School head teachers and SENCOs is the difficulty with communicating with Social Services

"When I ring with a concern about a child the first thing I ask is who am I speaking to and what is your direct telephone number, otherwise you never get to talk to the same social worker again" (Health Visitor).

The communication difficulties are heightened when social workers are off sick or leave as another health visitor commented;

"It was only by chance that I heard that the social worker had visited because one of my other mums was at the house when he called, before he (the social worker) had gone off sick." (Health Visitor).

These challenges can potentially be addressed by the Multi agency Safeguarding Hub (MASH) interventions, and reflects the Health Visitor role within the government's *Healthy Child Programme* (2012).

It is considered vital that professionals "hold the baton" (McCulloch, 2007, p. 37) rather than referring on and leaving protection to social workers. Perspectives on what constitutes early intervention and understanding levels of need have become hotly contested (Powell and Uppal, 2012) amidst the realisation that responsibility for prevention has landed on the shoulders of Universal professionals. For teachers, early years professionals and health visitors among others, the shift to safeguarding and the onus on early intervention represents a significant shift in expectation, as indicated by the different responses given within the case study interviews.

This small scale research captures the praxis experience of Universal practitioners working with the safeguarding agenda, their experience of action, concerns and their perceived successes and shortcomings of the system.

Findings and Analysis

Whilst this chapter focuses on early help for families, the connection between severe and complex cases and Universal Services is apparent in the literature and practice experience. Universal services, deal with "all" children, encompassing those who have few or transitory needs, as well as those who have extremely worrying needs, and all those in between. It is likely that the families with "worrying needs" are known to universal services over a long period of time. The ongoing knowledge of the family history is very significant when trying to understand their challenges and Universal Services may see key family members on a daily or frequent basis over some years. Furthermore, there is much evidence (Bradford et al., 1988; Grubin, 1998) that 80 per cent of harm to children is perpetrated within the family. It is likely, therefore, that the perpetrator and the child are well known to Universal Services. Brandon et al. (2011) state that while attention is drawn to the latter stages of high profile cases, it should be noted that such families are known throughout the system, and that the variety of professional roles should support all stages of concern for children. This is apparent in the case study data above, where practitioners identified complex cases and demonstrated a ready willingness to include safeguarding in their remit.

This positive acceptance of their role is supported by the work of Finklehor (1986), whose model of "intent to harm" children, considers the internal inhibitors of social vilification on the part of the perpetrator, and external inhibitors of the protective shield of effective and confident practice, and the child's own resilience (cited by Sanderson, 2004). Leaving the internal urge to harm to one side, the latter external inhibitors are critical to safeguarding children and relate to any form of risk across the spectrum of need (CWDC, 2009, p. 31); any form of abuse must first permeate these layers of protection and self-assurance. Thus, it is imperative to consider what it is that enables children themselves, and the practitioners which surround them, to establish these powerful protective forces. Surely there is something inherent here about prevention of vulnerability itself; not just the willingness to worry (Cleaver and Cawson,

2009), but the ability to foresee possible risk factors and ensure children know where to turn to. This is further extended by the recent National Society for the Prevention of Cruelty to Children (NSPCC) *Underwear Campaign* aimed at preventing risk of sexual abuse by enhancing the knowledge and confidence of all children in recognising when abuse might be happening to them. The identified role of schools and early years' settings in the daily and involved contact with children and their families is an essential feeding ground for such protection.

Working Together to Safeguard Children (DfE, 2015) points out the duty of early years providers, thus ensuring early years staffs take note of the importance of safeguarding training to enable them to recognise signs and symptoms of potential abuse and neglect. All early years' settings are required to identify a designated officer for safeguarding who has responsibility to co-ordinate and liaise over any relevant concern. These practitioners are trained in child protection and their role should be highly regarded in the context of multi-agency safeguarding practice. Both early years practitioners in the above case study were clearly complying with these rules and ensuring their practice is up-to-date and relevant. Whilst early years practitioners hold the same responsibility as other agencies, some of our data indicated a lack of confidence, or belief in their concerns being taken seriously.

Effective Safeguarding of children must mean "putting children at the centre of the system". This appears a challenge in a workforce embroiled with bureaucratic systems and practices. To overcome system barriers, Universal practitioners need ways of working which encourage the building of trusting relationships in order to make multi-agency practice effective for vulnerable children. Several high-profile child deaths from Victoria Climbié to Daniel Pelka have highlighted the tragic consequences when information, indicating a serious risk to a child is held by one agency, but is not shared and responded to by other agencies involved in safeguarding children. To aid with inter-agency information sharing, and assessing the risk to a child, several local authorities have established MASHs to mitigate the risk of a child slipping through the safeguarding net (www.gov.uk/working-together-to-safeguard-children-multi-agency-safe guarding-hub).

Following the Munro et al. report (DfE, 2011) "MASHs" are seen as the most effective approach with one central point of contact for referrals, manned by staff from Education, Health, Police Probation and Children's Services together with voluntary organisations involved directly with safeguarding children. MASH provides triage and multi-agency assessment of safeguarding concerns in respect of vulnerable children. It also takes decisions depending on statutory need, child protection, or early help. The sharing of information between these agencies enables decisions to be made as to the most appropriate intervention, in response to the child's identified needs. This ensures that vulnerable children and adults are responded to quickly and efficiently by the most appropriate professional. Timescales are agreed, depending on whether it is a statutory need, child protection, or early help. This process is dependent on those professionals involved in responding to a referral having a very clear understanding of the different roles and responsibilities of those professionals implementing the action plan.

The Home Office Review of 2014 concluded that MASHs support professionals involved with children to "join the dots" and understand the potential risks to a child, so that appropriate action can be taken to prevent harm. Multi-agency working is essential in timely, early, and effective identification of risk, by improved information sharing, joint decision making, and coordinated action and intervention (Gurrey and Brazil 2014). However, the review also concluded that multi-agency approaches, instigated by MASH, should not supersede a single agency's duty to identify, protect, and support a child. Hence the MASH response should identify where and how different professionals fit together, but avoid interventions with unrealistic expectations beyond a professional's capacity, role, and responsibility to safeguard children. The MASH team shares information from all relevant agencies to decide the most appropriate intervention in response to the child's identified needs. This collaborative approach produces a faster, more coordinated and consistent response to safeguarding concerns. It will improve the "journey" for the child with greater emphasis on early help and better informed services delivering intervention at the right time. This, in turn, will give a clearer process for the professional raising a concern about a child and result in a better coordinated approach to resources, as each agency will operate more effectively and efficiently within their field of practice (www3.hants.gov. uk/mash.htm).

The development of MASH has generated a discussion regarding the aspirations for this new collaborative approach which fits the realities of practice (Gurrey and Brazil 2014), but a question remains as to whether this requirement fits with the professional roles of other universal services practitioners?

Figure 1.2 CAF (Common Assessment Framework) Continuum of Need

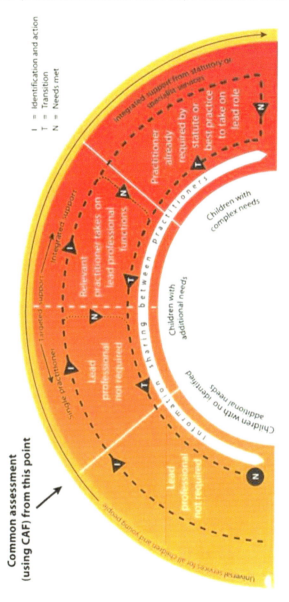

Source: CWDC, 2009, p. 31.

Conclusion

We began this chapter by identifying safeguarding of children as a social issue and considered the responsibilities of Universal Services professionals in that task. We reflected on the concerns held about the issue as articulated through media discourse and public policy and noted the constant refrain that communication between professionals is not effective, and that thresholds are too high for help to be given to families at an early enough stage. However, our analysis of the literature and our case study interview data suggest a more complex position on these issues.

Practitioners speak of their commitment to safeguarding the children in their care at all levels of need. Their frustration appears to be with the limits of what they can achieve. The long-term knowledge of families and the ability to monitor trends and concerns over time is evident in both the literature (Brandon et al., 2011; Cleaver and Cawson, 2009) and our research interviews. The professionals' care, concern, and commitment to these children came across strongly, where the professionals spoke emotively about trust, consistency, communication, and relationships with one another. These themes are also present in the literature surrounding the safeguarding agenda, which allows us to take a more positive view of what does work, rather than emphasising the obstacles which prevent effective early help. The recent findings of Ofsted (2015), however, are of significant concern, and we are mindful that this may present an ongoing debate within the new MASH frameworks.

We found a resonance between the literature discussion of cultural practices, the need for informed decision making and trust between practitioners, and the views of the practitioners themselves as reported here. The point made by Richardson and Asthana (2006), and Leese (2011) that subtle hierarchies exist across the system are echoed in the interview data too, although Watson (2010) considers these hierarchies to be somewhat inflated. We acknowledge the political undercurrent of high profile cases paraded across the media, which authors like Ayre (2001); Fook (2006); Nelson (2009) and; DfE (2011) suggest have actively stirred negativity towards social care professionals. In response to this, we would ask readers to reflect on the impact this has on the sector itself, and on the practitioners working within it. The times when multi-agency practice are most effective are when there is enough consistency, and a regular interface, to enable multi-agency professionals to know each other as individuals. This is typified by the quote in the title of this chapter; "You share coffee, you share cases". Such familiarity helps form a basis from which to negotiate the thorny issues of professional language, perspectives, and thresholds, and creates an environment in which misconceptions about roles and skills might eventually be replaced by inherent understanding and trust.

Bibliography

Akister, J. (2011). Protecting Children: the central role of knowledge. *Practice: Social Work in Action*, Vol.23, 5. DOI: 10.1080/09503153.2011.620090

Ayre, P. (2001). Child Protection and the Media; Lessons from the Last 3 Decades. *British Journal of Social Work*. Vol. 31, pp 887-901.

Braun, V. and Clarke, V. (2006). Using thematic analysis in psychology, *Qualitative Research Psychology*, Vol. 3 (2), pp 7-101.

Bradford, J., Bloomberg, D., and Bourget, D. (1988), The heterogeneity/ homogeneity of paedophilia. *Psychiatric Journal of the University of Ottawa*, Vol.13, pp. 217-226.

Brandon, M, Sidebotham, P., Ellis, C., Bailey, S., Belderson, P. (2011). *Child and Family Practitioners Understanding of Child Development; Lessons Learnt from a Small Sample of Serious Case Reviews*. Retrieved from: https://www.gov.uk/government/uploads/system/uploads/attachment_data/file/182520/DFE-RR110.pdf

Baginsky, M. (2008). Placing Schools at the Centre of Safeguarding Children. In M Baginsky (Ed). *Safeguarding Children and Schools*. London: Jessica Kingsley Publishers.

Burke, C. (2013). Sharon Shoesmith: Social workers should not be blamed for child murders. *Guardian* online accessed, 13 December, 2013.

Care Quality Commission. (2014). *Provider Handbook Consultation. NHS GP practices and GP out-of-hours services*. Retrieved from: http://www.cqc.org.uk/sites/default/files/20140409_provider_handbook_consultation_gp_practices_final_for_web.pdf

Children Workforce Development Council (2009). *Common Assessment Framework*. London: CWDC.

Cohen, L., Manion, L., and Morrison K. (2000). *Research Methods in Education* (5th Ed). London: Routledge.

Cleaver, H., and Cawson, P. (2009). *Safeguarding Children: A Shared Responsibility*. London: Wiley-Blackwell.

Cronin, M. and Smith, C. (2010). From safeguarding to Safeguarding. In G. Brotherton, H. Davies, and G. McGillivray. (2011). *Working with Children, Young People and Families*. London: Sage.

Department for Education. (2015). *Working Together to Safeguard Children: A Guide to Inter-agency Working to Safeguard and Promote the Welfare of Children*. London: TSO.

Department for Education. (2014). *Keeping Children Safe in Education. Statutory Guidance for Schools and Colleges*. London: Department for Education. Retrieved from:

https://www.gov.uk/government/uploads/system/uploads/attachment_data/file/
350747/Keeping_children_safe_in_education.pdf

Department for Education. (2014). *Statutory framework for the early years foundation stage. Setting the standards for learning, development and care for children from birth to five.* London: Department for Education. Retrieved from:
https://www.gov.uk/government/uploads/system/uploads/attachment_data/file/
335504/EYFS_framework_from_1_September_2014__with_clarification_note
.pdf

Department for Education. (2011). *Munro Review of Child Protection: final report – A child-centred system.* London; TSO.

Department for Education and Skills. (2003). *Every Child Matters,* Green Paper. London: HMSO.

Department of Education (2004). *Children Act 2004.* Chapter 31. Retrieved from:
http://www.legislation.gov.uk/ukpga/2004/31/contents; pdf version:
http://www.legislation.gov.uk/ukpga/2004/31/pdfs/ukpga_20040031_en.pdf

Department of Health (2000). *Framework for the Assessment of Children in Need and their Families.* London: HMSO.

Duck, S.(2007). *Human Relationships.* London; Sage.

Floyd, A, and Morrison, M. (2014). Exploring Identities and Cultures in Inter-Professional Education and Collaborative Professional Practice. *Studies in Continuing Education.* Vol. 36; 1, pp.38-53.

Finkelhor, D. (1984). *Child Sexual Abuse: New Theory and Research.* New York: Free Press.

Fook, J., and White, S. (2006). *Critical Reflection in Health & Social Care.* Maidenhead; McGraw Hill.

Gardner, F, Fook, J., and White, S. (2006). Critical Reflection; A review of contemporary literature and understandings. In F. Gardner., J. Fook, and S. White. *Critical Reflection in Health & Social Care.* Maidenhead: McGraw Hill.

Gilligan, P. and Manby, M. (2008). The Common Assessment Framework; does the reality match the rhetoric? *Child & Family Social Work* Vol.13, pp. 177-187.

Grubin, D. (1998). *Sex offending against children: Understanding the risk.* Research Development Statistics, Home Office.

Gurrey, M. and Brazil, E. (2014). Getting the right things right. In M. Blyth. *Moving on from Munro.* Bristol: Policy Press.

Home Office. (2006). *Safeguarding Vulnerable Groups Act.* Retrieved from:
http://www.legislation.gov.uk/ukpga/2006/47/contents; pdf version:
http://www.legislation.gov.uk/ukpga/2006/47/pdfs/ukpga_20060047_en.pdf.

Home Office. (2014). *The Disclosure and Barring Service* (Core Functions) (Amendment) Order (2014). London: TSO. Retrieved from:
http://www.legislation.gov.uk/uksi/2014/238/contents/made,
Pdf version:
http://www.legislation.gov.uk/uksi/2014/238/pdfs/uksi_20140238_en.pdf

Horwarth, J. (2009). Working Effectively in a Multi-Agency Context. In H. Cleaver, P. Cawson, S. Gorin, and S. Walker (Eds.) *Safeguarding Children; A Shared Responsibility.* Chichester: Wiley-Blackwell.

Kendrick, D., Elkan, R., Hewitt, M., Dewey, M., Blair, J., Robinson, D., Williams, and Brummell, K. (2000). Does home visiting improve parenting and the quality of the home environment? A systematic review and meta-analysis. *Archives of Disease in Childhood.* Vol. 82, pp. 443-451. DOI: 10.1136/adc.82.6.443.

Laming, W and Herbert B. (2009). The Protection of Children in England: A Progress Report. House of Commons, March 2009.HC 330.

Laming, W.and Herbert, B. (2013). *The Victoria Climbié Inquiry.* . Norwich: HMSO.

Lord Laming. (2003). *The Victoria Climbié Inquiry: Report of an Inquiry by Lord Laming,* (Cmnd 5730). London: HMSO.

Lord Laming. (2009). *The Protection of Children in England. A Progress Report.* London: TSO.

Leese, M. (2011). Child well-being: understanding children's lives, *Professional Development in Education* Vol. 37(3)*, pp. 472-473.

Local Safeguarding Children Board, Haringey. (2009). Serious Case Review: Baby Peter. Executive Summary February 2009. Haringey: LSCB

McCulloch, M. (2007). Integrating Children's Services: The Case for Child Protection. In K.Siraj-Blatchford, Clarke, and M.Needham. *The Team around the Child; Multi Agency Working in the early Years.* Stoke on Trent: Trentham.

Moran, P., Jacobs, C., Bunn, A. and Bifulco, A. (2007). Multi Agency Working: Implications for an Early Intervention Social Work Team. *Child and Family Social Work.* Vol. 12, pp.143-151.

Mukherji, P., and Albon, D. (2010). *Research Methods in Early Childhood. An Introductory Guide.* London: Sage.

Munro, E. (2008). *Effective Child Protection* (2nd. Edition). London: Sage.

Nelson, S. (2009). Preparing for the Special Challenge of Sexual Abuse. In J. Taylor, M. Themessl-Huber. *Safeguarding Children in Primary Health Care.* London; Jessica Kingsley Publishers.

OFSTED. (2015). *Early help. Whose responsibility?* London: OFSTED.

Parton, N. (2011). Child Protection and Safeguarding in England: Changing and Competing Conceptions of Risk and their Implications for Social Work, *British Journal of Social Work* Vol.41, pp. 854–875.

Powell, J., and Uppal, E. (2012). *Safeguarding Babies and Young Children. A Guide for Early Years Professionals.* Maidenhead: Open University Press.

Reder, P. (1993). *Beyond Blame: Child Abuse Tragedies Revisited.* East Sussex: Routledge.

Richardson, S., and Asthana, S. (2006). Interagency Information Sharing in Health & Social Care Services: The Role of Professional Culture, *British Journal of Social Work* Vol. 36, pp. 657-669.

Royal College of Paediatrics and Child Health. (2014). *Safeguarding children and young people: roles and competences for health care staff.* 3rd Edition. London: RCPCH.

Sanderson, C. (2004). *The Seduction of Children*. London: Jessica Kingsley Publishers.

Siraj-Blatchford, I., Clarke, K., and Needham, M. (2007). *The Team around the Child; Multi Agency Working in the Early Years*. Stoke on Trent: Trentham Books.

Stafford, A., Smith, C., and Vincent, S. (2011). *Child Protection Systems in the UK; A Comparative Analysis*. London: Jessica Kingsley Publishers.

Taylor, J., Lauder, W., Moy, M., and Corlett, J. (2009). Practitioner Assessments of "Good Enough" parenting; factorial survey *Journal of Clinical Nursing*. Vol.18, pp.1180-1189.

The Treasury. (2003). *Every Child Matters,* (Cm 5860). London: HMSO.

Tucker, S., and Trotman, D. (2010). Interpreting Risk: Factors, Fears and Judgement. In G. Brotherton, H. Davies and G. McGillivray (2011). *Working with Children, Young People and Families*. London: Sage.

Warner, J. (2015). *The Emotional Politics of Social Work and Child Protection*. Bristol: Policy Press.

Watson, A. (2010). Sharing or Shifting Responsibility? The Multi –agency approach to safeguarding children. In A.Pycroft and D. Gough. *Multi Agency Working in Criminal Justice*. Bristol: The Policy Press.

Webber, M., McCree, C., and Angeli, P. (2013). Inter-Agency Joint Protocols for Safeguarding Children in Social Care and Adult Mental Health Agencies; a cross sectional survey of practitioner experience. *Child & Family Social Work*. Vol. 18, pp. 149-158.

Winnicott, D.W. (1988). *Babies and their Mothers*. London: Free Association Books.

Websites

www3.hants.gov. uk/mash.htm

CHAPTER TWO

CHILDHOOD OBESITY, HEALTH AND EMBODIMENT: FROM INTERVENTION MODELS TO BODY-IMAGE AND BODY-BULLYING

WENDY SIMS-SCHOUTEN AND EMMA MAYNARD

Introduction

This chapter seeks to understand the complexities of how narratives and discourses around health circulate relationally and affectively in home and school contexts making links with our previous research (Maynard and Sims-Schouten, 2015; Sims-Schouten, 2015; Sims-Schouten and Cowie, 2016; Sims-Schouten and Edwards, 2016). Schools facilitate the monitoring of children's height and weight through the National Child Measurement Programme (www.hscic.gov.uk; Falconer et al., 2012), in an attempt to regulate childhood obesity. This involves categorising children's bodies as "underweight", "healthy weight", "overweight", "obese" and "overweight and obese combined" (www.hscic.gov.uk), and communicating this judgement to parents. The focus on childhood obesity stems from the apparent increase in health risks throughout childhood and into adult life, indicated as of concern for the individual but also for society at large. Lobstein (2010) anticipates an aging population in which a large proportion of families will experience serious long term illness, such as heart disease, diabetes and cancer, and will require long term medical intervention. Such concerns impact the individual in the context of family, work and education, but are also reported as being of great financial cost to the state. Lang and Rayner (2007) acknowledge that tackling obesity must be multifaceted, but they describe the current political and professional reaction as a "policy cacophony" (p166). Whilst

Falconer et al (2012), Peerson and Saunders (2009) and Sanders et al (2009) discuss the National Child Measurement Programme categories in regard to the benefits of health literacy, others suggest that the concern for children's weight is fuelled by the construction of obesity as a moral crisis (Rich and Perhamus, 2010; Riley et al., 2008). Brewer and Balen (2010) question why, if so many people find themselves identified as overweight or obese, do they face such stigma?

Children appear to be the key focus in obesity related policy because of the long term health implications of being either a healthy weight, or obese, but also because they are viewed as more open to learning and behaviour change, and if weight is not managed within given parameters, these are the people who pose greatest cost to the state and society in the future. Here, mixed messages are being sent out, from suggestions that "fat is bad" to messages indicating that children need to "eat well", and have a "good appetite" (Fielden, Sillence and Little, 2011). Yet, as neither children nor adults simply consume health messages in reductive and non-active ways, it is important to note that the discourses of health, which circulate in schools and preschool settings, impact significantly on children's embodied consciousness (Rich, 2010). Turner-Cobb (2014) discusses the gaps between intended and actual health related behaviours. Here she refers to The Health Belief model which relates to how people perceive apparent threats as being relevant to their lives, while the Theory of Planned Behaviour model refers to motivations for purposeful change. Both these perspectives are relevant to the subject of obesity and to the strategies employed through public health, healthcare providers, and other campaigners. In addition, there is the notion of "body-bullying", with research showing that weight-related criticism (WRC) is specifically and uniquely associated with pre-adolescent children's body self-perceptions beyond its association with general, non-weight-related victimization (Armstrong et al., 2013).

This chapter does not set out to challenge the risks identified with childhood obesity, but rather to question whether current approaches adequately address the wider circumstances in which obesity happens, and whether a "blame" culture enables or prevents us accessing optimum health for children. It questions whether we see children and families as actively or passively responsible for their health, or as sufferers of illness, disease and disadvantage.

The Childhood Obesity crisis and Causal Factors

"...in this meeting yesterday, this woman was talking about obesity, was talking about it being the bowl of spaghetti and that you can't just talk about it in terms of, um healthy living, that actually you can't detach it from poverty. You can't detach it from exercise! You can't detach it from, um.... parenting issues.... that very often it's the whole mesh of things going on and it's about unpicking it one by one, and thinking about things broader than just obesity"

This extract from an interview with a manager of a children's centre very neatly summarises the key issues around childhood obesity, in particular in relation to the causes of what is now referred to as a "crisis". The "obesity crisis", includes debates around "childhood obesity", "healthy diets" and "exercise" in school-settings and at home, and is a recurrent theme in the British media. The suggestion is that childhood obesity has now reached epidemic proportions, and calls are being made for strategies to reverse this unhealthy trend, and deal with this crisis. Currently, concern about childhood obesity dominates public health discourse, with a specific focus on the need for early intervention. This included a proposal for a Sugar Tax, which was debated in health and political circles (Briggs et al., 2013) before being introduced in the Budget Speech 2016. It is also reflected in public policy and pedagogy, through the National Child Measurement Programme, the Change 4 Life public health campaign and a direct stipulation of hours of exercise each week. In addition, there is significant media coverage, through the involvement of celebrity chef Jamie Oliver, trying to improve the food habits of the nation (Hollows and Jones, 2010). Overall, the aim is to drive down the rate of overweight and obese children from the current level of 28 per cent by 2020 (DfE, 2012). Thus, seen as a social issue, Governments have responded in a variety of ways. Health policies and practices have become radically interventionist, ranging from adaptations to school health and physical education policy, to the threat of obese children being removed from their families and placed into social care (Fielden, Sillence and Little, 2011; Rich, 2010).

This exemplifies why interventions that proscribe behaviours for weight management and target individual families can be interpreted as a "blame culture" (Fielden et al., 2011; Schwartz and Puhl, 2003).This can also be seen as a gender issue as criticism of childhood obesity tends to target mothers and evokes and reinforces social expectations of women as slim. Having an obese child is conveyed in social discourse as a maternal failure (Zivkovic et al., 2010), indicating significant pressures on the shoulders of women to maintain a perfect regimen of diet and exercise from pregnancy onwards, as proscribed by academic, medical and political hierarchies.

In order to understand healthy eating practices and the related childhood "obesity crisis", it is imperative to view this in the light of a complex interplay of demographic, parental and child variables. By examining relational dynamics, social structures as well as material and embodied factors, it might be possible to construct an explanation of causal factors in relation to the current obesity crisis. The blame directed towards mothers and children sits within a context of cheap, high sugar, high carb food, with a clearly identified link between obesity and poverty. Therefore, the extent to which we are active agents in maintaining weight may be socially determined or influenced by financial constraints and food culture. It is plausible that routine behaviours go unnoticed by individuals, thereby making it difficult to obtain insight and understanding of the dangers of obesity and relevance to oneself.

The pre-school years have been identified as a critical period for the development of childhood obesity, because the eating and physical activity habits that contribute to later obesity become established during these formative years. Here again the focus is predominantly on parenting (and more specifically mothers), with research consistently pointing to the association between parenting styles and diet and weight in young children, as well as in adolescents (Parletta et al., 2012). Demir and colleagues (2012) argue that information about the ways in which the parent and the child can influence each other, as observed in parent–child interactions around food, provides greater insight into the aetiology of childhood obesity. Turner-Cobb (2014) discusses the pivotal role of parents in the health habits of children, especially in early years where parents set patterns for expected behaviours. Research suggests that being obese during pregnancy significantly increases the risk of obesity in the resulting infant, leading to calls for educating mums-to-be and making them aware of healthy eating practices, not just in relation to themselves, but also to protect their unborn child (Atkinson et al., 2013). Evidence of this can be seen in Government documentation and advice groups. The All-party Parliamentary Group on a Fit and Healthy Childhood (2014) have made suggestions on reducing childhood obesity through creating better playgrounds to get youngsters to exercise; fitness checks in schools; and the appointment of a cabinet minister responsible for preventing obesity. In addition to this, pregnant women are warned not to "eat for two" and urged to attend lessons in how to feed babies to prevent over-eating from birth.

Thus, obesity is treated not just as an issue to do with health and the health-risks associated with being overweight, but also as a social issue with a value-laden, moral element linked to "bad parenting", as childhood obesity goes against the dominant conception of the "good mother" who looks after her child's health and wellbeing (Sims-Schouten et al., 2007, 2014; Zivkovic et al., 2010). This is also addressed by Lupton (2014) who argues that a moral panic has developed around this issue of "childhood obesity", and that when small children are considered to be overweight, these moral judgements are transferred to their mothers. She gives the example of Chrissie Swan, an Australian celebrity who appeared in a cover story of a women's magazine with her two sons, one of whom was overweight. What followed was an eruption on social media with debates focussing on whether Swan should have let her son become fat, leading eventually to Swan being forced to defend herself, noting that she had struggled with weight throughout her life.

This raises other issues including the question highlighted in the British media, of whether DNA tests at five can tell if a child will be fat at 14. There is some evidence that non-modifiable genetic factors related to energy storage patterns, might play a role in obesity (Skouteris, 2012), but this is insufficient to explain the increase in overweight and obese children in recent years. Turner-Cobb (2014) discusses the identified gap between health related intentions and behaviours, citing two models of understanding health related behaviour. The Health Belief Model links people's perception of threats, such as healthy/non-healthy eating, smoking and sexually transmitted infection (STI), to their health beliefs and self-determination. Alternatively, the Theory of Planned Behaviour relates to individuals' motivations for change in combination with their enacted behaviour. The latter is influenced by social constructs and relationships – what is normal, acceptable, and expected thus raising the issue of a moralised agenda regarding eating and weight management. Furthermore, Gillespie and Johnson-Askew (2009) consider the cultural practices which influence food choices and practices. They highlight that people construct reality by processing ideas, experiences and meanings together; thus families have their own food culture which they recognise as "normal". In addition to this, families actively make decisions about food, which has logic – i.e. there may be a reason behind "poor" food choices and people may actively change their practices without intervention due to their own aspirations and circumstances (Hepburn and Potter, 2011). Gillespie and Johnson-Askew's (2009) findings suggest that parents respond to emerging trends and influences in health, but this is set firmly in the context of their own food experiences as children, and their practical circumstances. Other research (Chivers, 2012) found that maternal education, parental birth weight, and parental BMI were the strongest influences on their child's BMI from birth to adolescence. The Body Mass Index (BMI) now occupies a central position in dominant discourse about body size and its relationship to health, and recent calls have been made to challenge the discourse concerning the relationship between body size, health, and personal value (Anderson, 2012).

It follows that relational influences, social structures, material environments and embodiment play a constitutive role, rather than merely a supplementary role in health-related practices in childhood. As well as focussing on parenting skills, and the role of the early home environment, socio-economic status (SES) is also highlighted in research, with the suggestion that a higher proportion of socially disadvantaged children tend to be overweight compared with socially advantaged children (Krombholz, 2012). Here the focus is specifically on improving ways in which parents communicate with their children, through the development of parent-targeted treatment programmes for child diet quality and subsequent adolescent overweight/obesity. For example, Kaufman and Karpiti (2007) discuss responses to weight interventions in the Latino community of Brooklyn, New York. They present a case study of Yolanda, who initially rejected health professionals concerns over her overweight toddler as she believed her child was normal given the body shapes of generations of Yolanda's family. Yolanda eventually sought support because of inner turmoil, potentially a response to a moralised judgement on her parenting. She was noted to engage with dietary support when the doctor reassured her that the child was fine, and Yolanda gained affirmation that she was a good parent because she was concerned about her daughter's weight. Thus, the moralised issue of obesity, referred to above, is set in the context of genuine restrictions. This is an example of how unhealthy eating practices and subsequent childhood obesity tend to be constructed as a result of dysfunctional parenting, rather than a family's material circumstances and life events, together with the inability of the family to engage in (sometimes expensive) physical activity programmes (Rich, 2010). Papaioannou et al. (2013) considered the connection between parenting styles and the prevalence of fruit and vegetable intake in disadvantaged families. They honed in on the emotional climate and food related parenting in the home and found that a higher rate of overweight/obese children were exposed to "indulgent parents", where treats were in abundance, whilst '"uninvolved parents" scored lowest in making use of teachable moments where healthy eating habits can be capitalised on. Authoritative parents, more frequently correlated with middle class families, are found to have a higher usage of teachable strategies, access to facilities, and are also able to limit treats, thus resulting in lower obesity rates and a connection between, weight, parenting and social class (see also Rich and Perhamus, 2010).

The 'Obesity Crisis' – Reality and Perceptions

The social construction of weight, fatness and in particular childhood obesity has been the subject of a number of critical studies in recent years. Viewed from a health perspective, the World Health Organization (WHO) regards childhood obesity as one of the most serious global public health challenges for the 21st century. At the same time, obesity sceptics, such as Gard and Wright (2005) argue that the "obesity epidemic" should be perceived as a complex hotchpotch of science, morality and ideological assumptions about people and their lives, with ethically questionable effects. They question the existence of an "obesity epidemic" and argue that people have latched on to this because it conforms to the familiar story of Western decadence and decline. They argue that "obesity talk" has more to do with preconceived moralities and ideologies regarding "fatness" as no more than a comprehensive assessment of the existing evidence. Yet, the assertions and critiques of obesity sceptics have failed to make an impact on mainstream obesity science, government health policy and anti-obesity public health efforts (Lupton, 2014; Sims-Schouten and Cowie, 2016). Instead, there appears to be a continued focus on the fact that British children are getting fatter, with calls from the Department of Health (2012) to deal with the child obesity crisis, combined with a constant stream of information from the National Child Measurement Programme (NCMP), providing data about childhood obesity. Statistics for 2013/14 show that 19% of children in Year 6 (aged 10-11) were obese and a further 14.4% were overweight. Amongst children in Reception (aged 4-5), 9.3% were obese and another 13.0% were overweight. This suggests that almost a third of 10-11 year olds and over a fifth of 4-5 year olds were perceived as overweight or obese. There is also a wide gap between the most deprived and least deprived children. Data from the Health Survey for England (HSE), which includes a smaller sample of children than the NCMP but covers a wider age range, show that in 2012 around 28% of children aged 2 to 15 were classed as either overweight or obese (DoH, 2012). Interestingly, whilst there appears to be an increased focus on how British children are "getting fatter", the Department of Health (2012) indicates that the increase in childhood obesity appears to be levelling off, and that rates of childhood obesity have actually decreased since 2004.

In addition to the focus on childhood obesity within Government health policies, academic journals point to the dangers of obesity. Skouteris (2012) argues that more research is needed urgently to combat the alarming rates of childhood obesity, especially rates of overweight and obesity in pre-school children. Other researchers raise the issue of how being 'obese' is perceived in society, not only from a health perspective, but general stigma and stereotypes, such as that "fat people are lazy". Lupton (2014) argues that "fat bodies" are culturally represented as inferior, deficient, ugly and disgusting. People who are "fat" are viewed as deserving their fate due to their lack of self-control, but they are also perceived as a burden on society and costly. Fat children, Lupton (2014) argues, are subjected to greater harassment and prejudice than other children, and experience ostracism, teasing and bullying to a greater extent (see also Sims-Schouten and Cowie, 2015). Here, self-worth, self-esteem and body dissatisfaction mediate the paths between weight, status and being a victim of bullying (Fox and Farrow, 2011). Research also strengthens and highlights the stigmas that are already there in society, with medical journals and research consistently highlighting the health implications of being obese and fat, whilst social sciences research points to inherent causes (bad parenting) and effects of being obese. Thus, issues of obesity appear to evoke a blame culture rather than the empathy and sympathy shown to other health conditions. Some research (Fielden, Silence and Little, 2011; Schwartz and Puhl, 2003) locates interventions into child obesity on changing the behaviours of children and parents themselves. O'Dea (2005, p. 259) sets this in the context of an inherent tension between some public health messages and the cornerstone of medical and research ethics to "first do no harm". O'Dea suggests public health messages have failed to effectively communicate the need to manage a healthy weight as part of a healthy mind and body by placing too much emphasis on thinness as a desirable goal. She cites an example of the positioning of smoking as being a useful slimming aid in the 1950s and 1960s, now known to be dangerously flawed advice (O'Dea, 2005). Like Schwartz and Puhl (2003), O'Dea (2005) acknowledges the moral shaming of obese people and, given the social expectations that adults provide protection and nurture for children, the shame associated with being, or having an obese child is magnified. The effect on children is also multi-faceted. Childhood obesity has an impact on all areas of a child's life, including their self-worth, through the social construction of "fat is bad" (i.e. unappealing, ugly and morally wrong), physical health, and their general development. The associated blame directed towards families hints at a further correlation with issues of well-being. This focus on obesity as a disease, and something that needs to be treated provides an impetus for the close monitoring of those who might be at risk in the name of prevention (Wright, 2009). This is discussed further in the next section.

Regulating Childhood Obesity – from Intervention to Monitoring

There are multiple factors that play a role in regulating childhood obesity, from family conditions to intervention models and biopedagogics. Mothers of young children have been positioned as key targets in anti-obesity campaigns. In 2009, the Department of Health launched the "Change4Life" campaign to raise awareness about diet and physical activity, and encouraged families to "eat well, move more and live longer". In addition, the National Child Measurement Programme (NCMP) played a role in reducing childhood obesity by providing local health commissioners with the aim to promote healthy weight in children (DoH, 2012). Since September 2008 local health authorities have been sharing information from the NCMP. Letters are sent out to parents, determined by the child's BMI percentile, and parents/carers are encouraged to contact the Local Primary Care Trust for further advice and assistance (DoH, 2012). In addition, there has been an increased focus on educating children and families in terms of physical activity at an increasingly younger age in order to protect them from the threat of future ill health. Tackling obesity is a priority for the current Conservative Government and Public Health England (PHE), which focuses on preventative measures arguing that 'physical inactivity' is now a national epidemic with the prediction that this generation of young people will live five years less than their parents.

Obesity is not just a British phenomenon. In schools across Western societies, curricula and pedagogies are being drastically re-shaped by policies concerned with tackling the so-called childhood "obesity epidemic" (Lupton, 2014). The OECD (2013) found that, based on self-reported data, more than 20% of boys and girls are defined as overweight in Greece, Italy, Slovenia, the United States and Canada. In these countries, a strong positive relationship appears to exist between social deprivation and obesity, as obesity prevalence is significantly higher in deprived areas. In addition, childhood obesity prevalence is also significantly higher in urban areas than rural areas (HSCIC, 2014).

Childhood obesity awareness and intervention campaigns are targeting families and educational settings, as socialization of children into healthy food practices takes place in nurseries and schools as well as in homes. The Early Years Foundation Stage, which is the early years curriculum in England (DfE, 2012), provides guidelines and regulations on promoting healthy eating and physical exercise. Here, the focus is on an educational programme that involves activities and experiences for children that help them understand the importance of physical activity and make healthy choices in relation to food (DfE, 2012). Other programmes, such as Sure Start and the Healthy Child Programme, have more indirect approaches towards healthy eating. For example, according to Shribman and Billingham (2009) effective implementation of the Healthy Child Programme, a preventative programme produced by the Department of Health in 2009, should lead to healthy eating and increased activity. Sure Start uses measures such as the 2 year developmental check to support families. Other initiatives include HENRY (Health Exercise and Nutrition for the Really Young), which aims to tackle childhood obesity through training practitioners to work more effectively with parents of pre-school children, around issues to do with obesity and lifestyle (Brown et al, 2013). The Healthy Schools toolkit (2012) is designed to help schools plan health and wellbeing improvements for children and young people by identifying and selecting effective activities and interventions to discourage children from eating 'naughty' food, such as crisps. It has been pointed out that the latter may actually be counter-productive and play a role in the rise in eating disorders among children and teenagers.

Although educators and practitioners are now playing an increasingly important role in monitoring and regulating healthy eating practices and childhood obesity, they are dealing with highly sensitive issues that can sometimes be difficult to raise with parents. Redsell et al. (2016) argue that informing parents about healthy diets is far easier than addressing issues to do with an infant being overweight. Furthermore, teachers' and practitioners' perceptions of healthy food and obesity can differ from those of children and parents. For example, in a study on lunchtime interactions between minority students and majority teachers in a Danish classroom, Karrebaek (2012) found that cultural and personal preferences were disregarded if at odds with dominant understandings of healthy food.

Thus, the current emphasis on reducing childhood obesity raises issues to do with stigmas and stereotypes, not just in relation to "fat children", but also in relation to economically disadvantaged families. One Early Years Practitioner stated to one of the authors *"it is usually the poor parents who don't know how to provide a healthy diet to their children"*

Links are also made between children's behaviour (in relation to watching
TV and playing computer games), physical inactivity and childhood
obesity. Yet, so far no link has been found between physical education in
schools and long-term health and body weight (Gard and Wright, 2005;
Wright, 2009).

Obesity sceptics refer to the normalising and modifiable practices,
discussed above, as "bio-pedagogies" generated by claims of a global
epidemic. They suggest that this is driving the monitoring of those who
might be at risk, but in the name of prevention (Wright, 2009). Set against
a backdrop of neo-liberalism, parents are encouraged to seek out social
opportunities for their children through a mixture of state and private
institutions, engaging with the market as a means to do so (Rich, 2010).
Yet, this suggests that drawing on facilities in relation to physical activity
and healthy eating may only be an option for those who have the cultural
desire to use them and the means to afford them. Some parents are clearly
better placed than others, in terms of symbolic and economic resources, to
read and take advantage of opportunities for physical activity and health
outside of school (Rich and Perhamus, 2010). It is questionable whether
the increased emphasis on physical activities and healthy eating in schools
and early years settings is enough to compensate for the many other
inequities influencing peoples' lives.

Embodiment, Body-Image and Body-Bullying

Not only do the healthy eating and childhood obesity campaigns raise
issues to do with parenting, they also raise issues to do with the "body"
(fat, thin and obese) and "embodiment" within contemporary society.
Notions to do with healthy eating, obesity and embodiment are
intrinsically linked. There also appears to be a link between the social and
personal worth of a person and their weight (Halse, 2009; Murray, 2009).
Leahy (2009) found that 'disgust' is an affect commonly mobilised by
both teachers and students in health classes and by other health strategies
designed to address childhood obesity.

Research has also found links between eating practices, body image,
childhood obesity and being a victim of bullying, particularly in girls
(Farrow and Fox, 2011). Here, the notion of 'body-bullying' is
highlighted, with research showing that weight-related criticism (WRC) is
specifically and uniquely associated with pre-adolescent children's body
self-perceptions, beyond its association with general, non-weight-related
victimization (Armstrong et al., 2013). It is important to note that the
discourses of health which circulate in society impact significantly on

children's embodied consciousness (Rich, 2010). Here, 'discourse' refers to both external, spoken formulations and inner speech. Inner speech, which is private and personal, mirrors the conversational forms of previous social interactions and can be traced back to instructional episodes (Cromby and Harper, 2009). Here two factors and conceptions in relation to the 'body' are at play. One stimulated by concerns regarding children's physical health and future, with a focus on healthy eating practices and exercise. The other factor links to body-perceptions and the construction of overweight bodies as indulgent and somehow wrong (Sims-Schouten and Cowie, 2016). An example of the first is the current policy and Public Health focus discussed earlier, constructing physical inactivity as an epidemic with the predicted result that the current generation of children will live five years less than their parents' generation. Here, a direct link is made between child obesity and life expectancy. Yet, the body is not just another object in the world; it is the "medium by which there is a world for us all" (Cromby and Harper, 2009, p. 345). This links with the second issue, namely body-bullying, disordered eating and a focus on 'fatness', and it could be argued that to some extent all result from experiences where bodies have been subject to surveillance techniques inside and outside of school contexts and in the media.

Thus, perceptions play a key role in the multidimensional nature of young people's lives. In one focus group interview with young mothers (Sims-Schouten and Cowie, 2016), the conversation revolved around the behaviour of young children (aged 3-5) in early years settings. One mother mentioned that she witnessed one child say to another child *"you are fat"*, and that the mother of the first child responded by saying *"we don't use that word!"* Within the focus group the question was raised whether this was an appropriate reaction, as by making this (i.e. "you are fat") an issue, it can then become instrumental and a weapon.

In society today, rightly or wrongly, childhood obesity is an issue and the approach towards monitoring and intervention in and of itself is resulting in segregation, with some being the "good" (slim, healthy) people and others being "fat" and "bad". Thus, following Cromby and Harper (2009, p. 345) what we see is not simply out there in the world but it is also what is "in here" (our embodied feelings). This singles out families who, for whatever reason, are less able to provide their children with "healthy diets" and physical activity. A distinction needs to be made here, between obesity and disordered eating and eating disorders. Although there is a link between the former and SES there are no such direct links with eating disorders, such as anorexia nervosa, and research suggests that this affects children from all backgrounds (Rich, 2010).

Nevertheless, one cannot deny the link between the heightened/increased focus on childhood obesity and disordered eating and eating disorders. In both the "body" takes central position/place, together with the perception that being slim/slender/thin is beautiful and desirable. As such, the body, health and weight have become moral issues, leading to a negative approach towards people perceived as not fulfilling this moral and desirable ideal. One of our participants, in an interview with young people based around bullying and resilience (Sims-Schouten and Edwards, 2016), said: *"And, so this kid tried to bully me, he is a fat shit, so I punched him"*. Pro-anorexia (also referred to as 'pro-ana') websites have sprung up supporting a need in young people to fit in with the slim and slenderness ideal (Riley, 2008). Wannarexia is one website used by individuals, especially teenage girls, ambitious to become anorexic but have not yet achieved a BMI low enough. A culture of competitive weight loss has emerged, supported by a wide variety of weight and fitness management apps, social networking and peer pressure. This combination is producing a pseudo-supportive culture of extreme weight-loss, with shared language and aspirations, providing verification and an environment to share practices which are moralised – the polar extreme of childhood obesity (Boero and Pascoe, 2012).

Conclusion: A way forward

This chapter has shown that obesity is not just an issue to do with healthy eating practices; there is also a value-laden, moral element to it. The "obesity crisis" is multi-faceted, and constructed within health, social and psychological frameworks. From a health perspective the focus has been on the health challenges associated with obesity and physical inactivity, including the anticipated reduced life-expectancy of the current generation of young people. Socially, the focus has been on educating parents and children, and specifically addressing deprived communities. Here, a link is made between obesity and "bad parenting", something that goes against the dominant conception of the "good mother" who looks after her child's health and wellbeing. Fat, overweight and/or obese children, are subjected to harassment and prejudice and experience ostracism, teasing and bullying to a greater extent than other children. This links with psychological constructions of self-worth; self-esteem, physical appearance and body dissatisfaction mediate the paths between weight status and being a victim of bullying. As such, the current emphasis on reducing childhood obesity also raises huge issues to do with stigmas and stereotypes, not just in relation to "fat children", but also in relation to economically disadvantaged families.

What all three frameworks have in common is the assignment of blame to obese children and their families. First, obese people are blamed for causing a drain on our health-services. Second, parents are blamed for not providing healthy foods for their children. Thirdly, obese people are blamed for being indulgent and lacking in self-control. Fourth, blame is also put upon the obese body itself, for being unappealing and unattractive. Yet, this distracts from the fact that policy-makers have consistently failed to curb the excessive use of fats and sugar in many products that are promoted in the media and in supermarkets in ways that make them attractive to children. The recent Sugar Tax, long debated in health and political circles, has yet to be implemented.

This raises questions about the way forward in this contradictory and conflicting world of healthy eating – how can we protect our children and young people from the confusion that is out there to do with healthy eating, "super-foods", balanced diets, nutrition and "eating well"? With the rise in social media use, especially among teenagers (and more recently primary school children) this can only add to the hotchpotch of information on the body (good, bad, healthy, smelly, and obese). Yet, at the same time with more researchers interested in this area and an ever increasing governmental focus, there is a promise of creating a better, more balanced response. But, more research is needed into what websites children access when it comes to weight-loss and healthy eating and lifestyle, and how this impacts on their lives. In addition, effort needs to be made in getting rid of stigmas, and schools could play a significant role here.

In conclusion, on the continuum running from large to overweight and clinically obese there will be points where it is in the child's best interest to intervene in order to prevent later acute health problems. Yet any solution must take account of the complex interacting social factors that contribute to one particular child's body size, including social circumstances, cultural reference and perceived relevance to individual lives in the context of a moralized discourse body (see also Sims Schouten and Cowie, 2016).

Bibliography

All-Party Parliamentary Group. (2014). On a fit and healthy childhood. Clark, H. Retrieved from: http://www.activematters.org/news/694/88/Report-by-APPG-on-a-fit-and-healthy-childhood/d,library/

Anderson, J. (2012). Whose Voice Counts? A Critical Examination of Discourses
    Surrounding the Body Mass Index, *Fat Studies*, Vol. 1(2), 195-207, DOI:
    10.1080/21604851.2012.656500
Armstrong, G., Oeffinger, K., Chen, Y., Kawashima, T., Yasui, Y., Leisenring, W.,
    Stovall, M., Chow, C., Mulrooney, D., Mertens, A., Border, W., Durand, JB.,
    Robison, L., Meacham, L. (2013). Modifiable risk factors and major cardiac
    events among adult survivors of childhood cancer. *Journal of Clinical
    Oncology.* DOI: 10.1200/JCO.2013.49.3205
Atkinson, L., Olander, E.K. and French, D.P. (2013). Why don't many obese
    pregnant and post-natal women engage with a weight management service?
    Journal of Reproductive and Infant Psychology, Vol. 31(3), pp. 245-256.
Bell, K., McNaughton, D. and Salmon, A. (2009). Medicine, morality and
    mothering: public health discourses on foetal alcohol exposure, smoking
    around children and childhood overnutrition. *Critical Public Health*, Vol.
    19(2), pp. 155- 170.
Boero, N. and Pascoe, C. (2012). Pro-Anorexia Communities and Online
    Interaction; Bringing the Pro-Ana Body Online *Body & Society,* Vol. 18, pp.
    27.
Brewer, C., and Balen, A. (2010). The adverse effects of obesity on conception and
    implantation. *Society for reproduction and fertility.* Vol. 140(3), pp. 347-64.
    DOI: 10.1530/REP-09-0568
Briggs, A., Mytton, O., Kehlbacher, A., Tiffin, R., and Rayner, M. (2013). Overall
    and income specific effect on prevalence of overweight and obesity of 20%
    sugar sweetened drink tax in UK: econometric and comparative risk
    assessment modelling study. *British Medical Journal,* Vol. 347, pp. 1-17.
    Retrieved from: http://dx.doi.org/10.1136/bmj.f6189
Brown, R.E., Willis, T.A., Aspinall, N., Hunt, C., George, J. and Rudolf, M.
    (2013). Preventing Child Obesity: A long-term evaluation of the HENRY
    approach. *Community Practitioner,* Vol.87 (7), pp. 23-27.
Chivers, P., Parker, H., Bulsara, M., Beilin, L. and Hands, B. (2012). Parental and
    early childhood influences on adolescent obesity: a longitudinal study, *Early
    Child Development and Care,* Vol.182 (8), pp. 1071-1087.
Cromby, J. and Harper, D.J. (2009). 'Paranoia: a social account.' *Theory &
    Psychology*, Vol.19 (3), pp. 335–361.
Department for Education. (2012). *Statutory Framework for the Early Years
    Foundation Stage. Setting the Standards for Learning, Development and Care
    for children from birth to five.* Retrieved from:
    http://webarchive.nationalarchives.gov.uk/20130401151715/https://www.educ
    ation.gov.uk/publications/standard/AllPublications/Page1/DFE-00023-2012
Department of Education. (2012). *The Healthy Schools Toolkit.* Department of
    Education. Retrieved from http://www.activematters.org/news/694/88/Report-
    by-APPG-on-a-fit-and-healthy-childhood/d,library/
Demir, D, Skouteris, H., Dell-Aquila, D, Akson, N. McCabe, M.P., Ricciardelli,
    L.A., Milgrom, D. and Baur, L.A. (2012). An observational approach to testing
    bi-directional parent–child interactions as influential to child eating and

weight. *Early Child Development and Care,* Vol. 182(8), pp. 943-950. DOI: 10.1080/03004430.2012.678591

Department of Health. (2012). An update on the government's approach to tackling obesity. Memorandum for the committee of public accounts, National Audit Office. Retrieved from: http://www.nao.org.uk/wp-content/uploads/2012/07/tackling_obesity_update.pdf

Falconer, C., Park, M., Skow, A, Sovio, U., Saxena, S., Kessel, A., Croker, H., Morris, S., Viner, R., and Kinra, S. (2012). Scoping the impact of the national child measurement programme feedback on the child obesity pathway: study protocol. *BMC Public Health.* Vol.12, p.:783. DOI: 10.1186/1471-2458-12-783

Farrow, C.V. and Fox, C.L. (2011). "Gender differences in the relationships between bullying at school and unhealthy eating and shape-related attitudes and behaviours". *British Journal of Educational Psychology,* Vol. 81, (3), pp. 409-420.

Fielden, A.L., Sillence, E. and Little, L. (2011). Children's understandings of obesity: A thematic analysis. *International Journal of Studies on Health and Well-Being,* Vol. 6 (3), pp 1-17.

Flewitt, R. (2005). Conducting research with young children: some ethical considerations. *Early Child Development and Care*, Vol. 175(6), pp. 553–565.

Gard, M. and Wright, J. (2005). *The Obesity Epidemic.* London: Routledge.

Gillespie, A and Johnson-Askew, W. (2009). Changing Family Food and Eating Practices: The Family-Food Decision Making System. *Annals of Behavioural Medicine* 38, (Suppl. 1):S31–S36. DOI: 10.1007/s12160-009-9122-7

Hallam, J., Lee, H., and Das Gupta, M. (2012). Multiple interpretations of child art- the importance of context and perspective. *Psychology of Aesthetics, Creativity, and the Arts.* Vol. 6 (2), pp. 185-193.

Halse, C. (2009). Bio-Citizenship: Virtue Discourses and the Birth of the Bio-Citizen. In J. Wright and V. Harwood (Eds.). *Biopolitics and the Obesity Epidemic.* New York: Routledge, pp. 45-59.

Hepburn, A. and Potter, J. (2011). Threats: Power, family mealtimes and social influence. *British Journal of Social Psychology*, Vol. 50, part1, pp. 99-120. DOI: 10.1348/014466610X500791

HISCIC (Health and Social Care Information Centre). (2014). *Statistics on Obesity, Physical Activity and Diet: England, 2014.* Retrieved from: www.hscic.gov.uk

Hollows, J., and Jones, S. (2010). 'At least he's doing something': Moral entrepreneurship and individual responsibility in Jamie's Ministry of Food. *European Journal of Cultural Studies.* Vol. 13 (3), pp. 307-322.

Kaufman, L and Karpati, A. (2007). Understanding the Sociocultural roots of Childhood Obesity: Food Practices among Latino families of Bushwick, Brooklyn. *Social Science & Medicine* Vol.64 (11), pp.2177-2188. DOI: 10.1016.2007.02.019

Karrebaek, M. S. (2012). "What's in Your Lunch Box Today?" Health, Respectability, and Ethnicity in the Primary Classroom. *Journal of Linguistic Anthropology*, Vol. 22(1), PP. 1–22. DOI: 10.1111/j.15481395.2012.01129.x.

Krombholz, H. (2012). The motor and cognitive development of overweight pre-school children. *Early Years: An International Research Journal.* Vol. 32 (1), pp.61-70.

Lang, T. and Rayner, G. (2007). Overcoming policy cacophony on obesity. *Obesity Reviews.* Vol.8 (1), pp. 165-181.

Leahy, D. (2009). Disgusting Pedagogies, in: Wright, J. and Harwood, V. (Eds.), *Biopolitics and the Obesity Epidemic.* New York: Routledge. Pp.172-182.

Lobstein, T. (2010). "The Size and Risks of the International Epidemic of Child Obesity". In F. Sassi (eds.), *Obesity and the Economics of Prevention: Fit Not Fat*, Paris: OECD Publishing, pp. 107-114. Retrieved from: http://dx.doi.org/10.1787/9789264084865-en

Lupton, D. (2011). 'The best thing for the baby': mothers' concepts and experiences related to promoting their infants' health and development. *Health, Risk and Society*, Vol.13 (7/8), pp. 637-651.

Lupton, D. (2014). 'How do you measure up?' Assumptions about 'obesity' and health-related behaviors in 'obesity' prevention campaigns. *Fat Studies*, Vol. 3(1), pp. 32-44.

Maynard, E. and Sims-Schouten, W. (2015). Early Support and Home Learning. *Report for Portsmouth City Council.*

Murray, S. (2009), Marked as 'Pathological': 'Fat' Bodies as Virtual Confessors. In: Wright, J. and Harwood, V. (Eds.), *Biopolitics and the Obesity Epidemic.* New York: Routledge. PP. 78-92.

O'Dea, J.A. (2005). "School-based health education strategies for the improvement of body image and prevention of eating problems: An overview of safe and successful interventions". *Health Education.* Vol. 105 (1), pp. 11-33.

OECD (2013). *Health at a Glance.* Retrieved from: http://www.oecd.org/els/health-systems/Health-at-a-Glance-2013.pdf

Papaioannou, M., Cross, M., Power, T., Liu, Y., Qu, H., Shewchuk, R., and Hughes, S. (2013). Feeding Style Differences in Food Parenting Practices Associated With Fruit and Vegetable Intake in Children From Low-income Families. *Journal of Nutrition Education and Behaviour.*Vol.45 (6), pp.643-65.

Parletta, N., Peters, J., Owen, A, Tsiros, M.D. and Brennan, L. (2012). Parenting styles, communication and child/adolescent diets and weight status: let's talk about it. *Early Child Development and Care.* Vol.182 (8), pp. 1089-1103.

Peerson, A. and Saunders, M. (2009). Health literacy revisited: what do we mean and why does it matter? *Health Promotion International.* Vol.24 (3), pp. 285-296.

Redsell, S.A., Edmonds, B., Swift, J.A, Weng, S., Nathan, D. and Glazebro, C. (2016). Systematic review of randomised controlled trials of interventions that aim to reduce the risk, either directly or indirectly, of overweight and obesity in infancy and early childhood. *Maternal & Child Nutrition.* Vol.12, pp. 24-38.

Rich, E. (2010). Obesity assemblages and surveillance in schools, *International Journal of Qualitative Studies in Education.* Vol.23 (7), pp. 803-821.

Rich, E. and Perhamus, L.M. (2010). Health surveillance, the body and schooling. *International Journal of Qualitative Studies in Education.* Vol. 23 (7), pp. 759-764.

Riley, S. Burns, M., Frith, H. and Markula, P. (Eds). (2008). *Critical bodies: Representations, Practices and Identities of Weight and Body Management.* London: Palgrave/ MacMillan.

Robinson· E. and Kirkham· T.C. (2014). Is he a healthy weight? Exposure to obesity changes: perception of the weight status of others, *International Journal of Obesity.* Vol.38, pp. 663–667.

Sanders, L., Shaw, J., Guez, G., Baur, C., and Rudd, R. (2009). Health Literacy and Child Health Promotion: Implications for Research, Clinical Care and Public Policy. *Paediatrics.* Vol.124 (3). DOI: 10.1542/peds.2009-1162G

Schwartz, M.B. and Puhl, R. (2003). Childhood Obesity: A societal problem to solve. *Obesity Reviews.* Vol.4 (1), pp. 57-71.

Shribman, S. and Billingham, K. (2009). Healthy Child Programme – Pregnancy and the first five years. Retrieved from: www.dh.gov.uk

Sims-Schouten, W. and Cowie, H. (2016). Ideologies & narratives in relation to 'fat' children as bullies, 'easy targets' and victims. *Children and Society.* DOI: 10.1111/chso.12147

Sims-Schouten, W. and Edwards, S. (2016). 'Man Up!' Bullying and Resilience within a Neoliberal Framework. *Journal of Youth Studies.* DOI: 10.1080/13676261.2016.1171831

Sims-Schouten, W., Riley, S.C.E. and Willig, C. (2007). Critical Realism: A presentation of a systematic method of analysis using women's talk of motherhood, childcare and female employment as an example. *Theory & Psychology.* Vol. 17(1), pp.127-150.

Sims-Schouten, W and Riley, S.E. (2013). Employing a form of critical realist discourse analysis for identity research: An example from women's talk of motherhood, childcare and employment. In: Edwards, P., O'Mahoney, J. and Vincent, S. (Eds.). *Putting Critical Realism into Practice: A Guide to Research Methods in Organization Studies.* Oxford: UOP.

Skouteris, H. (2012). Parental influences of childhood obesity. *Early Child Development and Care.* Vol. 184 (5), p. 941, DOI: 10.1080/03004430.2012.678589

Turner-Cobb, J. (2014). *Child Health Psychology.* London. Sage.

Wright, J. (2009). Biopower, Biopedagogics and the Obesity Epidemic. In: Wright, J. and Harwood, V. (Eds.). *Biopolitics and Obesity Epidemic.* New York: Routledge. PPs. 1-15.

Zivkovic, T., Warin, M., Davies, M., Moore, V., (2010). In the name of the child; the gendered politics of childhood obesity. *Journal of Sociology.* Vol.46 (4), pp. 375-392.

Chapter Three

Rethinking Literacy Policy: Race, Ethnicity and the "Poor Reader"

Alexandra Scherer

"People learn and get better with reading at home. Not me. Cos I have to teach my mum how to speak English better. She is speaking English so BAD". (Tina, Chinese, 7 years old)

Introduction

Reading is a foundation skill and practice and remains central to success both in school and subsequently in the labour market. In spite of the increase in the use of digital technology, reading remains a key skill for accessing text both virtual and on paper. Literacy has the potential for empowerment and can open doors to social mobility; it also offers those who are literate opportunities to make decisions about their own lives. Literacy is not a panacea, but it is a powerful example of something which facilitates learning, the acquisition of knowledge and the ability to influence the rules of play within society's organisations. Additionally, reading is positioned as a tool for social justice (Blackledge, 2000).

There are many children in the UK today who have very poor reading ability. Sometimes this is due to a mental or physical disability or learning difficulty, but often it is a fact of underachievement. This chapter examines children's underachievement in reading at school with specific reference to race and ethnicity. It challenges neo-liberal discourses which positions underachievement as the 'fault' or responsibility of individuals. It argues that reading and literacy is an important social issue which is cut through by intersections of race and ethnicity. These intersections are explored through both the literature and government policy. Institutional racism is often positioned by governments as a concern which has been resolved but within the academic literature debates continue to rage (Rollock, 2012; Ball et al., 2011; Gillborn, 2010; Reay, 2006).

This chapter starts with a brief history of reading policy to map out the debate around race, reading and attainment at school and the ways in which this is part of wider debates within left wing and neo-liberal discourses. A research project in which pupil voice was consulted about reading demonstrates how the debates can gain a new perspective through taking account of children's and teacher's opinions. This enables us to rethink the issue of race and class attainment in reading at school and look to the future.

Early reading policy

Ball argues (2010) that policy is performative and the key to rethinking the issues involved. What this rethinking involves is an excavation of historical policies to explore the way in which what went before influences policy today. Uncovering the historical tracks of reading policy shows how poverty and poor reading go hand in hand. Ball (2010) argues that to think of policy as something habitual which iterates and repeats itself, can provide useful insights into its role. A backward glance of education policy and specifically on reading reveals that Conservative governments have traditionally opted for monitoring, targeting, and accountability strategies, while Labour governments have chosen more laissez-faire approaches to policy, giving greater professional autonomy to individual teachers. The complex reasons for this are outside the scope of this chapter, but the broader issues involve attitudes on the right (Conservative) towards a small state in favour of the private sector and a competitive labour market. In contrast, attitudes on the left (Labour) have traditionally favoured an interventionist state committed to redistribution of wealth, raising the standard of living, in a regulated labour market. New Labour in the 1990s made a break with this pattern choosing to adhere to neo-liberal discourses more generally associated with conservative ideology. To reiterate, neo-liberalism places responsibility on the individual and in the case of reading on the individual child and his or her parents (carers). When the individual is seen as responsible then they have to create the conditions for their own success rather than it being the responsibility of the education system. Neo-liberal discourse is central to this chapter but also to other issues addressed in this book including obesity, dyslexia, and bullying where similar individualistic discourses can be found.

Contemporary reading policy can be traced back to the 1818 Report of the Parliamentary Select Committee on the Education of the Lower Orders of Society. It concluded that children in England were the worst educated in Europe, because poor English children and their families could not afford schooling (West, 1970). The implication was that if government provided schooling it would be for children of the poor not the rich, as the education of children of wealthy families was already adequate (Stephens and Unwin, 1987). The education for children in the 19th century came largely through humanitarian, religious, and social philanthropists' efforts, rather than those of government (Darnton, 2014). However, from the inception of reading policy, the "poor reader" was the poorly educated child, but also the child from a poor background (Sanderson, 1995).

There were Education Acts/Codes of Regulation, which focused on reading in the nineteenth century (1838, 1841-42, 1845), but in the Code of 1862 the figure of the "poor reader" surfaced. This Code was contentious at the time, as it enforced a 'payment by results' system whereby children who achieved age appropriate "levels" in reading earned money for the school (28P in modern money). Schools in poorer areas tended to perform less well, and therefore risked being closed down due to lack of funding. As the assessment focus narrowed, so too did the curriculum, as teachers taught to the test.

The 1862 Code saw the appointment of inspectors to visit schools and administer tests. There was no 'value added' measure to show the progress achieved by the school or teachers in augmenting the children's skills. Similar debates circulated at the time to those raised today in the context of testing children for SATs (Standard Attainment Tests taken at seven and eleven years old). These debates were about how testing leaves the least able children, and the poorest readers, behind and how a narrowing of the curriculum disadvantages all children, but especially those who are already disadvantaged academically and socially. Holding back funding to schools that did less well in poorer areas also fulfilled the role of "punishing the poor" (Wacquant, 2008, p.1), as these schools often failed and closed. Ball's (2010) discussion of the ability of policy to exert power "at a distance" (p.135) in today's children's lives, shows parallels between the past and today. The 1862 Code worked in much the same way as individual SATS targets today to track pupil grades, monitoring student's academic attainment from term to term. In both cases, policy iterates itself through making schools, teachers, and children "show" or produce evidence that they have met targets or reached certain levels, without necessarily improving overall learning (Ball, 2010).

From 1900 to 1944 there were only minor amendments to the Reading Code. The 1944 Education Act, which introduced radical structural reforms, did not explicitly make provision for reading. Some, like Apple (1986), however, argue that it segregated children in terms of ability, so that "poor readers" in the new tripartite system went into the Secondary Modern school, rather than Technical Colleges or Grammar Schools. The former were schools for children who failed the "Eleven Plus" examination, This examination was composed in part of reading, and some Marxist critics and historians (Apple, 1986; Sharp and Green, 1975) suggest this examination system was a way of keeping "working class" children out of Grammar Schools and away from opportunities for social mobility which both Technical Schools and Grammar Schools offered.

Race, at this point in the story of education policy, and in relation to literacy and attainment, still remains silent as it had done throughout the nineteenth century. There were some children from non-white backgrounds in the education system, but it was not until the 1970s that academics such as Carby (1982) and campaigners such as Coard (1971) began to discuss the issue of institutional racism as a way in which children from non-white backgrounds were kept out of educational institutions such as grammar schools and universities. Reay (2006) argues that the system was set up as a meritocracy whereby high grades meant being able to attend Grammar School. This, however, enabled a myth to be created that with hard work, bright, but poor or minority ethnic children could succeed. So the poor child could slip the identity of "poor reader" and perhaps pass as "good" if they were able to perform well in the Eleven Plus examination. The 1944 Education Act, it can be argued, discriminated against the "poor reader", though the "poor reader" is invisible in this policy.

Migration, literacy policy, and race

Between the 1950s and 1970s there was a "great debate" over reading generated by concern over literacy standards (Hall et al., 2010, p. 1). This debate coincided with waves of immigration from ex-colonies including India, the West Indies and Africa. Immediately on joining the British education system, the "Black" child, and particularly "Black boys" were labelled as the new "poor readers". The figure of the child underachieving in literacy ceased to be "class-based" and became "race-based", but also gendered as "Black girls" tended to do better. Cultural difference at this time became synonymous with arguments about "assimilation", and rather than different varieties of English being celebrated, policy and mainstream discourses positioned these children and their backgrounds as a "problem" for literacy learning.

There was, however, an atmosphere of experimentation, with different methods for teaching reading in schools, promoted in the academic literature and practiced in the classroom. Such debates became known as the "Literacy Wars" (Meek, 1996, p. 45). They raged between researchers and academics rather, than policy or decision makers, and were evidence of a more laissez-faire era with a Labour government and many Labour controlled local authorities responsible for education. The two key 'camps' in the debate were the "whole book" approach (Meek, 1996, p.45) which emphasised the importance of narrative and enjoying stories and pictures and the "phonics" camp (Stahl and Miller, 1989). In general, teachers were given autonomy to use which method they thought best with a particular child, or a combination of methods.

One strand of debate came from within experimental behavioural psychology with its: claims to be scientific and the concept of literacy as neutral - claims which were backed up by 'objective' data (Hall et al., 2010, p.1). The power of such scientific discourses is that they position themselves as "true" and therefore do not create space for alternative explanations about reading or solutions to help the "poor reader". For example, the argument that Black and African Caribbean children had inherently lower IQs than children from other backgrounds. Such "findings" remained salient for another 10 years, and caused large numbers of Black children to be labelled educationally subnormal, illiterate, and unable to read at all in some cases. These children were not only labelled as "poor readers"; they were also positioned as "not intelligent".

Researchers such as Carrington and Troyna (1988), Rogers and Christian (2007) and Picower (2009) discredit Jensen's findings suggesting that the social conditions in which the tests took place unfairly disadvantaged the children whose IQs were being tested. They were asked questions using language that they did not understand, or were intimidated by the researcher and the setting in which the tests took place. In Rogers and Christian's (2007) work, where Black children understood what was being asked of them, they performed just as well as children from other groups. The significance of such "scientific" approaches, as long as they are held up as "true", is that if practitioners are not seen to be following them, then they could be held responsible for lowering standards. Whilst there was not a strong discourse of accountability in the policy at the time, notions of assisting "poor readers" as much as possible remained salient.

There was a backlash in the press against such relative freedom for teaching reading at the end of the 1970s. Whitty and Menter cite that schools and teachers were labelled "Loony Left", and children were described as running riot because of a lack of school discipline and no clear focus on the crucial skill of reading (Coulby and Bash, 1991). Partly in response to this, the Assessment for Progress Unit (APU) was set up in

1974. This marked the end of the laissez-faire period in the teaching of reading and a return to monitoring children and reducing teachers' autonomy. The Pupil Progress Monitoring Act introduced individual reading targets and levels, as a way of differentiating the "poor reader" from the "better reader".

The 1988 Education Reform Act of the Conservative Government under Margaret Thatcher was contentious for many reasons including the national curriculum; the loss of power of Local Education Authorities (LEAs) and the transfer of management responsibilities to schools (LMS). In 1992, Ofsted was created to monitor and inspect schools and league tables were published to increase transparency and accountability. After these most radical reforms since the 1944 Education Act, the Black child remained positioned as the "poor reader" and the new policy ignored the issue of race and cultural differences in its provision. Troyna (1987) describes the Christian focus, and the Euro-centric curriculum as "embarrassing" (p.250).

Post 1944 the autonomy of LEAs in relation to race, reading and attainment had resulted in funding for sensitive resourcing and community-based services. For example ILEA (the Inner London Education Authority) produced books and resources to be used with young children, who represented Black and ethnic minority children in a range of everyday contexts. ILEA, however, was perceived by the Conservative government as too powerful and was disbanded in the 1988 Act. There were strong parallels here between the 1988 Education Act and the 1862 Code, as both were put in place by Conservative governments, and both sought reform through accountability, monitoring and competition.

The end of 18 years of Conservatives in power came with New Labour's election in 1997. Their manifesto included improving literacy and supporting "poor readers", now made visible as children being "failed" by schools. The promise was that no child would leave primary school unable to read. A Literacy Task Force (1997) was established, which saw a return to the scientism of the 1970s with a focus on "best practice" (Hall, 2010, p.7). The approach to the teaching of reading was set down in a national strategy where "one size fits all". It was not about diverse methods for diverse children, but race surfaced here as children from ethnic minorities and EAL (English as an additional language) backgrounds were monitored, to ensure they were not slipping behind. Such monitoring, however, rarely sought to monitor success, but to look for failure amongst children who displayed problems in learning to read.

What was notable was the convergence between Conservative and Labour government's policies and emphasis on accountability and monitoring-evidence of New Labour's shift in ideology toward neo-liberalism. Ball (2010) observes that such shifts are not new, and that while each incoming government "seeks to render the previous one's policies absurd" (p.216) and unthinkable, their own policies will build on those which went before. In terms of reading policy, and the "poor reader", such processes work to hide or make invisible the institutional power of the school. Whilst the Conservative and Liberal Democrat Coalition government (2010-2015) harnessed such discourses, it did not introduce policy that applied specifically to reading. A "no problem here" (Gaine, 1987) hegemonic discourse prevailed where individuals, rather than the system and its power structures, are blamed for poor reading.

Critical whiteness

There is an assumption in much of the literature on race and ethnicity that race must mean "blackness" or refer to "non-white" groups. "Critical Whiteness Studies", however, remain a marginal field in the study of race and ethnicity. There is little of this work which focuses empirically on children's experiences apart from Copenhaver-Johnson's research (2006) on reading and whiteness. Still less research theorises about children's understandings of, and place in, whiteness studies. In such theoretical work, the idea that it is important to challenge the notion that race always starts from blackness-as-difference is crucial. The ways in which whiteness is absent, and power is invisible are key to decoupling race and "blackness", but also to making clear the power of the school, and the normalising and normative hierarchies it creates. For example, schools create "good" and "poor" readers, and "good" and "not good" pupils, and these labels tend to stick throughout a child's schooling, and even throughout their lifetime. It is important to query the taken for granted assumption that race always means "blackness" when this is not the case. Debates have raged in the media and academic literature since the 1960s about race, inequality and education. Coard (1971) highlighted racial inequalities while the Rampton Report (1981) "highlighted widespread concern about the poor performance of West Indian children in schools" (p. 1).

Conservative and critical social science approaches place responsibility for the "problem" of academic disparities between ethnic groups on specific aspects of the social world. Some, in particular those with a conservative stance, adopt an essentialist approach blaming particular "races'' for their inherent, hereditary inadequacies. In social policy:

"Black Caribbean pupils, despite notable exceptions [are]…generally underrepresented in higher levels [of achievement] at both Key stage one [5-7 year olds] and Key stage two [7-11 year olds] (Parker-Jenkins, 2007, p.36)".

There have been long-standing debates in the media and research literature about institutional racism within the British education system. Policy and practice have changed significantly from a time where "too many" Black children in one school were seen as an overwhelming threat [and] who were removed and bussed to different schools (Blackledge, 2000; Carby, 1982; Coard, 1971). There remain today a disproportionately high number of children of African Caribbean heritage excluded from school (Blackledge, 2000). The main focus of critical sociological work about underachievement is on the position of the Black child at school and that institutional racism is still operating in English schools (Davies, 1993) and profoundly affects how children perform. A number of studies highlight the combination of low expectations and discrimination communicated by schools and their cultures. British researchers draw attention to the underlying assumptions of the school curriculum and the appropriateness of the metrics on which government testing is based (Gaine, 1995; Troyna, 1987; Gillborn, 2005, 2008), teacher expectations (Gillborn, 2008, Rollock, 2012), and the discursive practices in schools which privilege middle class values and regulatory frameworks (Reay, 1998 and 2006; Davies, 1993; Nind et al., 2003) have historically been identified as important in positioning the Black child as "the" underachiever in reading.

Gillborn's research theorising race and education is concerned with how "racism has always played favourites" (2008, p.34) and what children achieve is dependent in part upon teacher expectations. He considers the way children from particular ethnic groups are perceived hierarchically and receive distinctively different and more/less favourable treatment. His research suggests that the impact of this is pervasive. The informal curriculum (Gaine, 1995) is also seen to have a significant impact on producing inequality. Gillborn draws attention to the ways the British primary school curriculum remains Eurocentric and ethnocentric, in spite of the commitment to multiculturalism (Pollard and Triggs, 2001). The English Primary curriculum remains focused on homogeneously white views of Britain, which Gillborn (2005) argues contributes to low achievement of other groups who feel "outside" such a worldview. In particular the life experiences of ethnic groups are not articulated by the curriculum's language, referents, or content which influences individual children's literacy success and attainment, or lack of it. Research has also been critical of metrics for assessment, arguing they produce a hierarchy of "readers". The London Development Agency's (LDA) statistics show the variations in reading skills of children in their schools highlighting "Black boys". They start their schooling at broadly the same level as other pupils, but in the course of their studies they fall further and further behind. There is also a problem with seeing "Black" children as one homogenous group, when such a label refers to a broad range of ethnicities and backgrounds, and begs the question what is "real" Blackness.

The debates above tend to sit on the left of the political spectrum, denouncing society and its racist structures and practices for the persistence of the problem of inequalities in reading achievement (Troyna, 1987; Gaine, 1995; Gillborn, 2005; Rollock, 2012). Another focus in the literature is on "the home" and understanding its contribution to different academic results. A number of studies highlight issues such as different expectations in home and school. Neo-liberals and right wing policy makers see "problem homes" as culpable rather than schools or teachers (Gaine, 1987). Sewell re-positions the responsibility for educational failure upon attitudes that "Black boys" absorb from home where the masculinities they aspire to are not concerned with "hard work" at school. He employs discourses of individualism, which put forward the idea that endeavour and responsibility are there for the taking if the child is only willing. New research, however, indicates that institutional racism remains a very real aspect of young Black children and their families' experiences with the education system. Rollock (2012) shows self-described Black middle class children, despite their linguistic and cultural capital, and the advantages, both material and cultural, of their home upbringing, felt "outside" the school system, and these children continue to underachieve in literacy. Her work re-introduces the aspect of social class to the debate and suggests social class does not mitigate race.

Those in government use statistics to indicate overall improvements, such as the increased number of children achieving higher 'levels' in literacy. They point to spending on the Pupil Premium, which targets disadvantaged pupils as narrowing the gap, according to Middlemas and Easby (cited in Department for Education, 2014).The statistics are also used by some to suggest not enough is being done. Community groups and campaigners look to data on ethnicity which indicates some groups are attaining more than others, in order to promote inclusion and as reasons to set up community language schools:

> "Indian or mixed white and Asian backgrounds had the highest proportion of pupils achieving a good level of development…Pakistani pupils have a notably lower than average percentage points achieving a good level of development (50%)." (Marshall, 2014, p.6).

There is yet another approach taken to such statistics by Gillborn (2008) who argues that the testing itself is the problem, and the thing which needs to be changed. He suggests that children's achievement is marred by the social conditions in which testing takes place and by teacher expectations. To look at attainment statistics based on ethnicity is to ask the wrong question: the right one is about how to stop institutional racism and refocus an ethnocentric curriculum, to make it and teaching methods more inclusive. Certainly the use of statistics writes children's individual stories and voices out of the debate about race, ethnicity, and reading. The statistics in which the children are enmeshed, as well as the polarised debates discussed above, show a different picture of reading from the issues which children and teachers render salient.

Data from the field

This chapter ends with a discussion of data from a field study which took place in a multi-cultural community school in London over one school year. It provides fresh insights into debates about race, reading, and attainment by consulting pupil and teacher voices. The research design encompassed semi-structured interviews with pairs of children; peer interviews, where older children were first trained and then invited to interview younger children; and thirdly visual methods, where children were given picture diaries to draw and write about their experiences of being interviewed. Finally, interviews were held with teachers. The aim of the research was to consider reading and the ways in which children from ethnic minority backgrounds constructed their sense of self, and the identity which took place through the activity of reading picture books, and learning to read at school (Scherer, 2016).

The research involved 58 children but this report extracts responses from children in Year 2 (aged six and seven) only. The children were each interviewed twice, and participant observation took place. Parents and teachers were also interviewed. The children were asked open questions about the books they read at school, about what they thought of reading, and about what made a good reader. The books were used as "trigger materials" (Carrington and Troyna, 1988, p.9) and as a springboard for discussion. The books selected were from the 'Oxford Reading Tree' scheme used in schools for reading instruction. The books were deliberately at a low level of textual difficulty, in order not to disadvantage poor readers or cause any unnecessary decoding difficulties.

The context in which the research took place is pertinent. First, the school was in Special Measures and at risk of being closed down, and it was also failing in literacy. The children were predominantly from ethnic minority backgrounds with 98 per cent having English as an additional language (EAL). The way in which this affected teacher narratives, and impacted on children and their reading, was noteworthy as teachers sought to protect themselves against the blemish of poor results. The "reading" which government policy and the school focused on was the reading of English school books, and the "measuring" was of children's ability to decode text, along with comprehending it. It was worth framing reading in this way, as many children at the school attended Arabic community language classes. By the end of Primary school, many were proficient enough to take GCSE Arabic, usually taken at 16 years old. This, however, was not the "literacy" OFSTED inspectors measured. In the context of cultural diversity it is worth positioning reading at school as school-based literacy (Davies, 1993) rather than other literacies children may demonstrate outside school.

What follows is an excerpt from field notes of the first day spent in the school and the very first conversation between the researcher and the Year 2 teacher:

> Miss West said she thought it was a shame [the school] was a mostly Muslim school. She explained that lots of the children had a few weeks off at the end of the summer to go home to see family, who live abroad in the children's home countries, as the flights are so much cheaper, and then they don't come back until after Eid [in the second week of the autumn term] and so effectively missed an entire term of school. Whatever OFSTED say about having to enforce children's school attendance, you cannot make this happen, she pointed out. One of the measures against which schools are graded is school attendance. She suggested that it was for this reason that the school will never be very good.

Miss West linked the failing school with children's Muslim faith. The connection was somewhat tenuous as visiting family overseas and faith were not necessarily connected; children with family abroad came from a range of faith backgrounds including Hindu, Christian and no-religion. Here, the market economics of flight prices, a religious calendar not matching the schedule of a school system set up with a latently Christian ethos, was fused with school failure. There was no recognition that in English schools half terms coincide with All Souls day, Maundy Tuesday and Whitsun respectively while longer holidays are timed around Christmas and Easter. To celebrate Eid by taking the day off school is seen here as both a transgression of the law (children should be in school every day) and also a problem for reading attainment in Miss west's account. Her comment, harks back to an old argument about assimilation; should children at school in England be permitted to maintain their cultural, linguistic and religious identity, or conform to the system of the country which is their 'new' home? Place and family were inextricably linked for the children, who spoke of family living elsewhere whom they visited: "I go to Bangladesh summer times and stay with my uncle" (Nawaz, 7, Bangladeshi). "I am so excited when I go to Russia, to see my family" (Kylie, 6, Russian).

Miss West suggested that because children like Kylie and Nawaz missed school to visit family, the school was failing. Such an explanation operated as "symbolic self-protection" (Wacquant, 2008, p.274) in the sense that Miss West's culpability as a teacher for progressing the children's reading skills was under no question if the children did not attend school. Significantly, some six children did arrive a week or so after the start of term, but they were not in the group who were the lowest achievers, according to school based metrics. Also, three of these children were not Muslims, and two of the late arrivers were positioned in the 'top group' and were exceeding age related national curriculum expectations. The rest worked at national averages.

Lesley (aged 7, Indian) was one of the late arrivers, having been in India over the summer. She was a child who exceeded national levels for her age in reading, and discussed what work she did whilst "at home" in India:

"In my country, India, yeah, my mum made me do Key Stage one [academic comprehension exercises] books. I like to read novels, I like ones about horses. When it's too hot outside, I read every day with my cousins".

We see the way in which Lesley is both encouraged to read by her mother who sees the value of extra homework, and how she is internally motivated to read for leisure, enjoying books about horses, an activity which was part of her daily routine while abroad.

Returning to the quote at the start of this chapter, from Tina, one of the children positioned in the bottom reading group in her class. We see the way in which a philosophy toward learning at home, as well as a parents' skill in English, was key to Lesley's success and Tina's failure at reading. A match between home and school ethos on reading helps children succeed more than the effects of race or gender. This is central to rethinking the social issue of literacy and underachievement. Following research on working class children's educational failure, the children did not critique the way that, if "home" could not help, school had also failed to teach them to read well. The same could be said for Tina and her classmates.

Such an argument does not prove that "blame the home" discourses are "right", but rather that it is important to examine the system in place, in order to effectively revisit underachievement as a "social" issue in education. Lesley, who had cultural and literary capital at home, and Tina, who did not, enable us to examine the ways in which social class and being able to speak English, as well as parenting skills, interface with other factors such as race, ethnicity, culture and gender, in order to show that approaches in policy and the literature should be rethought. We also gain a sense that the focus on Muslim children missing school, the teacher's "reason" for these children's underachievement, do not stand up when examined further. While assimilation discourses ring through Miss West's analysis of the issues in the school, so does latent Islamophobia.

However, before writing white teachers off as racist and seeing this as a case of institutional racism, it is worth considering the position in which teachers, such as Miss West, find themselves. As we have seen, neo-liberal discourses at their core are concerned with accountability. In a school faced with imminent closure, the teacher had a huge responsibility for children meeting targets, where they had previously failed. The power of the institution, and relative powerlessness of the teacher to critique or resist this, is evident in Miss West's narrative. She sought to indicate that the issue with the children was "out there", rather than something she had created, or caused. We see here how accountability can create a culture of blame. The consequences of such blame are severe for individuals; as if they fail or succeed to teach children to read, the school remains open or can be closed down.

Conclusion

This chapter has considered links between the child, social class, race, ethnicity, and underachievement in reading. Having initially mapped the history of reading policy, we were able to see the way in which the figure of the "poor reader" surfaced over time, and how this figure was initially linked to "class" and then came to be strongly linked to the male, "Black child". Drawing upon these points, it was possible to see how political discourses across time have influenced reading policy, and that there are patterns in political ethos which repeat and circulate rather than change, so that the same issues are revisited rather than resolved.

The two key points made in the literature review were how politicised the debate is, and how neo-liberal discourses seek to erase the issue of broader inequality and underachievement, seeing it as the responsibility of the individual and the family, not society. Race, ethnicity, attainment, and reading can only come back into sharp focus if dominant neo-liberal discourses are critiqued, in order to see the part the system has to play. Ball's (2010) notion of "policy as "performative" provides a useful vantage point for exploring the issue. Having considered the polarised debates on race, reading, and attainment, we gained a sense of how statistics are manipulated particularly by those on the right of the argument to make it appear that the issue has been resolved. Those on the left in the debate argue that if you accept that "Black" children are underachieving, you are positioning yourself as right wing and not taking a critical enough approach. Repositioning "race" as something in the "Critical Whiteness" field enables us to see the way in which race, as "Blackness", is positioned as a "problem" in much of the literature. The final section explored teachers' and children's narratives, and provided a different lens through which to view the issues of race, reading, and attainment.

Future work on issues affecting children's lives should seek to consult children. In the Sociology of Childhood, the idea of involving children in the research process and seeing them as socially competent (Prout and James, 1990) are taken for granted assumptions. These notions have not mapped across to education policy, or race and ethnicity research, especially where researching younger children is concerned. Positioning the debates around this area as inherently political and politically motivated is key. It is through such positioning, and also through foregrounding children's voices, that we are able to revisit the social issue of reading and 'race' in schools, and the ways in which it interacts with class and gender. Reading success depends upon the readers' stance whether we see it as the failure of the child or the system failing the child. This remains in dispute!

Bibliography

Apple, M. (1986). *Teachers and Texts: A Political Economy of Class and gender relations in education.* London: Routledge.

Ball. (2010). 'New voices new knowledges and the new politics of education research: the gathering of a perfect storm?' *European Educational Research Journal,* Vol. 9 (2), pp.124-137.

Ball, S. Vincent, C., Gillborn, D., and Ruddock, N. (2011). *The Educational Strategies of the Black Middle Classes.* London: Institute of Education.

Blackledge, A. (2000). *Primary School Literacy Power and Social Justice.* Stoke on Trent: Trentham Books.

Carby, H. (1982). 'Schooling in Babylon', in CCCS (Ed). *The Empire Strikes Back: race and racism in 70s Britain, Birmingham*. London: Routledge.

Carrington, B. and Troyna, B. (Eds.) (1988). *Children and controversial issues: Strategies for the early and middle years of schooling*. Hove: Psychology Press.

Coard, B. (1971). *How the West Indian child is made educationally subnormal in the British School system: the scandal of the Black child in schools in Britain.* London: New Beacon for the Caribbean Education and Community Worker's Association.

Copenhaver-Johnson, J. (2006). 'Talking to children about race: The importance of inviting difficult conversations'. *Childhood Education,* Vol. 83 (1), pp. 12-22.

Coulby, D. and Bash, L. (1991). *Contradiction and conflict: the 1988 Education Act in action.*

Darnton, R. (2014). 'First steps toward a history of reading'. *Australian Journal of French Studies,* Vol. 51(2), pp.152-177.

Davies, B. (1993). *Shards of glass: Children reading and writing beyond gendered identities.* Cresskill, NJ: Hampton Press

Department for Education. (2014). *National curriculum assessments at key   2 in England, 2014 (Revised).* London, TSO.

Gain, C. (1987). *No problem here: a practical approach to education and" race" in white schools.* London: Hutchinson.

Gaine, C. (1995). *Still no problem here.* Stoke on Trent: Trentham Books.

Gillborn, D. (2005). 'Education policy as an act of white supremacy: Whiteness, critical race theory and education reform'. *Journal of Education Policy,* Vol. 20(4), pp. 485-505.

Gillborn, D. (2008). *Racism and education: Coincidence or conspiracy?* London: Routledge.

Gillborn, D. (2010). 'The colour of numbers, surveys, statistics and deficit-thinking about race and class'. *Journal of Education Policy,* Vol. 25(2), pp.253-276.

Hall, K., Goswami, U., Harrison, C., Ellis, S., and Soler (Eds.). (2010). *Interdisciplinary perspectives on learning to read: Culture, cognition and pedagogy.* London: Routledge.

Marshall, S. (2014). *Early Years Foundation Stage Profile attainment by pupil characteristics, England.* London: DfES.

Meek, M. 'Book Learning and Literacy Information'. In Baker, D., Clay, J., and Fox, C. (1996). *Challenging ways of knowing: in English, Mathematics and Science.* London: Routledge.

Middlemas, J., Easby, J. (cited in DoE 2014 Retrieved from: https://www.gov.uk/government/uploads/system/uploads/.../SFR50_2014_Text .pdf

Nind, M., Sheehy, K., Rix, J., and Simmons, K. (2003). *Inclusive education: Diverse perspectives.* London: David Fulton Publishers Ltd.

Parker-Jenkins, M. (2007). *Raising attainment of pupils from culturally diverse backgrounds: aiming high.* Thousand Oaks California: Paul Chapman.

Picower, B. (2009). 'The unexamined whiteness of teaching: how white teachers maintain and enact dominant racial ideologies'. *Race, Ethnicity and Education*, Vol.12 (2), pp.197-215.

Pollard, A., and Triggs, P. (2001). *What pupils say: Changing policy and practice in primary education*. London: Bloomsbury Publishing.

Prout, A., James, A. (1990). *Constructing and reconstructing childhood: New directions in the sociological study of childhood* (2nd Ed (1997) Published by Routledge Ed.). Oxford: Routledge.

Rampton, B. (1981). *The Rampton Report: West Indian children in our schools*. London: HMSO.

Reay, D. (2006). The zombie stalking English schools: social class and educational inequality. *British Journal of Educational Studies,* Vol.54 (3), pp 288-307. DOI: 10.1111/j.1467-8527.2006.00351.x

Rogers, R., and Christian, J. (2007). ''What could I say?' A critical discourse analysis of the construction of race in children's literature'. *Race Ethnicity and Education*, Vol. 10(1), pp. 21-46.

Rollock, N. (2012). 'The invisibility of race: Intersectional reflections on the liminal space of alterity'. *Race Ethnicity and Education*, Vol. 15(1), pp.65-84.

Scherer, A. (2016). *Children, Literacy and Ethnicity: Reading Identities in the Primary School*. London: Palgrave Macmillan.

Sharp, R. and Green, A. (1975). *Education and Social Control: A Study in Progressive Primary Education*. London: Routledge.

Stahl, S., and Miller, P. (1989). 'Whole language and language experience approaches for beginning reading: A quantitative research synthesis'. *Review of Educational Research*, Vol. 59(1), pp. 87-116.

Troyna, B. (1987). 'Beyond Multiculturalism: towards the enactment of anti-racist education in policy, provision and pedagogy'. *Oxford Review of Education,* Vol. 13(3), pp.307-320.

Wacquant, L. (2008). *Urban outcasts: A comparative sociology of advanced marginality*. New York: Polity.

PART 2

CHAPTER FOUR

DIGITAL SOCIAL NETWORKING IN SECONDARY SCHOOLS

SIMON EDWARDS

Introduction

Significant research over the last 35 years has investigated bullying, and more recently cyberbullying, amongst children and young people, particularly in schools (Fanti, Demetriou and Hawa, 2012; Schneider, O'Donnell, et al., 2012; Davies, 2010; Kowalski, Limber and Agatson, 2012). Cyberbullying in particular, has become the focus of debate as this broad umbrella term covers a range of online activities (Paul, Smith and Blumberg, 2012; Davies, 2010; DfE, 2014) and is largely undefined. It is broadly summarised in UK government policy using the same terms as offline bullying; "behaviour by an individual or group, repeated over time, that intentionally hurts another individual or group either physically or emotionally" (DfE, 2014, p. 6). The same document further states "cyber-bullying is a different form of bullying and can happen at all times of the day, with a potentially bigger audience, and more accessories as people forward on content at a click" (p. 6). This definition, however, is not precise and what constitutes harm and how intentions are understood, is largely left to interpretation.

In addition, much of this research has focused on interpreting bullying and cyberbullying based on a definition signified within a politicised understanding of language and behaviours. For example, language used to interpret incidents perceived as cyberbullying often focusses on notions of perpetrator, victim, aggression, and unjustified intent to harm (DfE, 2014; Kowalski et al., 2012; Tokuma, 2010; Ttofi and Farrington, 2011). However, a young person's practice, which is defined by practitioners and adults as cyberbullying might not be seen by the young person as cyberbullying.

This chapter responds to concerns that current fears surrounding the umbrella term cyberbullying may amount to a moral panic (Cesaroni, Downing, and Alvi, 2012). Furthermore, Cesaroni et al. (2012) argue that some activities interpreted as cyberbullying may be normal to young people (e.g. friends who have fallen out sending hurtful messages online or a young person sending a message to another young person who has upset their friend). Other researchers have called for new interpretative frameworks for young people's use of digital social networking media and issues related to their use (Livingstone, Mascheroni and Murru, 2011; Paul, Smith and Blumberg, 2010). Yet, although there is a growing response to this call these frameworks still draw on language of aggression, perpetrator and victim (Kernaghan and Elwood, 2013; Paul et al., 2010).

The chapter re-thinks some young people's digital social networking practices, which are interpreted negatively and in some cases as cyberbullying. It first sets the context of current research and debates around cyberbullying and then presents the findings from a small ethnographic doctoral study in which a group of young people's socialising practices and language codes managed offline and online (text messaging and sms) were explored. Their social practices are viewed through the lens of Giddens (1991), who claims the self-project has become a highly reflexive and collaborative task co-constructed within the daily routines of managing relationships. This condition has emerged as a consequence of gradually discarding the fixities of the past (class based affinities and traditional notions of institutions including the family) from which the self-project was once orientated (Bauman, 2000).

The emergence of digital social networking media; text messaging, MSN messenger (1999), Myspace (2003), Facebook (2004), Bebo (2005), Twitter (2006), WhatsApp (2009), Instagram (2010) and Snapchat (2011), has motivated young people in particular to use these media as an extension of their offline socialising practices and fulfil the desire to maintain and affirm their self-identity with peers (Livingstone and Brake, 2010). Thus, young people's social practices observed online and offline are understood to be part of a wider strategy to manage their self-identities and narratives.

In summary, the chapter re-thinks young people's digital social networking practices, which might currently be seen in some cases by practitioners and policy makers as negative or as cyberbullying. It challenges some current perceptions of cyberbullying, underpinned by notions of unjustified aggression and intent to harm, and adopts the premise that young people's communication online is motivated by the desire to *construct,* rather than *deconstruct* relationships. It recognises their need to manage social practices and relationships online as an intrinsic condition of their existence in order to maintain their self-identities and narrative.

A historical overview of cyberbullying research; approaches to risk and intent to harm

The current focus on school sites as a genesis of bullying issues has its origins in early research which focused on bullying between school aged young people (Nansel et al., 2001). Correlations were drawn between age, gender, frequency, types of bullying and the considerable impact bullying had on the victim's mental health and academic attainment (Kowalski et al., 2012). Subsequently a significant proportion of research focused on bullying in school sites (Fanti et al., 2012), but the focus then shifted towards a psycho-educational approach characterised by risk and protective factors and where a range of cognitive and effective variables were analysed (Ortega-Ruiz and Nunez, 2012). Assumed victims' and perpetrators' perceptions of threat and control, and the consequences of being involved in bullying, were explored and analysed.

This psycho-educational approach further explored how victims might be supported, for example, by developing coping skills, in order to feel less helpless when bullied. Interventions were designed particularly to develop resilience amongst victims of bullying. Support for the victim, through encouraging resilience or reparation through dialogue, such as restorative justice approaches, became central.

However, as young people started using digital media and social networking sites issues related to what was perceived as cyberbullying on these sites emerged. Although researchers increasingly saw cyberbullying as an online social problem (Ortega-Ruiz and Nunez 2012, p. 605) there has been a growing understanding that young people's online social networking is linked to offline relationships often originating within school environments (Paul et al., 2010). Hence school sites have become a primary context for research and intervention. Although, this is largely because the school has a duty to intervene (DfE, 2014) when parents or a child complain that another child in the school is making unpleasant remarks about them, even if this occurs via social media and outside of school time.

Subsequently, cyberbullying has become defined using similar terms as offline bullying (Gorzig and Frumkin, 2013). Yet, drawing a consensus on what cyberbullying actually is and what it involves has proved problematic (Marczak and Coyne, 2010). Ortega-Ruiz and Nunez (2012, p. 605) recognise this and draw on a number of researchers and commentators to summarise cyberbullying as:

"a social problem of harassment, intimidation, bullying, and unjustified aggressiveness, using digital devices, which one person or group inflicts upon another person (the victim), either protracted over time or short-term, but whose harassment effects remain and are diffused exponentially, and the victim cannot defend him or herself alone quickly and effectively".

Further attempts to define cyberbullying (Kowalski et al., 2012) also reflect definitions of bullying in physical sites but locate these behaviours on digital networking sites. Drawing on interpretations of bullying presented by Olweus (1993) and Nansel et al. (2001) they identify a further feature of cyberbullying as "aggressive behaviour that involves an imbalance of power" (cited in Kowalski, Limber and Agatston 2012, p. 17). They argue this aggressive behaviour can be defined by strength or social status and is repeated over a period of time. It is this definition which is currently summarised in UK government policy as "behaviour by an individual or group, repeated over time that intentionally hurts another individual or group either physically or emotionally" (DfE, 2014, p. 6). It will be referred to in this chapter, as it is used to guide practitioners within the school setting.

Taking this broad definition of cyberbullying as its starting point a growing body of research is underpinned by the assumption that a significant proportion of online incidents occur between friendship groups originating either within the school environment or outside the school context, but which "often relates to school-based relationships" (Paul, Smith and Blumberg, 2010, p. 158). Guidance for practitioners and parents (such as Child Exploitation and Online Protection) developed in response to this. Research subsequently focuses on identifying protective factors and developing interventions, which seek to either reduce risk of cyberbullying by educating young people and adults (primarily parents) about the risks and safer use of digital media (Byron, 2008; Byron, 2010) or by offering guidance and support for young people once they encounter issues perceived as cyberbullying (Think-U-Know, Kidsmart and Cybermentors). Subsequent interventions related to cyberbullying, particularly in secondary schools, offer censoring and protective measures based on the premise that young people's actions are underpinned by "intent to harm", "unjustified aggression", "poor inter-personal relationships" or "risk taking behaviours" (DfE, 2014; Ofcom, 2008; Ofcom, 2014; Livingstone and Brake, 2010).

Conceptual understandings of cyberbullying by school-based practitioners are therefore understood within the limitations of this interpretative framework and its assumptions related to notions of perpetrator, victim and aggression, unjustified intent to harm and an imbalance of power (Kowalski et al., 2012; Tokuma, 2010; Ttofi and Farrington, 2011; Ortega-Ruiz and Nunez, 2012). Moreover, this interpretative framework largely ignores the young people's interpretations of their practices and experiences and does not view their practices from a wider sociological perspective. Furthermore, assumptions and interventions responding to this interpretative framework focus on surveillance, control and censorship (Marczak and Coyne, 2010), which limits the possibilities for developing more appropriate interventions.

Researching young peoples' relationship building strategies

The following section considers the findings of a small ethnographic study, which formed part of a larger doctoral project in a youth centre and secondary school site. The larger doctoral project (Edwards, 2013) was designed to explore young people's social practices in order to understand more fully issues related to conflict between the young peoples' and a school curricula understanding of language. The findings from the research provide a useful interpretative framework for some of their practices online and challenge assumptions underpinning interpretations of some of their practices, which might be otherwise viewed as bullying or cyberbullying.

The doctoral project explored the cultural world of 11 secondary school students attending an alternative curriculum programme. The study was sited in a school-based youth centre and was carried out by the author of this chapter, who was also the youth centre manager. Issues, which led to the research, were encountered when the young people attempted a GCSE teamwork assessment. Teamwork was conceptualised by them as managing relationships whilst completing a task as a group. The young people primarily viewed the task as a vehicle for managing interpersonal relationships, where there were no perceived individual roles; tasks were shared and swapped according to their value in supporting a friendship. Language was subsequently made problematic where the young people's and school based discourses and conceptual understandings of activities and practices appeared to conflict. The initial study forms the research basis for this chapter and an interpretative lens through which to view issues related to cyberbullying. The study aimed to explore the linguistic dimensions of the young people's practices in order to develop an intervention, and interpret processes, and roles related to their conceptual understanding of teamwork, and enable them to complete the teamwork assessment and the GCSE.

In order to gain insight into how the young people conceptualised teamwork and how they understood this in relation to their social practices, the linguistic and behavioural dimensions of those social practices were explored both online and offline. It is this insight which is useful when discussing issues related to cyberbullying. The researcher took the position of participant-observer, where the young people's perspectives of their worlds were being talked about during informal discussions. The socializing practices and language codes of the young people attending the alternative curriculum sessions were not disassociated from their basic sociality and cultural group norms. Therefore, the research extended to observing 300 of their peers social practices across a range of youth club sessions, which many of the alternative curriculum group members attended, in order to locate the latter's practices within their peers' wider social norms.

Observations were made by sitting with groups of young people as they socialized and by asking junior youth leaders to video record their peers. This approach enabled the researcher to observe and record the young people's practices and language codes without disrupting his established youth worker role as sitting and talking with young people whilst observing them, and with peers video recording each other, which was part of the normal session activities. Observations did not include noting the content of digital social networking at this stage, other than noting that text messaging was being used to communicate during the sessions. Two of the young people attending the alternative curriculum sessions and eight junior youth leaders participated in focus group interviews in order to help the researcher interpret observation recordings.

Findings – Social networking

The junior youth leaders and the researcher identified six relationship building behaviour categories negotiated during the sessions, which could be interpreted as negative or positive behaviors. Figure 4.1 describes these behaviours. Once the young people's relationship building behaviours had been categorised the language codes used in each behaviour were examined. The researcher used Bernstein's (1971) theory of language codes as a guide, which contain mediate (verbal) and immediate (non-verbal) gestures. Bernstein claims that mediate and immediate gestures form either formal or public language codes, and although all codes are open and are understood and used by all social classes, some codes characteristically reflect different social groups; specifically middle and working classes. A public language code is used primarily by working class groups and

> "(...) contains a high proportion of short commands, simple statements and questions where the symbolism is descriptive, tangible, concrete, visual and of low order of generality, where the emphasis is on the emotive rather than the logical implications".(Bernstein, 1971, p. 28)

The characteristics of a formal language code is used primarily by middle class groups and reflects

> "...accurate grammatical order and syntax regulate what is said. Individual qualification is verbally mediated through the structure and relationships within and between sentences. That is, it is explicit". (Bernstein, 1971, p. 55).

Figure 4.1. Behaviour categories

Behaviour	Description
Building	Two or more students pulling together to overcome a situation or complete a task. Tasks as vehicles for achieving goals where immediate gestures indicated calm, focused attention with little mutual eye contact. Joking formed a significant part of this behaviour between peers; short sentences but mainly full sentences used.
Maintaining	Free expression of peers within a group of friends where body language is presented as open and relaxed working towards a common goal. Immediate gestures; open, relaxed postures with eye contact, low to medium volume chatter focusing on social activities. Full sentences primarily.
Protecting	Assertive claiming of social space by a person or persons towards peers such that they affirm themselves and their identity. Medium volume short statements with arm waving and exaggerated gestures used to make peers aware of danger. Walking away from threat or turning towards each other.
Supporting	Extending support to a peer or peers to help them be

Behaviour	Description
	themselves. An action depicting the words 'I accept you.' Calm and relaxed, consistent eye contact or maintaining spatial position in relation to peers. Words of encouragement to peers using full sentences.
Exploring	Conscious decision to wait (in social space) until you feel safe and ready to move into another vacant social space or mingle with another crowd of peers. High volume and excitable statements but slow and deliberate actions.
Welcoming	Negotiated invite to peers to join a group or individual creating a sense of wellbeing ('thumbs up'). Huddling together or close contact within personal space. High volume statements and jokes towards one another with some full sentences.

Source: Edwards (2013).

Bernstein's ideas were used as an analytical tool to help the researcher frame the young peoples' language codes within each behaviour category. Each conversation and behaviour was analysed across a range of social relationship building activities. This helped the researcher understand how language was used by young people to socially position themselves with peers and signify their intent within these relationships. Essentially the emerging framework enabled the researcher to understand how the young people signified and conceptualised teamwork activities in their social practices. The researcher then discussed these activities with the young people and helped them interpret their understanding of teamwork into the language needed to complete the GCSE assessment.

When analysed against school post code data, the findings indicated that a public language code was used by young people from both middle and working class backgrounds in either restricted or elaborated forms. A restricted form of code Bernstein claims "facilitates the construction and exchange of 'social' symbols (…) an elaborated code facilitates the construction and exchange of 'individuated' symbols." (1971, p. 78). For example the following statements made by the young people represent restricted public codes:

"Cos if it's good, I'll like it"

"Go away titch no-one likes you, go home"

The following statements represent a more elaborated public code;

> *"Like when Liam was on the computer, I went to the computer to see if he was doing it"*

> *"Oh go on Sue can you send me pictures of him?"*

Language it seemed was not necessarily located within class based affinities as Bernstein claimed. However, the young people's use of an elaborated and restricted public code did vary according to the behaviours they signified and the level of relationship in which they were used.

A restricted public code, where sentences were short, using explicit expressions and words known between each person, was often used within **protecting** and **exploring** behaviours. Young people were observed **protecting** and **exploring** primarily when positioning themselves relationally with peers and adults within an established social group. Tones of voice and other non-verbal gestures signified subjective intent, which corresponded with the behaviour descriptors in Table 4.1 above. For example, the statement below reflects, according to the young people helping with the research, the behaviour descriptor for **protecting** and was observed where a group of junior leaders were planning a Big Brother (mimicking the television program at the time) youth event, during a youth club session. The young people had been members of the group for approximately 18 months but were not close friends;

> *"Go away titch no-one likes you, go home"*

Spoken assertively with firm, loud tone by a male to another male after the male referred to as "titch" tried to joke with the other male's female friend) - **Protecting**
The following examples of **exploring** were observed in an alternative curriculum session which a group of young people had attended for 10 months;

> *"It's got little turns – twists inside and then (giggling)…"*

Female young person describing a sausage to male young person when she was cooking- **Exploring**

> *"that's a bit perverted ….I'm joking ha'*

Male young person responding to comment above loudly and excitedly - **Exploring**

A more elaborated, or tacit public code, was primarily used during conversations related to future orientated goals (such as talking about future plans). It was observed being used in *building* behaviours between staff, young people and peers or *maintaining* conversations between groups of young people who were close friends or family members. Below are examples of *building* and *maintaining* conversations where a group of young people are chatting during an alternative curriculum session;

> *"Oh go on Sue can you send me pictures of him?"*

Female young person to female staff member about staff fiancé – sitting relaxed with legs folded – *Building*

> *"I'm getting an xport (*mini-motorcycle*) on Saturday."*

Male young person speaking calmly with eye contact to male staff member – *Building*

> *"Josh is alright, he is allowed to"*

Calm tone of voice, sitting relaxed on seat - female young person to male friend – *Maintaining*

Language signified behaviours being managed within specific individual or group relationships. For example, language signified differences between a range of behaviours when observed over 10 to 15 minute periods. Language, including tone of voice, facial expressions, words used and sentence structure changed as each behaviour changed, making each behaviour distinct. For example, language would change as young people made a transition from *welcoming,* when first meeting each other at a club session, to chatting and *maintaining* their relationships. A young person's language would also change as they momentarily supported a friend who was upset and who had just joined a group or when *protecting* the group from someone who was butting in on a conversation. This practice was seen in both of the above sessions where the young people helping with the observations said the behaviours they primarily observed were *building* (Big Brother) and *maintaining* relationships (alternative curriculum session) but some of the young people in each group momentarily *explored* and *protected* their individual relationships and social positions within the group activity (Seigler, DeLoache and Eisenburg, 2011; Erikson, 1986; Duck, 2011).

A further example of this social positioning can be seen below where a young person, Kim, was observed managing multiple and multi-directional relationships online and offline with a peer, close friend on a mobile phone, and me whilst completing a short piece of coursework in an alternative curriculum session. She had asked me for permission to answer her phone because her close friend, who attended another school, was in hospital. Four different behaviours were identified by me, and the young people helping with the research. Kim was primarily *maintaining* her relationship with me

> Kim *"Hello I'm in school Rachel...Hello ...I'm at school ...no I've got work experience"* – *Maintaining*
>
> Lance – (shouts from across the room): *"Is that Ruth?* - *Exploring*
>
> Kim to Rachel – *"all right bye"* – *Maintaining*
>
> Lance - (Walks past Kim) *"Was that Rachel?"* - *Exploring*
>
> Researcher to Lance – *"It was"*
>
> Researcher turns to Kim) *"how is she?"* - *Building*
>
> Kim – *"yeah alright"* – *Maintaining*
>
> Researcher to Kim – *"I haven't seen her for a while"* – *Maintaining*
>
> Kim to researcher – *" Well she's not going back to Davison's no more she's refusing to go cos she wants to move back here"* – *Maintaining*.
>
> One minute later Lance tries to get Kim's attention and plays a song on his mobile phone – *Exploring*
>
> Kim to Lance – *"you can send that to me Lance"* – *Protecting* by not being too friendly

In the above example language regulates transitions; that is, language signifies what Deleuze calls subjective intent (cited in Colebrook, 2002) within and between behaviours and within and between relationships.

Each observed session consisted of a series of behaviours acted out between individuals and groups and language signified collectively shared intensities emerging from multiple perceptions of social practices, thus creating and sustaining their reality. Their reality, however, was not solely identified within organisational discourse engaged in the school environment; an assumption embedded in organisational interpretations of issues related to social networking both online and offline. Reality, for these young people was primarily identified within relational discourse, managed within a multi-directional narrative where *building* and *maintaining* with peers and significant others enabled them to build social capacity.

Digital social networking; reconstructing behaviours online

The following section presents data from further research, which explored the signifying contexts and linguistic dimensions of the young people's social practices online. An assumption underpinning this research was that offline relationship building practices and linguistic structures were being reconstructed online in order to maintain a shared reality. Two focus group sessions were conducted, each with six females and six males who attended alternative curriculum sessions, and the interviews lasted an hour, The aim was to explore how the young people communicated online using the tools available at the time (Text messaging, MSN, Bebo and Facebook).

Two key findings emerged and are presented below. They guide the discussion later when re-thinking issues related to cyberbullying in schools;

1) *Reconstructing reality;* Language and relationship building strategies are not self-referential online. Language codes and behaviours managed offline are constantly being reconstructed and maintained online.

2) *Signifying a shared self-project;* Language online signifies transitions between levels of relationship and behaviours and manages the continuity of shared narratives.

Although only two focus groups were carried out, the findings provide some insight into young people's use of digital media as a vehicle for reconstructing their socialising practices and maintaining their perspective of reality. The males said that they didn't use social media very often but preferred just to meet up offline in pre-arranged sites such as a park. At other times they would text each other and arrange to meet. When they did 'meet' online, using Facebook, they said they would joke a lot with each other but wouldn't specifically go online in order to talk to new people;

"We joke a lot"

"I wouldn't talk to anyone new"

"Whatever comes out, it's random"

Joking, they explained, functioned to test relationships, develop trust and reduce anxiety. In addition to this, joking online and offline was described by the young males as either *building* or *welcoming* people within their existing friendship group, which had initially been established in the community, as they all lived near each other.

Data findings from the female focus group also reflected offline socialising practices being reconstructed online. When discussing how they communicated on MSN, Bebo, Texting and Facebook, the girls explained that hugs, saying hello or goodbye offline would be re-constructed online by spelling words phonically and adding emoticons. They said they tried to use emoticons (hearts, faces or other symbols showing emotions) on digital social media which signified a range of emotions used offline. Care was taken to place them at various points in sentences and the choice of emoticon depended on the level of relationship and type of behaviour being managed between each person. These helped to signify subjective intent, but within significant other relationships. One participant explained:

> *"(....) let me get the point across, say if you like are annoyed with somebody but then you are not too annoyed with them to not be their friend ...you know like every things still alright it's like that I guess".*

Phonic spelling of words was used in established relationships in order to signify relationship behaviour transitions within a conversation online. The conversation below reflects a more restricted public code used for initial *welcoming*. The participant said this welcome reflected a common set of communally shared online communications:

> *"How R U m8"*

> *"Yeah not bad thanks"*

> *"KL"*

The young people explained that 'KL' (cool) signified the offline relationship that had been re-established online and implied a transition to further communication could be made. This *welcoming* language checked the level of relationship between each person before the conversation could develop further. Language here regulated and signified a transition between behaviours and subjective intent in order for the young people to further *build* or *maintain* their shared narrative online.

These behaviours and language codes were reconstructed online, using the characters and tools available on media at the time. The young people said that once the relationship had been re-established online they would then ask each other what they were doing later. The example below was a typical individualised, tacit expression used between friends when communicating online:

> *"probs goin outage".*

It was explained that adding the term *age* to a word was a friendly term, also used to develop the relationships between close and not so close friends. The term "age" signified a friendly personality and the intention to *build* a relationship and socialise further;

> Leanne - *"Yeah yeah lovage is like the main one ...see you soonage"*

> Sarah - *"...I say lovage as being friendly yeah to my boy... mates and some of my girlfriends"*

Data findings also showed that when communicating online with people whose identity was not immediately known, language codes similarly reflected those used offline. For example, a more restricted code, using explicit language with no emoticons, was used to *protect* one-self. Jess was asked how she might respond to someone she didn't know who had contacted her online. Her language was restricted and explicit, not allowing any emotions to be shown but neither to appear rude

> *"Yes you go like hi who's this?" – Protecting*

Sarah added that if she were the unknown person who was attempting to develop a new relationship with Jess online, she would reply to Jess's question with

> *"...and like hey I got your number off someone who's this? ... My name's Sarah." - Building*

Sarah and Jess both said Sarah's communication was an attempt to *build* a new relationship. The language used shows a more elaborate code being used by Sarah to *build* the relationship than the restricted code being used to *protect* the relationship by Jess. However, at this stage of the relationship the elaborated code did not use tacit expressions associated with *maintaining* or *building* an established relationship.

Whether offline or online, the primary socialising behaviours being managed were *building* and *maintaining* and *supporting, exploring, welcoming* and *protecting* were subservient to these. The young people, regardless of social background, used a public language code within the youth centre and school environment which showed a mixing of once defined class based language codes used to manage and regulate a multi-directional self-narrative. There was no immediately recognisable distinction between 'class' uses of elaborated or restricted public codes. What became recognisable though, as a distinction in their application, was the use of elaborated codes to signify *building* and *maintaining* behaviours within conversations related to, 1) an ongoing shared narrative, and 2) future orientated goals. The key value of a restricted code however, lay in its ability to signify strategic social positioning (*welcoming, exploring, protecting* and *supporting*) within these contexts.

Re-thinking issues to do with digital social networking in secondary schools

The findings above reflect Giddens' (1991) view of the self as a highly reflexive and future orientated project for which a shared narrative and self-identity is managed and co-constructed within the daily routines of managing relationships. Community bonds and cultural norms established within offline relationships enable the *building* and *maintaining* of social capital (Bourdieu, 1986). Digital social networking sites offer the opportunity to re-construct these routines online, creating "networks of informational and emotional exchange, and channels for establishing, building and maintaining social capital" (Wang, Tucker and Haines, 2013, p. 4). Indeed, as Livingstone et al. (2011) suggest:

> "In relation to social networking, it seems that the task of interpretation is highly focused on the 'developing self' – to borrow Mead's term (1934), both the 'I' as in, who am I in and for myself, and the 'me' as in, how do others see and respond to me, what community am I part of (p. 3)".

Managing multiple conversations with people located within and outside the youth centre (see Kim and Rachel's conversation) cannot though, be contained within the school site. Like fluids they "… neither fix space nor bind time …it is the flow of time that counts, more than the space they happen to occupy" (Bauman, 2000, p. 2). Maintaining ongoing multi-directional relationships is therefore critical to young people's relationship building strategies online and offline, within and outside the school site. Relationships managed online and offline must therefore be maintained constantly in order to sustain the narrative project and ultimately the construction of a self-identity.

What also emerges from the research findings is a perception of the collaboratively produced self, located in perpetual flux managed within historical and wider social contexts which extend beyond the space (whether physical or digital) which each young person occupies. As physical and digital social networking sites provide a shared space within which each young person can collaboratively create and manage their wider narrative and essentially their self-identity. Indeed identities, as Livingstone and Brake (2010) claim, are constructed through interaction with others, in this case family, friends and peers both online and offline.

The findings show, in line with Paul, Smith, and Blumberg (2010), Livingstone and Brake (2010), Ofcom (2014), Mesch and Talmud (2006), that there is no distinct divide between online and offline relationships and that where relationships are managed online these could be managed anytime and anywhere with a range of people. Entering the school site, including the youth centre sessions held during the school day, did not restrict young people managing interpersonal relations established offsite with peers, friends and family members. These did not stop at the school gates.

Observations

What the findings from this study therefore bring to discussions about young people, digital social networking in schools and issues surrounding cyberbullying is some understanding of the way that narrative and self-identity is regulated through the use of language and behaviours both offline and online. Language, it seems, is located in the production of the self where identity is constructed in spaces available online (Ahn, 2011) and within discourse (Livingstone and Brake, 2010). The study indicates that behaviours and an individual's subjective intent are signified in language codes which enable strategic positioning within their socialising practices in relation to significant others; i.e. those who are viewed by the individual as important in terms of helping to maintain their self-project. The importance of communication, both offline and online, lies in its ability to act as a vehicle to mediate an individual's subjective intent and signify strategic shifts within a corresponding framework of behaviours.

This raises the possibility that language and conversations signifying *building* and *maintaining* behaviours do ultimately reflect, as Livingstone et al. (2011) state, a set of underlying ontological questions (Taylor, 1989); i.e. 'who am I?', and 'who are we becoming together'? The findings here suggest *building* and *maintaining* behaviours are motivated by a future orientated self; that is how young people perceive themselves to be in the future. The present self is future orientated (i.e. located within the context of a family of their own, close friendships or in a particular type of job). Socialising, whether based in physical or digital sites, is therefore a strategic process which lays the relational foundations within which this future self can be orientated.

At this point Clemson (2015), using the more extreme example of clique formation within schools, offers some more concrete insights into how the need to maintain the self-project can influence young people's actions towards peers. These actions may well be considered bullying or cyberbullying from an outsider's perspective. In her discussion about cliques and friendship groups Clemson states:

> "Preteens and teens look to their peers to figure out their roles and identities within their peer groups and to find acceptance .... [They] bond over similar interests but also   for   the   support,   sympathy   and protection they offer" (p. 74).

An overriding theme she discusses in relation to cliques and which applies to the findings in this study, is that they offer spaces to develop one's identity. Opportunities come at a price though; namely, ongoing commitment to the group. Joining and leaving the group must be carefully negotiated and cannot be taken lightly. Members must remain vigilant to *protect* the group and each member's identity and collaboratively produced narrative. As a result Clemson claims, a person may be intimidated into joining the group and others may be intimidated (online or offline) when leaving the group.

Aggression, in this case, is not unjustified, from the "aggressor's" perspective, but necessary to protect their own narratives and feelings of ontological security which are, if Giddens (1991) is correct, inseparably linked within reflexive relationships. This does not necessarily make the actions of the person sending the message morally right or justifiable, from an organisational perspective, but it offers insight into how some perceived cyberbullying issues might be understood within the context of young people's social practices. This discussion and research findings coincide with Davies' (2010) and Sheer's (2011) views that social media tools provide contexts for managing relationship construction not deconstruction.

Constructing and managing relationships online is likely to become increasingly problematic and the risk of miscommunication exponentially increases. Some behaviour might be more frequently managed on some media than others, depending on their suitability for conveying messages within that behaviour. Managing relationships across an increasingly diverse range of media puts relationships at risk of not only fracturing (Ofcom, 2008), but of being misunderstood if behaviours and communications are viewed in isolation from the overall narrative and other behaviours. This is because in face-to-face interactions behaviours are carried out within the same physical site and can be understood within the context of previous and overriding behaviours. Being in physical proximity enables each person to see and experience transitions between behaviours within social practices. Each can more easily be understood within the context of the other. Moving from an offline site to meet someone at another offline site also requires the physical moving away from one social space to the next – creating the illusion of what Deleuze (in Colebrook, 2002) might describe as a scene within each individual's narrative. These scenes form Giddens' (1991) routines of normalcy.

Managing different behaviours across different social media arguably requires careful management in order to understand and remember 1) how behaviours on one social media relate to behaviours in another, and 2) the overall relationship building strategy being used across each media The risk of severing the flow of these behaviours and the complex interconnected relationships which form the self-project through miscommunication and misunderstanding is exponentially increased online. There is a greater risk of behaviours being interpreted and acted upon by teachers and other adults in isolation from other social behaviours.

If Arendt (1958) is correct in her claim that we are conditioned beings; conditioned to act by the conditions under which we exist, young people may well be increasingly placed in a catch 22 situation. The social conditions under which they exist require them to become increasingly vigilant and continually maintain their relationships across a diverse range of digital media. But in the process, this puts them at greater danger of fracturing the very relationships they are trying to build and maintain. Subsequently, if this is correct, when relationships fracture young people may well be driven by feelings of ontological insecurity to take more extreme and aggressive measures to ensure the relationships are re-established.

Conclusion

If the above findings and discussion reflect young people's digital social networking practices in secondary schools, then we need to re-think some issues online that are defined as cyberbullying. Consideration should be given to the context within which relationships are managed (online and offline) and some behaviours deemed more risky, i.e. *exploring* new relationships and *protecting* existing relationships, might be re-framed and considered within the context of overriding behaviours of *building* and *maintaining*. Hence, if the findings from this study reflect a general trend in young people's socialising practices in physical sites and on digital media, then issues related to assumed poor interpersonal relationships and unjustified aggression may well be located within a highly complex ethical framework orientated towards Taylor's (1989) existential questions; who am I? And who are we becoming together?

Although aggression and intent to harm others cannot be viewed ultimately as good they may be seen by some young people as morally right in order to *build* and *maintain* a collaboratively produced self-identity. Thus these behaviours would not necessarily imply a deficit of empathic morality but rather an intrinsic desire and need to re-establish and re-engage a fractured identity and narrative, albeit for the greater good of the self over the good of the other. Actions seen as aggressive and with intent to harm might therefore require a different form of intervention, one that enables young people to manage their relationships positively and within an environment which supports rather than censors or isolates each group member.

Certainly digital social networking sites are here to stay and will continue to have a significant impact on young people's lives. Attempts to manage these complex relationship systems must therefore be encouraged but they must also be supported and understood in order to provide young people with a challenging ground to practice relationship management strategies and develop their self-identity. Interventions may well be needed, to support young people's socialising and relationship building practices on digital social media and recognise that there is considerable scope for young people to engage in the use of social media for and with positive purposes and outcomes (Livingstone, 2011; Ofcom, 2008; Ofcom, 2014).

Bibliography

Ahn, J. (2011). The effect of social network sites on adolescents' social and academic development: Current theories and controversies. *Journal of the American Society for Information Science and Technology,* Vol. 62 (8), pp.1435-1445. DOI: 10.1002/asi.21540.

Arendt, H. (1958). *The Human Condition.* Chicago: University of Chicago Press.

Bauman, Z. (2000). *Liquid Modernity* London: Polity Press.

Bernstein, B. (1971). *Class, Codes and Control, Volume 1* London: Routledge and Kegan Paul.

Bourdieu, P. (1986). The Forms of Capital. In J. Richardson (Ed.). *Handbook of Theory and Research for the Sociology of Education.* New York: Greenwood, pp. 241-258.

Byron, T. (2008). *Safer Children in a Digital World: The Report of the Byron Review.* London: Department for Children, Schools and Families, and the Department for Culture, Media and Sport.

Byron, T. (2010). *Do we have Safer Children in a Digital World? A Review of Progress since the 2008 Byron Review.* London: Department for Children, Schools and Families.

Cesaroni, C., Downing, S. and Alvi, S. (2012). Bullying Enters the 21st Century? Turning a Critical Eye to Cyberbullying Research. *Youth Justice,* Vol. 12(3), pp. 199-211.

Clemson, C. (2015). *The Prison Path: School practices that hurt our youth.* Maryland: Rowman and Littlefield.

Colebrook, C. (2002). *Understanding Deleuze.* Crows Nest, Australia. Allen and Unwin.

Davies, M. (2010). *Children, Media and Culture (Issues in Cultural and Media Studies).* Berkshire: Open University Press.

Department for Education. (2014). *Preventing and tackling bullying. Advice for headteachers, staff and governing bodies.* London: DfE Publications.

Duck, S. (2011). *Rethinking Relationships.* London: Sage.

Edwards, S. (2013). The Social Construction of Pupils' Cultural Worlds: Negotiating Viable Selves from the Margin. University of Sussex: Unpublished PhD thesis.

Erikson, E. (1968). *Identity: Youth and Crisis.* New York: W.W. Norton.

Fanti, K., Demetriou, A., and Hawa, V. (2012). A longitudinal study of cyberbullying: Examining risk and protective factors. *European Journal of Developmental Psychology,* Vol. 9(2), pp. 1–181.

Giddens, A. (1991). *Modernity and Self-identity.* Cambridge: Polity Press.

Görzig, A. and Frumkin, L. (2013). Cyberbullying experiences on-the-go: When social media can become distressing. *Cyberpsychology: Journal of Psychosocial Research on Cyberspace,* Vol.7 (1), article 4.

Kernaghan, D., and Elwood, J. (2013). All the (cyber) world's a stage: Framing cyberbullying as a performance. *Cyberpsychology: Journal of Psychosocial Research on Cyberspace,* Vol.7 (1), article 5.
http://dx.doi.org/10.5817/CP2013-1-5

Kowalski, R., Limber, S. and Agatston, P. (2012). *Cyberbullying: bullying in the digital age.* Chichester: Wiley Blackwell.

Livingstone, S. and Brake, R. (2010). On the rapid rise of social networking tools: new findings and policy implications. *Children & Society*, Vol.24 (1), pp. 75-83.

Livingstone, S., Mascheroni, G. and Murru, M. (2011). Social networking among European children: new findings on privacy, identity and connection. *Hermes*, Vol. *59*, pp. 89-98. [In French].

Marczak, M., and Coyne, I. (2010). *Cyberbullying at School*: Good Practice and Legal Aspects in the United Kingdom. *Australian Journal of Guidance & Counselling*, Vol.20 (2), pp. 182–193.

Mesch, G., and Talmud, I. (2006), "Online Friendship Formation, Communication Channels, and Social Closeness". *International Journal of Internet Science,* Vol. 1 (1), pp. 29 – 44.

Nansel T., Overpeck, M., Pilla, R., Ruen, W., Simmons-Morton, B., and Scheidt, P. (2001). Bullying behaviour amongst US youth: Prevalence and association with psychosocial adjustments. *Journal of the American Medical Association*, Vol. 285(16), pp. 2094-2100.

Ofcom. (2008). Social Networking: A quantitative and qualitative research report into attitudes, behaviours and use.

Ofcom. (2014). Adults' Media Use and Attitudes Report 2014.

Olweus, D. (1993). *Bullying at School. What we know and what we can do.* New York: Blackwell.

Orteg-Ruiz, R., and Nunez, J. (2012). Bullying and cyberbullying: Research and intervention at school and social contexts. *Psicoitema*, 24(4), pp. 603-607.

Paul, S., Smith, P., and Blumberg, H. (2010). Addressing Cyberbullying in School Using the Quality Circle Approach. *Australian Journal of Guidance & Counselling.* Vol.20 (2), pp. 157–168.

Paul, S., Smith, P., and Blumberg, H. (2012). Comparing student perceptions of coping strategies and school interventions in managing bullying and cyberbullying incidents. *Pastoral Care in Education,* Vol., 30(2), pp. 127-146.

Seigler, R., DeLoache, J., and Eisenburg, N. (2011). *How Children Develop.* New York: Worth.

Schneider, S., O'Donnell, L., Stueve, A., and Coulter, R. (2012). Cyberbullying, School Bullying, and Psychological Distress: A Regional Census of High School Students. *American Journal of Public Health,* Vol.102 (1), pp. 171-177

Sheer, V. (2011). Teenagers' Use of MSN Features, Discussion Topics, and Online Friendship Development: The Impact of Media Richness and Communication Control. *Communication Quarterly,* Vol. 59(1), pp. 82–103.

Taylor, C. (1989). *Sources of the Self.* Cambridge: Cambridge University Press.

Tokuma, R. (2010). Following you home from school: A critical review and synthesis of research on cyberbullying victimization. *Computes in Human Behaviour,* Vol. 26(3), pp. 277-287.

Ttofi, M. and Farrington, D. (2011). Effectiveness of school-based programs to reduce bullying: a systematic and meta-analytic review. *Journal of Experimental Criminology,* Vol. 7, pp. 27-56.

Wang, V., Tucker, J., & Haines, K. (2013). Deviance in cybercommunities: the case of Second Life. *International Journal of Criminology and Sociological Theory*, Vol.6 *(3)*, pp. 29-42.

Websites

www.beatbullying
http://ceop.police.uk/
http://archive.beatbullying.org/dox/what-we-do/cybermentors.html
http://www.kidsmart.org.uk/
http://www.thinkuknow.co.uk/

CHAPTER FIVE

UNDERSTANDING ABSENCE FROM SCHOOL

MYRTE VAN VELDHUIZEN
AND CAROL HAYDEN

Introduction

With the introduction of compulsory schooling, the concept of absence from school, often referred to as 'non-attendance', arose:

> "Compulsory education and school non-attendance constitute two faces of the same coin: it would be inconceivable to imagine otherwise where education for all is required by law" (Carlen, Gleeson and Wardhaugh, 1992, p. 12).

The extent to which the state intervenes in family life through the provision of a service that must be used, with legal sanctions for not using the service, is the backdrop to this chapter. Compulsory schooling raises broader issues about the role of schools and social control (Hayden, 2011), and the resistance of children and young people (and some parents and carers) to this attempt by the state to exercise control over where they spend their time. Schools have a wide range of roles to play, but two of the overarching requirements are to keep children and young people purposefully occupied and to promote conforming and compliant behaviour. In this sense schooling has been referred to as a form of custody which keeps children and young people off the streets and out of trouble (Hayden, 2011). The role of schools in relation to promoting social conformity is perhaps more implicit in contemporary schools, than in the past. The role of institutions has changed in this respect. Whitney (1994) writes of how concern about 'absence' in early nineteenth century England, was about absence from church and whether educational opportunity should be made conditional on church attendance. The latter debate characterised schools as an opportunity that rewards conforming behaviour. Yet, as Carlen et al. (1992) and Whitney (1994) argue, in relation to England there has always been resistance to going to school, particularly from the poorest sections of the population.

This chapter draws on comparative research on persistent and serious absence from schools in England and the Netherlands. These countries illustrate different perspectives on the application of legal sanctions for serious and persistent absence from school. In England the focus of sanctions is on the parents, whereas in the Netherlands, it is primarily the young person. Sanctions include fines and imprisonment (in both countries) and community service in the Netherlands. The chapter concludes with a consideration of the implications for practice, specifically in relation to prevention and early intervention.

Absence from school – a complex and multi-faceted problem

Absence from school is a complex phenomenon that takes a number of forms and is referred to by several different terms. These terms relate both to the degree of control or choice exercised by the child and the parent(s)/carer(s), as well as the extent to which absence from school is primarily linked to problems at home or in school and, the severity of these problems.

The term 'truancy' is generally used to refer to the decision not to attend school being in the control of the child (Atkinson et al., 2000). Children who do not attend school for whole days are called "blanket truants". "Post-registration truancy" refers to children who do attend school, but miss particular lessons. The latter form of truancy can be harder to monitor and is likely to be underreported in official and national reports on school attendance data.

"School phobia", "separation anxiety" and "school refusal" are terms used to describe absence from school that is anxiety-based (Kearny, Turner and Gauger, 2010). For example, children who are afraid to go to school, are depressed, have separation anxiety disorder or are victims of abuse (Atkinson et al., 2000). Children who display school refusal behaviour are on average younger than truants and emotional problems play a major role in this type of absence. "Persistent or chronic absence" from school refers to a more serious or entrenched pattern of absence. Research has demonstrated that this is likely to be connected to a range of vulnerabilities and sometimes offending and anti-social behaviour (Hayden, 2011). On the other hand, absence from school may relate to family holidays taken during school term time (known as "luxury absence" in the Netherlands), and is not necessarily related to problematic circumstances at all. Recent legislation in England has enabled schools to impose fines on parents who take their children on holiday during term time. Persistent or chronic absence can develop into dropping out of school, or simply not returning to school after a summer holiday or moving home. Ofsted (2003) has estimated that around 10,000 children 'disappear' from the school role between years 10 and 11 (age 15 to 16 years) in England. Broadhurst, Paton and May-Chahala (2005) interviewed parents, carers and children who were 'missing' from education, in the sense that they had completely disengaged with going to school. They saw this issue as one that had "barely touched government agendas" (p.106) except when it is noted as a factor in the failure of authorities to prevent child death, as in the case of Victoria Climbié (1).

Balfanz and Byrnes (2012) characterise three broad types of absence; children and young people who:

Cannot attend school
- due to illness, family responsibilities, housing instability, the need to work or involvement with the juvenile justice system.
Avoid school
- to escape bullying, unsafe conditions, harassment and embarrassment.
Choose not to attend
- because they, or their parents, do not see the value in being there,
- they have something else they would rather do,
- or nothing stops them from skipping school (pp.4-5).

These three broad categorisations begin to capture the complexity of reasons and situations behind absence from school. This also illustrates the extent to which child and adult choice, indifference, or other more pressing issues play a part in the different situations behind school absence.

Is absence from school primarily a rich world problem?

According to Reid (2008) absence from school (he uses the term 'truancy') is primarily a rich world problem. Reid (2012) is of the view that:

"....we need a major research study to determine why truancy is such a major problem in the UK and parts of the USA, Canada and a few other "westernised" countries when it is not a serious problem in most developed nations in the world (Japan, Korea, Finland, etc.)" (p. 336).

Shimiz (2011) would disagree, in relation to his research in Japan, he writes:

"Throughout modern Japanese history, the issue of long-term non-attendance at school has been a recurring theme of discussion on education and society. The government continues to redefine the phenomenon and to include Japan's total number of absentee children in its annual statistics, often prompting sensational reports in the media. Expert opinions are eagerly sought, and the issue of non-attendance frequently becomes a major topic of seminars and symposia, not to mention novels, comics and films" (p.165).

Shimiz (2011) reviews official data and popular discourse in Japan from the 1950s onwards detailing a changing discourse over this time period, but with a sense that this is an intractable problem. Yoneyama (2000), focusing on school phobia in Japan, argues that:

"....there is an extremely large pool of 'would-be school phobics' in Japan who do their best to keep going to school. But, most significantly, Tôkôkyohi [School Phobia/Refusal] is the mode of school non-attendance in Japan, whereas it may manifest itself as truancy or dropout in other societies" (p.80).

So, it might be more accurate to say that there is relatively little evidence of a readily accessible official or research discourse on absence (particularly persistent or chronic absence) from school in some countries in the world. This may in part be due to language as well as access to some publications. But, we should also consider, as Yoneyama's (2000) analysis points out, whether this always means that there is no equivalent problem in another country. If we look to other concepts such as 'disaffection' with school, which is associated with some forms of absence, as well as 'disruptive behaviour' in school, we might see a different story. Disaffection simply put means that some students don't like school (or aspects of it) and respond (in some cases) by being absent, *if they can*. 'If they can' is a crucial qualifier to the last statement: sometimes the family, school or community and cultural conditions make absence more or less possible. 'Disruptive behaviour' refers to children who are rebellious, troublesome and so disturb lessons whilst at school. Some children who display 'disruptive' behaviour are also disaffected with school. Sometimes they misbehave in order to get excluded, which legitimates their absence from school (Hayden, 2007)

Yan and Jament (2008) write of the 'quiet disaffection' of some children in mainstream schools in China and India; they are described as withdrawn and not included in their classrooms. This could be seen as a different sort of absence, the children may be physically present but they are not engaged with or part of the classroom or the school. In other words there are different forms of resistance to school attendance and active presence and participation in school. Jonasson (2011) illustrates this type of issue in a Danish study, where students are described as "absent *in class*". One specific form of being "absent in class" is where students on several occasions actually fell asleep during class, with their head bent over the table (p.24). While these students who are '*absent in class*' are technically not serious or persistent absentees, the long-term consequences might be very similar to those of non-attendance at school. The requirement to attend school is generally associated with arguments about the need for a workforce with the requisite knowledge and skills to be employable. This latter view became visible from the mid-nineteenth century onwards in many rich countries and was often bound up with other concerns such as the desire to end child labour. In the United States, for example:

> "The first school attendance laws were passed in Massachusetts in 1852 as a way to combat child labour in that state. By 1900, 32 other states had also adopted school attendance laws, and by 1918 every state had followed suit. Unfortunately, these laws were seldom imposed and simply removed children from school instead of trying to address the problems or issues associated with their absenteeism" (Gleich-Bope, 2014, p.110-111).

Removing children from school as a response to absence (as in the quote above) clearly does not address the problem, and would now be seen as "archaic and counterproductive" (Gleich-Bope, 2014, p.111) in the United States and many other countries with compulsory schooling.

Responses to absence from school

Legislation and policy in relation to school attendance can be complex and in some ways contradictory, both revealing the limits of state power over families, as well as commitment to providing school-based education for all. The practises of home education and exclusion from school reveal these limits. Home education is not allowed in some countries, such as the Netherlands, whilst in others it is relatively well organised, as in the UK.

In the UK it is estimated that around 60,000 children (0.6% of children of school age) are home educated (see http://www.home-education.org.uk/). A key focus of the argument of Home Education UK (n.d.) is parental and children's rights, the primacy of the family in relation to education (Vis a Vis the state) and criticism of the role and motivation of state provision of education:

> "The right to home educate stems from the long standing right, and responsibility, of parents to determine the nature of the education of their own children. Without this responsibility children's education would become a state controlled monopoly in which a child's education would be subject to government policy. We believe that the state has interests other than those of the child's and while many of those interests may be important and worthy of consideration, the final decision should remain with the child and family" (paras 1 and 2).

So, home education can be argued to be a human right. Home Education UK (n.d.) makes a very pertinent point in saying that: "Education cannot take place against a person's wishes" (para 10). There is a legal framework to home education in the UK that varies slightly across England, Scotland, Wales and Northern Ireland. The counter to this parental rights argument focuses on concerns that are wider than whether a child, who is home educated, is being appropriately educated. There are also legitimate child protection concerns, because of the lack of routine (daily) professional surveillance of children who are home educated. The NSPCC (2009) argue that there should be better monitoring and that it needs to be wider than educational attainment. Children should be seen without their parents being present and should be made aware of organisations such as ChildLine.

Exclusion from school might be seen as the opposite problem to home education. One way of conceptualising exclusion is as a form of school refusal where the school is refusing to have the child in the school, for a time or permanently. Exclusion from school is possible in many countries, although there is usually some provision or expectation that the child will go to another school. The lack of national monitoring data and research in many countries makes this difficult to verify. In England there have been annual reports on exclusion from school for over 20 years (as well as a great deal of academic research), so this form of absence from school and the inter-connections with school attendance is well researched (see for example Hayden, 2007).

How big is the problem?

Estimates of the scale of absence from school in different countries vary partly because of the different terms used and how broadly (or narrowly) the issue is defined. For example, Balfanz and Byrnes (2012) focus on 'chronic absence' defined as missing 10% of the school year for any reason. They found limited data produced at state level in the United States, from which they say they can make "only an educated guess at the size of the nation's attendance challenge" (p.3). They estimate a national rate of at least 10% chronic absenteeism and up to 15%, equating to between 5 and 7.5 million students in the whole country. In England there is a great deal of annual monitoring data on absence from school, and this is reported separately from exclusion. However, there are frequent changes of definition, format and focus in government reports. The latest figures at the time of writing (DfE, 2015) show an overall absence rate of 4.4% across English schools, an improvement from 6.1% in 2010. There is an increasing focus on 'persistent absentees', who make up 3.6% of 'possible pupil enrolments'. This figure rises to 14.6% for pupils at special schools (DfE, 2015). 'Persistent absentee' is defined as pupils who miss around 15% or more of possible sessions (DfE, 2015). Overall 9.5% of 'possible pupil enrolments' in England miss more than 20 days schooling or 10% of the school year (DfE, 2014). Other DfE (2011) figures show that 184,000 pupils miss 20% of school (40 days or more) and more than 430,000 pupils miss 15% of school (around 30 days) a year. The 9.5% figure for England noted above (i.e. 9.5% of possible pupil enrolments) equates with the lower chronic absence level in the United States research by Balfanz and Byrnes (2012). Writing about Japan, Shimiz (2011) says that 3.8% of the junior high school population and 0.8% of the elementary school population are recorded as long-term absentees, i.e. they miss 30 days or more of school a year.

The national absence figures for the Netherlands are reported in absolute numbers rather than as a percentage of the total compulsory school-aged population. Furthermore, absence is not measured in total school days missed per academic year. Instead a distinction is made between 'relative absence from school' (at least 16 hours unauthorized absence during a period of 4 weeks) and 'absolute absence from school' (not being registered at any school). Official records do indicate a rise in absence from school in recent years. For instance, the 'relative absence from school' (which includes both 'signal absence' and 'luxury absence') rose from 84,750 in the year 2011/2012 to 88,655 in the year 2012/2013 (Ministerie van Onderwijs, Cultuur en Wetenschap (OCW), 2014). The

Dutch Government argues that this rise is at least partly due to increased attention being paid to absence from school and more accurate registration by schools and councils (OCW, 2014). This is confirmed by Lubberman, Mommers and Wester (2014) who argue that although growing attention and improved registration explain the rise in 'relative absence from school', these factors are only partially responsible for the rise in 'absolute absence from school' (not being registered at any school). The rise in the number of 'absolute absentees'(from 6,430 in 2011/2012 to 8,974 in 2012/13) also reflects a real increase in the number of Dutch children and young people who are not registered at any school.

We calculated percentage absence from school in the Netherlands using absolute numbers and the estimated total school-aged population (based on figures from the youth statline database). For the year 2011/2012 'absolute absence from school' was estimated at 0.23% of the total school-aged population and 'relative absence from school' at 3.06% of the total school-aged population (based on OCW, 2014 and jeugdmonitor (n.d.) youth monitor) (2). These percentages (even if added together) are considerably lower than the calculations for England and the United States (presented earlier). This could possibly be explained, however, by different ways of measuring and registering absence. Furthermore, in the Netherlands only unauthorised absences are counted, whereas in England both authorised and unauthorised absences are included.

However we define the issue, absence from school involves a lot of children, but they are still a minority within the school population. They are a minority that (in most cases) are likely to be vulnerable and/or get into trouble, partly because they are not in school and under the supervision of professionals. The next section outlines the existing research evidence on *persistent and serious absence* from school.

What do we know about persistent or serious absentees?

We have already established that absence from school covers a range of situations and circumstances. This section focuses on persistent or serious absentees, that is children who are regularly or chronically absent. The research evidence shows that these are often very vulnerable children who have problems on different levels. In the Netherlands this form of absence is called 'signaalverzuim' (signal absence) (Boekhoorn and Spellers, 2004), which suggests that children are sending out a signal about their situation by persistently not attending school. These 'signals' can include problems across a range of environments - including home, school and community, as well as psychological problems that may inter-relate with these problems in other environments.

Problematic home circumstances are very common among serious absentees. Problems can include: family breakdown, violence and conflict between parents, abuse and a range of other issues, including being isolated from others (Kearny, 2008b; Veenstra et al., 2010). The majority of persistent absentees, who are living in families where the birth parents have separated, are not in touch with one of their biological parents (Van Veldhuizen, 2010). According to Thornton, Darmody and McCoy (2013) the chance of children having attendance problems becomes twice as high when there are or have been many conflicts between the parents. Also being a witness to violence at home (especially between parents) and being subject to other forms of maltreatment are strongly related to persistent absence from school (Egger, Costello and Angold, 2003; Kearny, 2008b, Ramirez et al., 2012). In addition, families of absentees often show poor cohesion, detachment, and enmeshment and are isolated (Kearny, 2008a). The likelihood of absence from school increases when the level of parental involvement with the child is low and when the parental supervision is inadequate (Egger et al., 2003; Kearny, 2008b; Sheppard, 2009). These latter issues inter-relate with others; for example it is very common for persistent absentees to have parents with substance misuse issues, psychological or chronic physical health problems.

Some young people, facing the above mentioned problems at home, might enjoy attending school because it gives them the opportunity to escape their home situation, but others are anxious about what is happening at home. For many persistent absentees school is another area in their lives in which they encounter problems. School based problems relate to: a negative school climate, large class sizes, relationships with school staff and teachers, and bullying (Attwood and Croll, 2006; Kearny, 2008b; Lauchlan, 2003).

Many researchers have established a connection between bullying and absence from school (Egger et al., 2003; Kearny, 2008b; Lauchlan, 2003). However, Attwood and Croll (2006) indicate that while truancy increases in the later years of secondary school, concern over bullying decreases with age at secondary school. Moreover, although some of the persistent truants they interviewed did mention bullying as a reason for their non-attendance; they did not establish a significant relationship between bullying and truancy in their data from the British Household Panel Survey. Therefore, the relative importance and nature of the impact of bullying on persistent absence remains unclear.

Although it is well-established that peer groups have a strong social influence on young people during adolescence (Cook, Buehler and Henson, 2009), not much of the research on persistent absence from school has focused on the role of peers. Lauchlan (2003) argues that having troublesome peers is a risk factor for serious absence. This finding is confirmed by Van der Laan et al. (2009) who established in their research in the Netherlands that serious absentees have more friends with police contacts (i.e. young people that are known to the police because of crimes committed or anti-social behaviour on the streets) and are more often outside the house with their peers during the week compared to other young people. On the other hand, some persistent absentees seem unable to develop peer relationships and become very isolated (Dube and Orpinas, 2009).

Individual factors (emotional and behavioural) play a part in the onset of persistent absence from school, including anxiety disorders and depression (Egger et al, 2003; Kearny, 2008a), and conduct disorder, ADHD, tantrums, aggressive and deviant behaviour (Egger et al., 2003; Ingul et al., 2012; Veenstra et al., 2010). Furthermore, a strong correlation exists between internalising and externalising problems (Egger et al., 2003; Ingul et al., 2012; Wood et al., 2012). For example, a child might try to conceal an anxiety disorder by 'acting out' and 'playing up'. Wood et al. (2012) studied the direction of the relationship and conclude that in some cases absenteeism is a predictor for the development of psychopathology and in other cases the psychopathology predicts absenteeism. Furthermore, a strong relationship exists between sleep problems and school absenteeism, such as: refusal to sleep alone, nightmares, fatigue and insomnia are all connected to serious school absence (Egger et al., 2003). Chronic illness and somatic complaints are also associated with persistent and serious absence (Egger et al., 2003; Ingul et al., 2012). Learning difficulties are common, although they have not always been officially recognised (Ingul et al., 2012). When school absence has started at a young age or has been ongoing for a long time, the absence itself can explain the difficulties the young person is experiencing with the school work.

Serious or persistent absentees often experience an accumulation of these different risk factors and have very few protective factors (such as parental interest and supervision, positive school climate) in their environments (Van der Laan et al., 2009), which enhances their vulnerability. This accumulation of problems suggests that, although at first sight it might seem that young people choose not to attend school, many persistent absentees actually cannot attend school because of the numerous problems they encounter.

On the other hand, a strong correlation exists between persistent absence from school and juvenile delinquency (Dembo et al., 2012; Weerman and Van der Laan, 2006), although it remains unclear whether there is a causal relationship between serious absences from school and offending behaviour. As Weerman and van der Laan (2006) indicate, the correlation might be explained by the similarity of many of the factors that underlie both serious absence and juvenile offending behavior.

Persistent absence from school is characterised by the heterogeneity and diversity of the different symptoms involved (Dube and Orpinas, 2009) and is progressive in nature (Lyon and Cotler, 2007). Absence from school often starts with only missing a couple of hours during a school week, then moves to missing whole days and/or weeks and can end in not attending school at all (school drop-out). Absence from school is also transactional: the problems and risks experienced by many of the serious absentees increase the likelihood of serious absence from school, but the absence can also further expand the existing problems (Kearny, 2008a; Lyon and Cotler, 2007). For example, conflicts between parents might be one of the factors influencing the onset of absence from school, and then the absence from school may lead to further parental and family conflict. In this way, one can argue that persistent absence from school can become a vicious circle for the young people and families involved, and it is hard to change the pattern. Therefore, there is no single response by schools or governments that will tackle absence from school. The next section of this chapter examines the various measures taken by the Dutch and English governments in response to this issue.

Responding to absence from school in the Netherlands and England

The wide variety of problems associated with serious and persistent absence from school means that there are strong incentives to try and address the problem, for the young people themselves, their families (and carers) and for society as a whole. However, the complexity of the issue and the limited research into the effectiveness of alternative responses makes it difficult for governments, local authorities and schools to decide how to prioritise the different types of response available.

Interventions to reduce serious and persistent absence need to operate at different levels: the community, the school, the family, peer groups (school and community) and at the individual level. The responses are different in England and the Netherlands. Of particular note is the different focus of legal action: in the Netherlands it is young people (aged 12 years and over); whereas in England parents and carers of absentees are the target of government responses, whatever the age of the child. Table 1 provides an overview of the different responses in both countries to parents and children/young people.

Table 1 illustrates that there is a wider range of responses to parents in England, compared with the Netherlands, although both countries have a mixture of welfare and justice based responses. For example, in the Netherlands, prosecuting a young person because of persistent absence from school appears to be primarily a justice based response. Young people usually get a community sentence under the supervision of a probation officer. The probation officer also investigates the young person's problems and welfare needs and works with them to address their problems. Young people attend intervention programmes or have access to a psychologist, as a result of their prosecution. This illustrates that a judicial response can lead to welfare based assistance.

Table 5.1 Possible responses to parents and persistent absentees in England and the Netherlands

		Parents	Children and young people
School	Eng.	- Telephone call services, check with the home - Some schools employ the equivalent of welfare officers - Parenting contract -Penalty notices (£60-£120)	- Part-time timetable or dual registration at a college to study a vocational course - Education welfare officer will also work with the child
	NL	- Some schools will call parents when the child is not attending school or arrange a meeting with parents to discuss the absence of the child	-Care Advisory Team (CAT) – a multi-agency consultation in which all children who have problems at a school will be discussed -report serious absence to the local authority (education welfare officer)

Local authority/education welfare service	Eng.	- The 'Troubled Families' Programme - Warning letter - Parenting contract - Penalty notice (£60-£120) - Education Supervision Order (ESO) - School attendance order - Prosecution	-The 'Troubled Families' Programme works with the child and parents/carers within a whole family approach - Education welfare officer will also work with the child
	NL	-Prosecution	-Consultation with school -(final) warning -Send to Halt (3) -Referral to care -Prosecution
Justice system	Eng.	-Parenting order -Level 3 fine (up to £1000) -Level 4 fine (up to £2.500) -Imprisonment (up to 3 months)	
	NL	-Fine (up to €4050) -Imprisonment (up to 1 month)	-Fine -Community service sentence, work sentence or learning sentence -Youth probation – (assess, help and support, functional family therapy (FFT), multi-systemic therapy (MST)

Response of schools

Both in England and the Netherlands, schools are the first institution that will recognise the serious or persistent absence of a child or young person. In England all schools are required by law to have a written behaviour policy, which can include measures they can take against parents when their child is not behaving in compliance with the school rules or has irregular attendance (DFE, 2013a). One of the measures schools can use to improve attendance in England is a parenting contract. Parenting contracts are a voluntary agreement between parents and the school, in which parents agree to meet the requirements that are set out in the contract and the school promises to support the parents to comply with the contract (DFE, 2013a). Although parenting contracts are voluntary, schools record parental refusal to sign a contract, because this can be used as evidence in court when a parenting order is requested by the local authority.

Besides parenting contracts, English schools can use penalty notices to encourage parents to ensure their child's attendance at school. The circumstances under which head teachers can impose a penalty notice on parents are set out in The Education (Penalty Notices) (England) regulations 2007, to which some amendments were made in 2012 and 2013. Since 2013, the schools can impose a fine on parents of £60, which they must pay within 21 days. The fine increases to £120 if they do not pay within the 21 days. Schools have to notify the local authority when they issue a penalty notice to parents, and the fine has to be paid to the local authority. The penalty notice can be imposed on each of the adults liable for the offence, so both parents can individually receive a penalty notice for the same day(s)/period of unauthorised absence of their child. Schools can issue a penalty notice in cases of absence that they did not authorise, for example when parents take their children on a family holiday during term time. Furthermore, when parents allow their child to go to a public place within the first five days of an exclusion from school, a penalty notice can be imposed on the parents (DFE, 2013a).

In England there are no formal justice responses to the child or young person who is seriously absent from school – the focus is on welfare, encouragement and support. English schools encourage young people to attend school regularly and the DFE (2013b) advises that in exceptional circumstances schools can place a pupil on a part-time timetable with the goal of full-time reintegration. A school might use an individualised part-time timetable to encourage a persistent or serious absentee to attend school more regularly and to guide them back into attending full-time. In addition, secondary schools have a pastoral care system to offer children the help and support they need.

Dutch schools have very little power against parents of absentees compared to English schools. In the Netherlands, parenting contracts do not exist and therefore schools cannot use this measure to try to improve the attendance of a child or young person. Furthermore, schools cannot impose penalty notices on parents. When parents take their child on a holiday during term time, the education welfare officer can prosecute them. The fines are higher in the Netherlands compared with England: €100 per child per day with a maximum of €600 for the first week per family, and in the case of two weeks maximum €900 per family (OM, 2014).

In the Netherlands, almost every secondary school has a care advisory team (CAT) which consists of professionals from various backgrounds. The CAT comes together to confer on the situation of any young person in the school who is experiencing problems in one or more areas of their life at school. Children and young people with physical or mental health problems, learning difficulties or serious and persistent absence can be discussed in a CAT. In many schools, the education welfare officer of the local authority takes part in the CAT, which ensures that the wider background of young people is known by the education welfare service. When a child or young person is regularly absent from school, but it is not (yet) serious, the CAT will propose a plan to prevent them from becoming a serious or persistent absentee.

Response of the Local Authority

Schools in both countries do have to report serious absence from school to the local authority or the education welfare service. In England, the local authority has a range of actions they can take. They can apply to the court for an education supervision order (ESO). If this ESO gets accepted, it is placed on the child or young person and it means that the local authority will have to supervise their education (at school or at home) for a specified period of time (DFE, 2013a). The DFE (2013a) advises local authorities to apply for an ESO before prosecuting the parents, but it is also possible to do both simultaneously. The local authority can also send parents a warning letter in which they allow the parents some time to ensure an improvement in the school attendance of their child before going on to prosecute the parents. The local authority (like schools) can impose parenting contracts and penalty notices to encourage parents to ensure that their child attends school regularly. Finally, parents can be prosecuted by the local authority because of the persistent or serious absence of their child and in that case the court will decide on a sentence. Also, when a child or young person is not receiving suitable education (at school or in any other form) the local authority can issue a school attendance order. This order enforces the responsibility of parents to register their child at a named school, when parents fail to do this they can be prosecuted.

In the Netherlands, Article 21 (part 1) of the Compulsory Education Law 1969 states that a school has to report serious unauthorised absence to the local authority when a student of compulsory school age has missed a total of (at least) 16 school hours within a period of 4 consecutive weeks.

After the school refers the serious absentee to the local authority, the education welfare officer has a choice between various responses. Normally, a conversation with the young person will take place in which the education welfare officer investigates the situation, and might give a final warning to allow them some time to increase their school attendance.

The Dutch education welfare officer can conclude that the young person has many problems and needs professional help to deal with them, rather than a sanction for their absence from school. The Dutch Child Protection Service (Raad voor de Kinderbescherming (RvdK), 2013) argues that in these situations the education welfare officer should refer the child to organisations that can provide the young person or the family with (voluntary) care before legal action is taken. The RvdK (2013) believes this will prevent the criminalisation of serious absence from school caused by severe background problems.

There are a range of other responses from the local authority in the Netherlands. If the absence from school does not exceed 10 days and the young person admits to offending behaviour, the education welfare officer can refer them to HALT, which stands for 'Het ALTernatief' (translation: the alternative). HALT is an organisation which aims to prevent young people from becoming young offenders through a short-term intervention program. If a young person successfully completes the programme they avoid involvement with the justice system and a criminal record. A young person can only be sent to HALT once. The young person will be prosecuted when a second offence is committed or when the programme is not completed successfully. Finally, a young person can be prosecuted for persistent absence from school, if they are absent for more than 10 days or have already been through the HALT programme or received help for their problems.

Response of the Court

In both countries, the courts determine the punishment for parents who are prosecuted by the local authority for their child's persistent or serious absence from school. In England the court can impose a penalty order, a level 3 fine, a level 4 fine or imprison the parents for up to three months (DfEa, 2013). According to section 44f of the Education Act 1996, a level 3 fine (up to £1000) can be imposed on the parents when their child of compulsory school age, who is registered at a school, fails to attend that school regularly. A level 4 fine (up to £2500) or imprisonment can follow when the parent(s) know their child is not attending school regularly and without a reasonable justification fail to ensure their attendance. Because children and young people cannot be held legally responsible for their absence from school, the English court has no involvement with them because of persistent or serious absence.

Whereas parents in England, who are not aware of irregular attendance, can still be prosecuted and sentenced with a level 3 fine, Dutch parents who can demonstrate they cannot be held responsible (e.g. because they are not aware of their child's absence) will not be prosecuted. Yet, when Dutch parents are seen to be responsible for the serious or persistent absence from school they can be fined (2nd category) or imprisoned for up to one month (Article 26, part 1 of the Compulsory Education Law 1969). The maximum amount of a fine of the 2nd category is €4,050 (Article 23, part 4 of the (Dutch) Penal Code). Although the law allows the court to impose a prison sentence of up to one month on parents of persistent or serious absentees, in practice this (almost) never happens.

Other interventions and programmes aimed at reducing serious absence from school

The three absence types – cannot attend school, avoids school and chooses not to attend school – distinguished by Balfanz and Byrnes (2012) require a different response. It is possible that a response that is effective for someone who avoids school, will not have a positive impact on children who cannot or choose not to attend school, although there will also be some overlap between the three absence types. Therefore, interventions that allow space for professionals to adapt the intervention to the specific individual needs of the young person or the family are likely to be more successful. The English 'Troubled Families' Programme is an example of such an intervention. This programme focuses on whole families, and getting children back into school is one of the aims, other aims include reducing youth crime and antisocial behaviour, getting parents back into work, and reducing public expenditure on these families (Department for Communities and Local Government, 2012). In this programme a family intervention worker concentrates on key issues and problems that affect school attendance (as well as other issues within the family) using an individualised approach with a particular family. Families are not forced to participate in the programme, although it may be an alternative to a more punitive approach in some circumstances (such as a fine or court order). Early evidence suggests some success in reducing persistent absence from school (Hayden and Jenkins, 2014).

Both in the Netherlands and England there are special schools or alternative forms of education for children who cannot or do not attend mainstream school. These forms of education are for children with emotional or behavioural difficulties, as well as for children with serious absence problems. In the Netherlands, these facilities are called 'onderwijsopvangvoorzieningen' (OOVR). The goal of these OOVRs is to lead young people back to mainstream schooling. In England 'Pupil Referral Units' (PRUs) are comparable facilities.

Finally, it is interesting to discuss financial (dis)incentives that can be used to improve school attendance. In the Netherlands, the education welfare officer has the possibility to withhold child benefits for parents of 16 and 17 year old children, who are not attending school (Donkelaar and Schüller adviseurs by, 2009). This idea has also been discussed in England, but it has not been implemented. There are programmes in the United States where financial incentives are used to improve school attendance and/or performance (Slavin, 2010).

Conclusions and implications for practice

This chapter has shown that persistent and serious absence from school is a recognised social and educational problem in England and the Netherlands and in many other countries too. It is a complex and multi-faceted problem that is best responded to holistically, taking into account the individual, school, family and community based issues that may be important in a particular case. In this respect, the Troubled Families programme in England offers the possibility of seeing the individual issues within a whole family setting. Similarly the multi-agency fora of the CAP in the Netherlands, sets out to look at wider issues that relate to a young person's absence from school.

The problems and risks posed by persistent and serious absentees are varied: they include leaving school without qualifications, missing out on the development of vital personal and social skills, and potentially becoming involved in anti-social and criminal behaviour, both because of the lack of institutional and adult surveillance and because of restricted work opportunities after school leaving age.

England and the Netherlands have been used as more in-depth examples to illustrate the different responses to this issue. The evidence about effective responses to the problem is fairly limited, but generally emphasises early detection and intervention, before the problem becomes serious or persistent. The incentives to do so are clear, given the evidence of adverse outcomes, both in the short and the long run (Dube and Orpinas, 2009; Kearny, 2008a). The progressive nature of persistent or serious absence from school strongly suggests that early intervention is likely to be most beneficial and cost effective in the long run. Professionals who are working with persistent absentees (e.g. education welfare officers, youth probation workers, family intervention workers, psychologists) feel that it is hard to change the pattern at a later stage, because patterns of behaviour can become entrenched and bring with them additional problems.

A priority for early intervention should be persistent and serious absence from primary school. Serious and persistent absence at primary school is less common than at secondary school and so may well be an indicator of the most problematic circumstances. Furthermore, missing education in primary school is likely to lead to the child getting behind with their school work. Since this is a further risk factor for becoming persistently absent and leaving school without qualifications, intervention at this early stage could be more fruitful than intervening when children are already in secondary school. Another focus is the transition from primary to secondary school, when some children can become overwhelmed by the change and size of the secondary school. The 'Troubled Families' Programme in England, offers the possibility of more individualized, context-based family responses that can address this multi-faceted problem.

Notes

(1) In 2000, Victoria Climbié, an eight year old girl living in London, was tortured and murdered by her guardians. Her death led to a public inquiry and produced major changes in child protection policies in the United Kingdom.

(2) The total school population for the year 2011/2012 is calculated based on figures in a youth database from the Dutch Centraal Bureau voor Statistiek (CBS). Unfortunately, these figures include 4 year olds for whom education is not yet compulsory and 17-year olds who might already have obtained a 'start qualification' (and therefore do not have to attend school anymore). Furthermore, because absolute numbers are used to calculate the absence from school, it is possible that the absence from school from one pupil is counted more than once in the academic year 2011/2012.

(3) HALT stands for 'Het alternatief' (The alternative). Young people who commit a 'light' offence (persistent absence from school is seen as an offence in the Netherlands, because the young person violates the education law) can be sent to Halt by the police or the education welfare officer. At Halt the young person receives a short punishment/intervention, which aims to show the young person the consequences of his/her behaviour and to reduce recidivism. If the young person completes the Halt sanction successfully, the 'offence' will not be placed on a criminal record.

Bibliography

Atkinson, M., Halsey, K., Wilkin, A., and Kinder, K. (2000). *Raising Attendance 2. A detailed study of Education Welfare Service Working Practices.* Berkshire: The National Foundation for Educational Research.

Attwood, G., and Croll, P. (2006). Truancy in secondary school pupils: prevalence, trajectories and pupil perspectives. *Research Papers in Education,* Vol. 21(4), pp. 467-484. DOI: 10.1080/02671520600942446

Balfanz, R., and Byrnes, V. (2012). *Chronic Absenteeism: Summarizing What We Know From Nationally Available Data.* Baltimore: Johns Hopkins University Centre for Social Organization of Schools.

Boekhoorn, P., and Speller, T. (2004). *Interventies bij schoolverzuim. Inventarisatie van justitiële maatregelen spijbelgedrag.* Nijmegen: Bureau Boekhoorn Sociaal-wetenschappelijk Onderzoek.

Broadhurst, K., Paton, H. and May-Chahala, C. (2005). Children missing from school systems: exploring divergent patterns of disengagement in the narrative accounts of parents, carers, children and young people, *British Journal of Sociology of Education,* Vol. 26(1), pp. 105-119.

Carlen, P., Gleeson, D. and Wardhaugh, J. (1992). *Truancy. The Politics of Compulsory Schooling.* Buckingham: Open University Press.

Cook, E.C., Buehler, C., and Henson, R. (2009). Parents and Peers as Social Influences to Deter Antisocial Behaviour. *Journal of Youth and Adolescence,* Vol.38, pp.1240-1252.
DOI 10.1007/s10964-008-9348-x

Dembo, R., Briones-Robinson, R., Ungaro, R.A.., Gulledge, L.M.., Karas, L.M., Winters, K.C., Greenbaum, P.E. (2012). Emotional Psychological and Related Problems among Truant Youths: An Exploratory Latent Class Analysis. *Journal of Emotional and Behavioural Disorders,* Vol. 20 (3), pp.157-168.
DOI: 10.1177/1063426610396221

Department for Education (2015). *Pupil Absence in Schools in England: 2013-2014.* 25 March. SFR 10/2015. London: DfE

Department for Education (2014). *Pupil Absence in Schools in England: 2012-2013.* 25 March. SFR 09/2014. London: DfE

Department for Education (2013a). *Parental responsibility measures for school attendance and behaviour. Statutory guidance for maintained schools, academies, local authorities and the police.* Retrieved from the website of the UK Government:
https://www.gov.uk/government/uploads/system/uploads/attachment_data/file/268787/Parental_Responsibility_Measures_for_School_Attendance_and_Behaviour.pdf

Department for Education (2013b). *School attendance. Departmental advice for maintained schools, academies, independent schools and local authorities.* Retrieved from the website of the UK Government:
https://www.gov.uk/government/uploads/system/uploads/attachment_data/file/268648/advice_on_school_attendance_nov_2013.pdf

Department for Education (2011). *Persistent absence: government changes definition to deal with reality of pupil absenteeism in schools. 12 July. Press Release.* Retrieved from the website of the UK Government: https://www.gov.uk/government/news/persistent-absence-government-changes-definition-to-deal-with-reality-of-pupil-absenteeism-in-schools

Donkelaar and Schüller adviseurs bv (2009). *Richtlijn melding leerplicht in het kader van de algemene kinderbijslagwet.* Retrieved from the website of the Dutch Parliament (eerste kamer) in September 2014: http://www.eerstekamer.nl/behandeling/20091211/richtlijn_melding_leerplicht _in/document3/f=/viawfsutj1sr.pdf

Dube, S. R., and Orpinas, P. (2009). Understanding Excessive School Absenteeism as School Refusal Behaviour. *Children and Schools,* Vol. 31, pp. 87-95.

Egger, H.l., Costello, E.J. and Angold, A. (2003). School Refusal and Psychiatric disorders: A community study. *Journal of the American Academy of Child and Adolescent Psychiatry, Vol. 42, pp.* 797-807.

Gleich-Bope, D. (2014). Truancy Laws: How Are They Affecting Our Legal Systems, Our Schools, and the Students Involved? *The Clearing House: A Journal of Educational Strategies, Issues and Ideas*, Vol. 87(3), pp. 110-114.

Hayden, C. (2007). *Children in Trouble.* Basingstoke: Palgrave/MacMillan.

Hayden, C. (2011). *Schools and Social Control.* In Hayden, C. and Martin, D. (eds.) *Crime, Anti-Social Behaviour and Schools* Basingstoke: Palgrave/MacMillan.

Hayden, C. and Jenkins, C. (2014). 'Troubled Families' Programme in England: 'wicked problems' and policy based evidence. *Policy Studies* Vol. 35 (6), pp. 631-649.

Ingul, J.M., Klöckner, C.A., Silverman, W.K., and Nordahl, H.M. (2012). Adolescent school absenteeism: modelling social and individual risk factors. *Child and Adolescent Mental Health*, Vol. 17, pp. 93-100.

Jeugdmonitor (n.d.). *CBS statline jeugddatabase.* Retrieved from: http://jeugdstatline.cbs.nl/Jeugdmonitor/selection/?VW=T&DM=SLNL&PA= 71010NED&D1=a&D2=0&D3=2-4&D4=0&D5=0&D6=a&HDR=G1,G3,T&STB=G4,G5,G2

Jonasson, C. (2011). The dynamics of absence behaviour: interrelations between absence from class and absence in class, *Educational Research*, Vol.53 (1), pp.17-32.

Kearny, C. A. (2008a). School absenteeism and school refusal behaviour in youth: a contemporary review. *Clinical Psychological Review,* Vol. 28, pp. 451-471. DOI: 10.1016

Kearny, C.A. (2008b). An Interdisciplinary Model of School Absenteeism in Youth to Inform Professional Practice and Public Policy. *Educational Psychological Review,* Vol. 20, pp 257-282.

Kearney, C. A., Turner, D., and Gauger, M. (2010). *School refusal behaviour.* Chichester: John Wiley.

NSPCC (2009) *NSPCC Response to DCSF Call for Views on Home Education. Retrieved from:*

http://www.nspcc.org.uk/Inform/policyandpublicaffairs/Consultations/2009/Ho meEducation_wdf64376.pdf

Laan, A. M., van der, Schans, C. A., van der, Bogaerts, S., and Doreleijers, Th. A. H. (2009). *Criminogene en beschermende factoren bij jongeren die een basisraadonderzoek ondergaan.* Den Haag: Boom Juridische Uitgevers, WODC.

Lauchlan, F. (2003). Responding to chronic Non-attendance: a review of intervention approaches. *Educational Psychology in Practice,* Vol.19 (2), pp.133-146.

Lubberman, J., Mommers, A., and Wester, M. (2014). *Leerlingverzuim in beeld. Een studie naar de cijfers en registratie van absoluut en relatief verzuim.* Nijmegen: ITS Radboud Universiteit Nijmegen.

Lyon, A. R., and Cotler, S. (2007). Toward reduced bias and increased utility in the assessment of school refusal behaviour: the case for diverse samples and evaluations of context. *Psychology in the Schools,* Vol. 44 (6), pp.551-565.

Ministerie van Onderwijs Cultuur en Wetenschap (2014). Kamerbrief *voortgang aanpak schoolverzuim.* Retrieved from: *http://www.rijksoverheid.nl/documenten-en-publicaties/kamerstukken/2014/03/20/kamerbrief-over- aanpak-schoolverzuim.html*

OFSTED (2003). *Key Stage 4: towards a flexible curriculum.* London: TSO.

OM (2013*). Richtlijn voor strafvordering strafrechtelijke aanpak schoolverzuim* (2013R015). Retrieved from the website of the OM on 17 March 2016.

Raad voor de Kinderbescherming (2013). *Factsheet aanpak schoolverzuim.* Retrieved from: https://www.kinderbescherming.nl/wat_doet_de_raad/bescherming/overige_be schermingonderwerpen/

Ramirez, M., Wu, Y., Kataoka, S., Wong, M., Yang, J., Peek-Asa, C., and Stein, B. (2012). Youth Violence across Multiple Dimensions: A Study of Violence, Absenteeism, and Suspensions among Middle School Children. *The Journal of Pediatrics,* Vol, 161(3), pp. 542-546e2.:

Reid, K. (2008). The causes of non-attendance: an empirical study, *Educational Review,* Vol. 60 (4), pp. 345–357.

Reid, K. (2012). Reflections of being "A Man of Truancy": 40 years on, *Educational Studies,* Vol.38 (3), pp. 327-340.

Sheppard, A. (2009). School attendance and attainment: poor attenders' perceptions of schoolwork and parental involvement in their education. *British Journal of Special Education,* Vol.36 (2), pp. 104-111.

Shimiz, K. (2011). Defining and Interpreting Absence from School in Contemporary Japan: How the Ministry of Education has Framed School Non-attendance, *Social Science Japan Journal,* Vol. 14 (2), pp. 165–187.

Slavin, R. E. (2010). Can financial incentives enhance educational outcomes? Evidence from international experiments. *Educational Research Review,* Vol. 5, pp.68- 80. DOI:10.1016/j.edurev.2009.12 .0

Sumter, R.S., Bokhorst, C.L., Steinberg, L., and Westenberg, P.M. (2009). The developmental pattern of resistance to peer influence in adolescence: Will the teenager ever be able to resist? *Journal of adolescence,* Vol. 32, pp.1009-1021.

Thornton, M., Darmody, M. and McCoy, S. (2013). Persistent absenteeism among Irish primary school pupils. *Educational Review,* Vol. 65 (4) pp. 488-501.

Van Veldhuizen, M. (2010). *Schoolverzuim; een signaal voor achterliggende problematiek?* Masterthesis in het kader van de Master Maatschappelijke opvoedingsvraagstukken. Universiteit Utrecht.

Veenstra, R., Lindenberg, S., Tinga, F., and Ormel, J. (2010). Truancy in late elementary and early secondary education: The influence of social bonds and self-control – The TRAILS study. *International Journal of Behavioural Development,* Vol.34 (4), pp.302-310.

Weerman, F.M., and Laan A. M., van der (2006). Het verband tussen spijbelen, voortijdig schoolverlaten en criminaliteit. *Justitiële Verkenningen,* Vol. 32 (6), pp. 39-53.

Wood, J.J., Lynne-Landsman, S.D., Langer, D.A., Wood, P.A., Clark, S.L., Eddy, J.M., and Ialongo, N. (2012). School Attendance problems and Youth Psychopathology: Structural Cross-Lagged Regression Models in Three Longitudinal Data Sets. *Child Development,* Vol. 83(1), pp. 351-366.

Whitney, B. (1994). *The Truth about Truancy.* London: Kogan-Page.

Yan, F. and Jament, J. (2009). Integrated but mot included: exploring quiet disaffection in mainstream schools in China and India, *The International Journal on School Disaffection,* Vol.6 (1), pp. 12-18.

Yoneyama, S. (2000). Student Discourse on Tôkôkyohi (School Phobia/Refusal) in Japan: Burnout or Empowerment? *British Journal of Sociology of Education,* Vol. 21(1), pp. 77-94.

Websites

http://www.home-education.org.uk/

CHAPTER SIX

TEACHING STUDENTS WHO ARE GIFTED IN THE NATURAL SCIENCES AND MATHEMATICS TO STUDY LITERATURE: A VIETNAMESE PRACTITIONERS' RESEARCH

DAVID HOLLOWAY AND MI NGYEN

Introduction

On the 3rd December 2013 the outcomes of the most recent triennial Programme for International Student Assessment (PISA) tests carried out by the Organisation for Economic Co-operation and Development (OECD) were published for 510,000 participating students in all 34 OECD member countries and 31 partner countries. The PISA 2012 testing cycle covered Science, Reading and a particular focus on Mathematics. The results provoked concern in the UK from academics, some of whom questioned the PISA methodology (Goldstein, cited in TES 29 July, 2013), from teachers and their professional associations, the national media and not least from politicians, who were careful to blame their political opponents for what they perceived as a threat to the nation's economic future. UK schoolchildren are perceived, especially by the politicians, as participating in a life-long competition in the global economy against their peers in South Korea, Canada, China, numerous European countries, Singapore and other rapidly developing states. The UK is portrayed as being in a race, a competition, to improve educational attainment and through that to enhancing economic competitiveness, but it is a competition that according to PISA the UK is already losing thus leading politicians and policy advisers to the belief that what is required is further top-down, government–led reforms.

   This chapter explores ideas about education, teaching, learning and assessment. The approaches commonly found in the Confucian circle countries, namely China, Taiwan, Singapore, Vietnam and South Korea, are currently received sympathetically by English government ministers responsible for education and their policy advisers. This is well illustrated by the UK Secretary of State informing the Parliamentary Select Committee on Education that "I have been to Singapore and Hong Kong, and what is striking is that many of the lessons that apply there are lessons that we can apply here" (Gove, 2010 cited in Crossley, 2014). Mr. Gove told the World Education Forum in 2011 that "No nation that is serious about ensuring its children enjoy an education can afford to ignore the PISA (and McKinsey) studies" (Gove, 2011 cited in Crossley, 2014). But such developments are increasingly questioned in the best performing PISA test countries where the high scores are attributed to excessive student workloads and a focus on testing: " the Chinese education system is excellent in preparing outstanding test takers, just like other education systems within the Confucian cultural circle: Singapore, Korea, Japan and Hong Kong" (Zhao, 2011).

The Vietnamese secondary education system, particularly since the overthrow of the colonial powers and the reunification of the country in 1975, provides an interesting case for examining global policy and pedagogic developments and perhaps offers an insight and warning for the UK. In the PISA 2012 tests Vietnam, in common with other countries in the Confucian circle, out-performed the UK in Mathematics, Science and Reading. Teaching and learning in Vietnam is examination oriented. It can be argued that compulsory education in the English secondary sector increasingly demonstrates the same tendency with recent decisions to move away from course work to a greater use of summative examinations at GCSE and GCE A-Levels. Stemming from its peculiar history, Vietnamese education has been shaped by the education model of the former Soviet Union but earlier effects of the French colonial powers and, perhaps more significantly, Confucian philosophies have had a profound influence. Yet despite success in international tests there is now a growing recognition in educational circles in Vietnam of the need "to renovate the existing curriculum". This paper reports a small scale action orientated study, with a focus on the study of literature, carried out in a highly selective high school that educates "gifted and talented" young people aged from 16 to18 years in a provincial city in coastal central Vietnam.

Although it is a requirement of the Vietnamese national curriculum, the study of literature is not popular among gifted and talented science and mathematics students who prefer to study the subjects they specialise and excel in. Parents often share this view.

Context

Education in Vietnam

Vietnam is a multi-ethnic, multi-lingual society and culturally a blend of Buddhism and Confucianism. The country was dominated by its northern neighbour, China, until the mid-19th Century when the French imposed colonial rule. The Confucian influence is, however, still significant. China occupied much of Vietnam for 1000 years shaping many aspects of Vietnamese institutions. The Vietnamese adopted the Chinese practice of competitive examinations to recruit staff for the state bureaucracies. Formal education was restricted to a very small minority who memorised the content of books, Chinese Buddhist and Confucian classics, in preparation for the imperial examinations. Females were excluded. Contemporary commentators argue that this explains why teaching and learning at all levels in Vietnam and in other Confucian heritage nations, has long been and continues to be examination–orientated (Yong Zhao, 2011). The French colonial influence placed a greater emphasis on science and languages but the elitism remained and education provision for Vietnamese children continued to be extremely limited (Marr, 1981). From the early 20th century onwards anti-colonial activists advanced the idea that Vietnamese communities should encourage education and literacy to promote the national interest. The Soviet influence, post-unification, emphasised a narrow specialisation in the curriculum with a focus on science and mathematics. The role of the teacher was that of a moral guardian delivering standardized content to students who were expected to memorise. Arguably creativity and individualism were not encouraged.

Since 1986, and the unravelling of the socialist centrally planned economy, Vietnam has undertaken economic reforms not unlike those that have been implemented in neighbouring China; essentially a shift from a centrally planned economy towards a market economy. The result has been rapid economic growth, averaging 8 per cent per annum, since the millennium and considerable inward foreign investment including hi-tech manufacturers like Canon, Samsung, Hon Hai, and Intel (Hayton, 2010). The economic growth has, however, exposed major weaknesses not only in the country's infrastructure but also in its education system. London (2010, p.374) reports acute skills shortages facing Vietnamese employers and underdeveloped research capacities in the sciences, social sciences and humanities, stating that these will "limit the sustainability and global competitiveness of Vietnam's economy and may distort achievements in the social, political, and cultural spheres". The economic reforms have been used as a rationale for a move away from an elite model of education towards a mass model - the country shows impressive increases in enrolments at primary, secondary and tertiary levels since 1990. However, since 2005 the encouragement of educational elite has been enshrined in law with special provision for gifted and talented learners – again an enduring legacy of the Confucian and French educational traditions. The influence of Confucianism should not be under-estimated. Yong Zhao (2011) argues persuasively the effect on Vietnamese students: education is seen as a "meal ticket" and a mechanism for upward social mobility. The curriculum emphasises theoretical learning, arguably at the expense of practical application and experience.

The current Vietnamese curriculum was introduced in 2000 but was not implemented in the upper secondary schools until 2006/7. It was aimed at making significant changes:

- The curriculum should ensure all-round education, with balanced development of moral, intellectual, physical and aesthetic abilities, and basic skills, especially vocationally oriented skills.
- The curriculum should have content that is fundamental, simplified, practical, and up-to-date. In particular, the curriculum should be practical and strongly relevant to the context of Vietnam, reach the regional and international level, ensure proportional ratios between subjects on science and social/humanities, and provide integrated teaching and learning.
- The curriculum should ensure the implementation of innovative teaching and learning methods which would allow a shift from the one-way transfer of knowledge and skills – " the teachers read and the students write down" paradigm- to a form of teaching and learning where the learning activities of students become more active, and their thinking competencies are encouraged.
- The curriculum should have the highest level of uniformity throughout the country, in particular it should include relevant standards of knowledge, and skills to be learned, and at the same time should consider specific and unique features of local provinces and regions (Vu Trong Ry, 2005).

The curriculum also proposed changes to assessment by widening the focus from concentrating only on mastering of the knowledge and skills of students taking into account their developmental levels. Also advocated were new assessment techniques that could ensure higher levels of objectivity and reliability. Assessments should not be conducted only by teachers; self-assessment by students and peer assessment among students should also be encouraged (Vu Trong Ry, 2005).

But change has been slow. Nguyen (2006) attributes this to the inadequate implementation conditions such as the limited capabilities of teachers, insufficient teaching hours, poor school infrastructure and equipment. At this point it is possible to identify the key characteristics of Vietnamese education:

- Memorising of factual information in preparation for examinations.
- Uncritical acceptance of knowledge transmitted from the teacher.
- The teacher's role is didactic, to impart knowledge.
- Students are required to internalise what is taught regardless of its usefulness.
- Students show little interest in group work or teamwork, critical thinking and problem-solving activities.
- Students are diligent and adaptive but lack flexibility.
- Students tend to look for perfection and are, therefore, fearful of failure.
- Qualifications are more important than the quality of education. (Adapted from Saito and Tsukui, 2008 and Nguyen, 2000).

Nguyen (2002, p. 4) summarises this well: (Vietnamese learners) are very traditional in their learning styles. They are quiet and attentive, good at memorising and following directions, reluctant to participate (though knowing the answers); shy away from oral skills and from group interaction. They are meticulous in note-taking; they go "by the book" and rely on pointed information, and regard the teacher as the complete source of knowledge.

The research site

This study was seen as an opportunity to carry out a small scale educational action–oriented enquiry that would have benefits for the learners and for the teacher-researcher. The over-arching research question asked was:

How can we improve the teaching and learning for students who are gifted in the natural sciences and mathematics in the study of literature?

Whilst currently there are no written aims or statement of school mission, in the case study institution, there is widespread informal knowledge. Its most important function is to prepare high quality human resources for the city. Thus, the school's implicit goals include: to educate and train students for international and national academic contests; to prepare students for entry to prestigious international and national universities; and to nurture and preserve the moral qualities of each student. Such schools may appear unfamiliar to the UK reader but they share some of the characteristics of a UK 6th Form college. Such institutions are also found in the high performing Hong Kong and Singapore education systems. They perform well in national examinations offering advanced school level qualifications, usually academically oriented, like GCE "A" Levels and the International Baccalaureate.

The concept of "Gifted and Talented" is highly problematic since there is little consensus on what constitutes "giftedness" and no globally accepted definition of what a gifted student is. In the UK the National Association of Gifted Children refers to learning, social and emotional needs of children with high learning potential who demonstrate outstanding aptitude or competence in one or more domains of learning (NAGC 2011). In Vietnam the concept is used to include those students who have excellent academic achievements found in the general secondary school (Article 61, Vietnamese educational law, 2005).

The case study high school educates students age 16 to 18. Every year the school enrolls approximately 300 students to the following subjects.

Gifted in mathematics:	70	Gifted in literature:	02
Gifted in physics:	50	Gifted in history:	10
Gifted in chemistry:	35	Gifted in geography:	10
Gifted in informatics:	20	Gifted in English:	40
Gifted in biology:	35	Gifted in French:	05

The school selection process comprises two rounds. Round 1 involves a review of the academic and personal records of students and in Round 2 selected students from Round 1 take an examination in which they have to complete four tests in mathematics, Vietnamese literature, a foreign language (English or French), and the main subject of the gifted class that they intend to enroll in. Marks in the first three subjects are counted with a coefficient of 1 but the mark in the gifted subject has a coefficient of 2.

Students attend normal classes every morning of the week except Sunday. These classes are strictly based on the national curriculum. Gifted classes are held on two afternoons each week. Special classes for preparing students for national academic contests vary, but are mostly arranged in the afternoon. Afternoon is also the time for sports, gymnastic and art classes.

The current Vietnamese national curriculum is divided into two levels of study: fundamental and advanced. Students work with the textbooks determined by the subject group and level they belong to. For example, the students in the mathematics, physics, and chemistry gifted groups will use text books at advanced level while in all other subjects their text books will be at fundamental levels. This research paper reports on the students who study the fundamental literature curriculum. From a teaching and learning perspective, teachers in the school have a degree of professional autonomy and can be flexible in the way they design and deliver their lessons. The rationale underpinning this autonomy and flexibility is the belief that the students attending the school are intelligent, academically focused and aware of their own achievements and potential.

The students in this study were gifted in mathematics, physics, and informatics. The study covers four classes. The following data covers school year 2012 – 2013:

Class 10A1 (Gifted in math, 16 years old): total 35 students, 24 males, and 11 females

Class 10A2 (Gifted in math, 16 years old): total 34 students, 16 males, and 18 females.

Class 10A3 (Gifted in physics, 16 years old): total 25 students, 17 males, 8 females.

Class 10A5 (Gifted in informatics, 16 years old): total 20 students, 16 males, 4 females.

A significant feature of these classes was that the number of males was higher than females. It is possible that this gender characteristic had effects on the motivation to study. Moir and Moir cited by Gilbert (2002, p. 32 – 33), claim that "Males and females are drawn by the biases of their brains to learn in different ways and to have different interests and enthusiasms, any educational system that insists that boys and girls are the same, and must therefore be treated the same, is set to do damage." Thus, Gilbert (2002, p.33) poses and answers the question: "What does this mean for motivation in your classroom? For a start, make sure you have female-type learning opportunities – cooperative, collaborative, language-based – as well as male-type learning – competitive, physical and emotional, with an emphasis on symbols and things." In this situation, when male – type learning seems essential due to their greater number, the females still play a significant role in the classroom because they often volunteer to answer questions and share their views and feelings in literature classes. There is also a tacit knowledge that females are more comfortable studying literature than males because they are more open in expressing their feelings. Teachers of literature frequently believe that the standards that constitute a good essay involve a combination of "reason and emotion". Teachers tend to search for emotional expressions throughout students' work to judge whether students pour their hearts into it or not. The common word that features in much feedback in students' literature work is "dry", which means "little emotion". Is there a subtle bias against males in literature classes? This study has sought to be aware of and to avoid that bias.

From a teacher's perspective, the students from these classes have a learning style that shapes their perception of literature. Cottrell (2008, p. 59) describes the "logician learning style" that includes characteristics such as: "you like things to make sense; you like to know the reasons behind things; you are organised in your approach to study; you enjoy tackling complex problems; you are a perfectionist". The first, second and fourth characteristics are the most recognised features among the students of this study.

In addition to issues of gender and group characteristics, social and family pressure had been placed on the students. Students are required to participate in competitions and examinations, and their goals are not only to pass but to achieve high marks and to win prestigious titles in local, national, and ultimately international contests. During many conversations, parents state their views and describe their efforts in orienting their children to pay attention to their main subjects, especially in the case of students gifted in natural sciences, because it is widely believed that students gifted in these disciplines have more opportunities to gain places in prestigious universities and acquire better jobs. To some unknown and unmeasurable extent, these interventions affect students' perception of literature. Even though literature is officially recognised as one of the most important subjects in the curriculum, it does not have the status for the students of this study.

The above mentioned elements contribute to the students' attitudes towards the study of literature. Bright and academically focused, but in general, the students are not enthusiastic about studying literature. They show a reluctance to write essays and to answer questions. Their approach to the study of literature can be summarized as the following: they find it difficult to express their thoughts or feelings transparently and succinctly in words. This problem is revealed throughout their essays and some mentioned it during interviews. The students have difficulty transferring their learning from one situation to another and they find it difficult to analyse new material. The length of essays has become a challenge, since the students encounter problems in generating ideas and do not have an adequate knowledge base in the literature topics. Finally, the students do not understand the conventions for referencing. Plagiarism, intentional or otherwise, is a common error often identifiable in their essays.

Research design

The enquiry was essentially practitioner based research carried out in a country where such approaches are in their infancy. Practitioner based research has its roots in a seminal work by Stenhouse (1975) advocating the teacher-as-researcher model with its commitment to systematic questioning of one's own teaching as a basis for teacher professional development. Further contributions have emphasised the relationship between practitioner research and critical reflection, the systematic study of professional practice, practitioner control, and ownership of research (Elliot, 1991; Cochran-Smith and Lytle, 1993; Zeichner, 2001).

In Vietnam, whilst there is a growing recognition of the need to reform the curriculum, change approaches to teaching and learning and to improve assessment, little attention has been paid to the relationship between improving educational practices and encouraging teachers to engage in practitioner research in order to bring about change. Change is usually seen as a top-down process emanating from central government. This research involved two phases: the aim of Phase 1 of the enquiry was to obtain data about the students' reading activities. The teacher asked students in two classes of mathematics, one class of physics and one class of informatics a set of questions about their reading activities. The questions were arranged in the following order:

1.   Do you read books on mathematics/ physics/ informatics?
2.   Have you ever read any literature?
3.   Do you read any newspaper?
4.   Do you use online resources?
5.   Do you read comics?

The students who showed interest gave more details about their reading activities. The teacher asked further questions in order to clarify their favourite books and the number they read.

The aim of Phase 2 was to improve the motivation of the students when studying literature. This was achieved by the teacher making changes to the classroom assessment and teaching approaches.

Traditional literature tests in the Vietnamese classroom are often designed around one topic requiring students to undertake tasks including analysing a character from a story or their perceptions about a poem in their text books. While that appears to be a valid way to assess their knowledge and skills, in the Vietnamese context it also creates a passive approach to learning because students tend to learn – by – heart the notes that they took from the lessons and then reproduce what they memorised rather than their own thoughts. Therefore, the teacher designed a different test containing questions that allowed students to develop their literature skills such as summarising, comparing, identifying the key issues and analysing. The new test was based on new material that was not taken from the text book, had not been read by the students previously but came from the same literature genre and possessed similar features to the material in the text book. Due to the use of the new material, the students could neither memorise nor plagiarise. This also created additional challenges and competition between the students. Prior to the test, the teacher asked the students to review the skills they employed when reading the similar literature material in their text books. After the test, the teacher interviewed the students in order to elicit their judgments. When it was not possible to interview the students, the teacher-researcher made notes based on her observations of the class.

Regarding the teaching approaches, the teacher worked with the students to identify and clarify the purpose, relevance, and methods of the lesson before covering content. The intention was to give the students a sense of transparency and coherence as well as provide a rationale for the new approach. A case study was carried out during which the teacher used the comparative method for reading important literature material. The teacher also invited other colleagues to attend the class. The impact of the lesson was evaluated by using an unstructured focused interview with three students who were available for interview during a break period and semi-structured interviews with three colleagues who had attended the class.

Data analysis and findings

Phase 1: students' reading activities

Question 1: Do you read books about your main discipline?
All of the students from the four classes answered positively to the question. Students from class 10A1 and 10A2 (Gifted in Mathematics) showed enthusiasm for reading books on mathematics. Some students from class 10A3 (Gifted in Physics) said they had been told that reading physics books was necessary in order to achieve success in contests. Students from class 10A5, (Gifted in Informatics) said they read documents provided by their informatics teacher.

Question 2: Have you ever read any literature? The answers are listed below in table 6.1.

Table 6.1 - Student Responses to Question 2

Class	Number of students who answered yes to the question out of total number students
10A1	33/35
10A2	27/34
10A3	24/25
10A5	8/20

Question 3: Do you read any newspapers?
All students from the four classes responded yes to the question. Only two students, from class 10A1, claimed they never read books on literature. Students from 10A3: stated that they read Chinese and French fiction that were recommended by peers or by their parents. Two students in that group said they read Vietnamese poems. Students in 10A5, who read books on literature, were in a minority, but revealed that they enjoyed work by Nguyen Nhat Anh, a best- selling author on teenager fiction.
Students from classes 10A2, 10A3, and 10A5 enjoyed reading teenage magazines, but students from class 10A1 preferred more mature publications.

Question 4: Do you use online resources?

Again, the response from all students was positive. The websites that they often visited were online newspapers for teenagers and sport news.

Question 5: Do you read comics? The answers are listed in table 6.2.

Table 6.2 - Responses to Question 5

Class	Number of students who answered yes to the question out of total number students
10A1	6/35
10A2	32/34
10A3	23/25
10A5	20/20

Class 10A1: had the lowest number of students reading comics claiming they did not have time. One respondent stated that comics were poor quality and did not improve his language skills. The two students who did not read comics in class 10A2 responded that comics lacked sophistication.

Overall, the students in 10A3 considered reading comics was an entertainment whilst in 10A5 students were all enthusiastic about reading comics because they found them funny and entertaining.

Phase 1 of the enquiry was important in order to identify the students' reading activities and, arguably, to provide evidence and insight to underpin the teacher researcher's own beliefs about her students and to provide the basis for Phase 2 activities which involved assessment.

Assessment

Interviews were conducted with A2 Mathematics students. These students were presented with new material that had similarities to that already used in the curriculum but had not been read by them before. The students liked the new material claiming that they found it challenging, especially their ability to interpret it unassisted by the teacher. But three members of the group expressed fears that their marks would suffer stating that if they were to be tested, they would prefer to use the old curriculum. Others, however, preferred to be tested using the new material because they "could answer for themselves rather than memorise and reproduce what the teacher had told them. The students claimed that they were not afraid of learning new material but they did fear getting poor marks because of the problems that could arise and the consequences. This suggests that the students fully recognised the constraints imposed by the testing regime in the school and the pressure they were under to consistently gain high grades. An additional student from the A1 group was interviewed. He liked the new approach to assessment. He believed he had developed his own skills and answered for himself rather than in the way the teacher wanted him to think.

The Informatics Group was not formally interviewed due to the constraints of time. However, the teacher was able to observe and noted the following: when they received the new material they appeared to be worried and perplexed but after an explanation offered by the teacher they were more composed and focused. The Physics Group, who are perceived as able in the natural sciences but not interested in literature or the humanities, found the new material difficult and perceived it as having a negative effect on their marks. Some of the students did not appear to take the test seriously although others were more focused.

Teaching approaches

Three students were coded A, B and C. During the interview, student A said that he liked exploring literature works and judged himself as being "rational". He believed that "*deep emotions evoked from literature belong to teachers, I'm not sure students feel the same.*" He wanted to develop his learning skills and responded that he liked the comparative method used in the lesson, partly because he had the opportunity to work with new material.

Student B claimed she liked imagining and associating pictures and emotions as well as living the lives of the characters in different works. "*Sometimes when the teacher gave a good lecture, I was too deep in my imagination of the characters and I forgot what the teacher really said.*" She wanted to listen to interesting comments about literature from teachers. She found it difficult to express accurately some of her best ideas in words and consequently she believed that the teacher did not really understand them. In her opinion, the comparative method could broaden the meaning of the literature material but could not help her to explore the characters more deeply. Student C claimed that she preferred rational ideas and disliked rambling sentences. She liked to summarise the most important points of the literature lesson so that it was easier for her to remember them. She said that she liked the comparative method because it provided her with reasons to comment or analyse the material.

The three teachers who were interviewed were coded I, II, III. Teacher I stated that the application of the comparative method was clear and suitable for the lesson. Comparison was not only applied as a teaching method but also as a literature skill to the students. The teacher had widened the meanings of the literature material but the limitation was that the teacher could have given the students the comparative material in advance so that they were better prepared for the lesson.

Teacher II believed that the comparative method was well applied and that it highlighted the creativeness of the author being studied. She listed what she perceived as being the limitations of the lesson: some knowledge was not necessary for students of the standard literature curriculum; the method could be effective with high performing classes but would confuse students from the lower performance classes. She recommended that the teacher use other methods in the lesson and that the comparative method should only be applied to a few aspects of the literature curriculum.

Teacher III claimed that the comparative method was suitable for improving students' creative ability and motivation but that it would be even more effective if it was applied to teaching those students who were gifted in literature. She also thought that the teacher should have allowed the students to read the material in advance so that they would be more able to compare and contrast. Furthermore, comparative method is only one of the approaches to the study of literature and sometimes just a technique to explore literary materials.

Conclusions

Overall it is difficult to provide a full assessment of the initiative at this stage. Nevertheless, some tentative conclusions can be drawn. The students, on the whole, were positive because they appreciated a new pedagogic approach and were interested in the new elements, both the materials and the assessment. A major shortcoming for them was a lack of consistency between teaching and assessment. The students were under considerable pressure from both the school and their parents to achieve high grades in their specialist subjects and as a consequence were reluctant to adopt new approaches to other subjects.

The other literature teachers were only engaged in the final stages of Phase 2. Overall they appeared to be positive although one preferred the traditional approach. However, the teachers were more critical of the use of the comparative method in the study of literature rather than the traditional approach to teaching and learning. They all agreed that the teacher should have spent more time preparing the students in advance.

We suggest that the findings support the view that it is highly likely that students' motivation in the learning process, not only when studying literature, is influenced by the pedagogic approach adopted, the materials selected by the teacher for use in the lesson and by the students' level of interest in those materials. Student involvement cannot be imposed, especially in the Vietnamese context where students are expected to be more passive and didactic teaching approaches are commonplace. Involvement needs to stem from the materials and the pedagogic approach. Yet this is increasingly ignored in the UK by politicians and policy-makers when driving forward policies aimed at greater marketization and performativity. UK teachers respond by "teaching to the test" in order to prepare their students for standardised tests.

As researchers and practitioners we regard this small scale action oriented project as showing early signs of success. As indicated earlier there has been little emphasis on using practitioner-based research approaches to bring about curriculum change and teacher development in Vietnam. In the UK, Western Europe, North America, and Australasia, however, there is a growing body of evidence that suggests that by engaging in practitioner research teachers can derive a range of professional benefits. As indicated by the teacher in this study it is possible to gain a better understanding of pedagogic practice and ways to improve it (Dadds and Hart, 2001); that by engaging in this type of research and enquiry gives teachers an enhanced sense of the student's perspective in the classroom (McLaughlin & Black Hawkins, 2006); it reminds teachers of their intellectual capability and the importance of that capability to their professional lives allowing them to see that the work they carry out in the school matters. In this case the research enabled the teacher to examine theories and ideas and how they could be applied to educational practice and encouraged her to expand her sense of what could and ought to be done (Campbell, 2007).

Perhaps the most significant benefit of engaging in such initiatives, however, is that the result can be a renewed feeling of pride and excitement about teaching and in a revitalised sense of oneself as a teacher (Elliott, 1991; Dadds and Hart, 2001; Zeichner, 2003; McLaughlin et al., 2006). This can be contrasted with the initiatives promoted by the UK government, in part as a reaction to the outcomes of the PISA tests that only appear to lead to a demoralised profession. In Vietnam, on the other hand, there has been recognition of the shortcomings of pedagogic practices in their schools and, like other Asian countries, alternative approaches have been advocated to bring about improvements in teaching and learning to enhance creativity. In both the UK and Vietnam changes are required in teacher professional practice. Practitioner research approaches enable the teacher to acquire and develop pedagogical knowledge and research skills and competencies. It means teachers will pose questions about their professional practices but this questioning is more likely to bring about the improvements in the quality of teaching, learning and assessment than political rhetoric and top-down policy initiatives inspired by PISA outcomes.

Bibliography

Campbell, A. (2007). *Practitioner Research.* London: TLRP. Retrieved from: http://www.tlrp.org/capacity/rm/wt/campbell.

Cochran-Smith, M. and Lytle, S. (1993). *Inside-Outside: teacher research and knowledge.* New York: Teacher College Press.

Cottrell, S. (2008). *The Study Skills Handbook* (3rd Ed). Basingstoke: Palgrave Macmillan.

Crossley, M. (2014). Global league tables, big data and the international transfer of educational research modalities. *Comparative Education,* Vol.50 (1), pp. 15-26.

Dadds, M. and Hart, S. (2001). *Doing Practitioner Research Differently.* London: Falmer.

Elliot, J. (1991). *Action Research for Educational Change.* Buckingham: Open University Press.

Gilbert, I. (2002). *Essential Motivation in the Classroom.* London: Routledge.

Goldstein, H. cited by Stewart, S. (2013). Is PISA Fundamentally Flawed? *Times Educational Supplement 26 July 2013.*

Hayton, B. (2010). *Vietnam: Rising Dragon.* London: Yale University Press.

London, J. (2010). Globalisation and the governance of education in Viet Nam. *Asia Pacific Journal of Education,* Vol. 30 (4), pp. 361-379.

Marr, D.G. (1981). *Vietnamese Tradition on Trial.* Berkeley: University of California Press.

McLaughlin, C., Black-Hawkins, K., Brindley, S., McIntyre, D. and Tabor, K. (2006). *Researching Schools: Stories from a Schools-University Partnership for Educational Research.* London: Routledge.

Moir, A. and Moir, B. (n.d.) cited in Gilbert, I. (2002). *Essential Motivation in the Classroom.* London: Taylor and Francis.

National Association of Gifted Children. (2011). Redefining Giftedness for a new century: shifting the paradigm. (Position Paper). Retrieved from: http://nagc/index2.aspx?id=6404

Nguyen, Huu Chau. (2006). *Study on the evaluation of quality and effectiveness of the nationwide implementation of the new curriculum and textbooks in primary and lower secondary schools.* Hanoi: NIESAC cited in Yong, Zhao. (Ed.) (2011). *Handbook of Asian Education.* Abingdon: Routledge.

Nguyen Tuong, Lai. (2000). Opportunities and challenges for Vietnam in facing the knowledge-based economy. Cited in Yong, Zhao. (Ed.) (2011). *Handbook of Asian Education.* Abingdon: Routledge.

Saito, E and Tsukui, A. (2008). Challenging common sense: Cases of school reform for a learning community under an international cooperation project in Bac Giang province, Vietnam. *International Journal of Educational Development*, Vol. 28, pp. 571-584.

Vietnamese Ministry of Education and Training. (2005). Retrieved from: http://www.moet.gov.vn /? Page=6.21

Vu Trong Ry. (2005). *The Renovation of contents, teaching and learning methods and forms in school.* Hanoi: NIESAC.

Yong Zhao (Ed.) (2011).*Handbook of Asian Education.* Abingdon: Routledge.

Zeichner, K. and Noffke, S. (2001). Practitioner Research. In Richardson, A. (Ed.) *Handbook of Research on Teaching,* 4th ed. Washington, D.C.: AERA.

Zeichner, K. (2003). Teacher Research and Professional Development. In *Educational Action Research*, Vol.11 (2), pp. 301-326.

Chapter Seven

Why Dyslexia is a Social Issue

Chris Neanon

Introduction

"Useful as it may be, Dyslexia, or for that matter any other label, is not the problem here, but the deeply embedded fears that create anger and shame are" (Scurfield, 2014, p.344).

Is dyslexia a social issue or an educational issue or both and if so, why? As the comment from Scurfield (2014) suggests, naming this condition is only part of what is required to prevent dyslexia from being a major factor compromising the well-being of individuals in every sphere of life. There continues to be evidence (Dyslexia Action, 2012) that not adopting an early and systematic approach to identifying and remediating the learning and literacy challenges experienced by dyslexic children can have long term social and economic implications. Despite the raft of approaches to supporting literacy needs (Brooks, 2002), policies of inclusion and changes in definitions of need, which have proliferated since the Warnock Report (1978), the failure to identify and effectively support–those with dyslexia remains a key determining factor in their social, emotional and economic wellbeing.

This does not remain at the personal level but has consequences for the wider society and continue to impact on all aspects of life for those identified with dyslexia. An example of this becomes evident when reviewing literacy levels of those in prison. Hewitt-Main (2012, p.7) showed that 53 per cent of the prisoners at Chelmsford Prison (a prison for male offenders) were identified as dyslexic. This compares significantly with 10 per cent of the UK population (British Dyslexia Association (BDA, n.d). Hewitt-Main's research supported previous studies into prison populations (Rice, 1999; Clark and Dugdale, 2008) which suggests that there is a correlation between the failure to establish literacy skills and those who offend. Whilst dyslexia is not exclusively associated with illiteracy, it is a very common outcome and so the social consequences of failing to address the issue become very apparent. Hewitt-Main (2012, p.6) summarised the potential social impact of failing to address dyslexia stating:

> "those learners who had experienced difficulties in the classroom when they were children, moved through low self-esteem, a sense of failure and frustration, leading to behaviour problems, school exclusion, inability to find jobs, apply for benefits or pass theory driving tests, spiralling into petty offences, a life of crime, prison and serial reoffending" .

Whilst there are many individuals identified with dyslexia who create successful and fulfilling lives, there is no doubt that experiencing constant failure as a child is not the most positive of starts in life. The research by Hewitt-Main (2012) suggests that for some, experience of failure in school sets them on a path with negative outcomes. The challenge is how this cycle can be interrupted and how dyslexia can cease to be an issue with such grave social outcomes for some.

One major challenge is that dyslexia is a complex and confounding learning problem. Significantly more is known now about how it impacts on learning and the role that neurological differences play than previously. Gilger (2008, p.32) notes that one of the challenges with understanding dyslexia is that "no single cognitive or neurological model seems to fit all of the data" so interpretation needs to be cautious. Pennington et al (2011, cited by Carroll, 2014, p.95) support the understanding of dyslexia as a "multiple deficits model" and as unpicking a single cause or attribute becomes impossible there is the potential for an abnegation of responsibility on the part of classroom professionals. Consequently this can lead to a failure or reluctance to identify dyslexia in an individual, ultimately creating the situation where the learning needs of one in 10 of the population are not addressed whilst they are in school and when intervention is most appropriate (BDA, n.d.).

At the most extreme end of opinions these challenges have led to the claim that dyslexia is a "cruel fiction" allowing "Certified dyslexics [to] get longer in exams," (BBC news, 2009, citing Graham Stringer). This supports the apocryphal and clichéd view that 'dyslexia' is simply the term that middle class parents use when their children are simply not intelligent. However Ott (2007) refers to the inconsistency found in dyslexia as being its most consistent factor hence the one factor that can be anticipated. Unfortunately this unpredictability does not sit comfortably alongside the Government agenda for raising standards in schools - an agenda which seems to suggest that there is a simple and straightforward resolution to literacy acquisition.

In this chapter, three of the "inconsistencies" and the debate around Dyslexia and the social and emotional ramifications of failing to address the issues will be examined. First a clear understanding of the nature and definition of dyslexia will be explored. Second, an understanding of the emotional and social costs of dyslexia and associated limited literacy skills in the personal and societal context will be considered. Finally, the role that schools and the wider community could play to bring about effective changes at an individual and societal level for those identified as dyslexic will be discussed.

Understanding the nature of dyslexia

A Google search of 'What is dyslexia?' reveals 11,800, 000 results in 0.27 seconds.   Information comes from very different sources and includes medical, university, celebrity, local authority, education, employability, holistic therapy and dictionary and Wikipedia sites all within the first 20 pages. Ironically the ubiquity of information explains to some extent why there is still confusion as to what dyslexia is. In the UK, dyslexia is defined in law through the Equality Act (2010) as a disability. A person (P) has disability if

a) P has a physical or mental impairment, and
b) The impairment has a substantial and long-term adverse effect on P's ability to carry out normal day-to-day activities.
    (Equality Act, 2010)

Clearly there will be those with dyslexia where the challenges are not 'substantial' as the impact can be seen as a continuum. Nevertheless, even though there is this legal explanation and the terms 'substantial' and 'long term' are defined by law, there is still confusion. Table 7.1 gives some of the most commonly cited and recent definitions of dyslexia but even within these definitions there are significant differences.

Table 7.1 Definitions of Dyslexia

Rose Report (2009)

Dyslexia is a learning difficulty that primarily affects the skills involved in accurate and fluent word reading and spelling.

- Characteristic features of dyslexia are difficulties in phonological awareness, verbal memory and verbal processing speed.
- Dyslexia occurs across the range of intellectual abilities.
- It is best thought of as a continuum, not a distinct category, and there are no clear cut-off points.
- Co-occurring difficulties may be seen in aspects of language, motor co-ordination, mental calculation, concentration and personal organisation, but these are not, by themselves, markers of dyslexia.
- A good indication of the severity and persistence of dyslexic difficulties can be gained by examining how the individual responds or has responded to well-founded intervention.

Snowling (2012, p. 7)

"Dyslexia is a neurodevelopmental disorder with a probable genetic basis and it is generally agreed that more boys than girls are affected….The core feature of dyslexia is a problem with word decoding, which in turn impacts spelling performance and the development of reading fluency…..In addition problems with working memory, attention and organisation are frequently reported."

British Dyslexia Association (2015)

Dyslexia is a hidden disability thought to affect around 10% of the populations, 4% severely. It is the most common of the Specific Learning Difficulties (SpLDs). Dyslexia is usually hereditary. A student with dyslexia may mix up letters within words and words within sentences while reading. They may also have difficulty with spelling words correctly while writing; letter reversals are common. However, dyslexia is not only about literacy, although weaknesses in literacy are often the most visible sign. Dyslexia affects the way information is processed, stored and retrieved with problems of memory, speed of processing, time perception, organisation and sequencing. Some may also have difficulty navigating a route, left and right and compass directions.

Reid (2008)

"Dyslexia is a processing difference, often characterised by difficulties in literacy acquisition affecting reading, writing and spelling. It can also have an impact of cognitive process such as memory, speed of processing, time management, co-ordination and automaticity. There may be visual and/or phonological difficulties and usually some discrepancies in educational performances. There will be individual differences and individual variation and it is therefore important to consider learning styles and the learning and work context when planning intervention and accommodations."

Challenges with literacy are commonly recognised in these definitions but not all specify the other effects such as "time perceptions" identified by the BDA (2015) and yet this is a common feature of dyslexia which can have a serious impact on learning. The following is a real life example of what this can mean to an individual. Imagine that you have been identified as being at the 'significant' end of the dyslexia continuum, and have a Statement of Special Educational Needs (SEN)[1] which has been created to provide appropriate support and protection. You are in a secondary school which has a two week timetable and the specialist support allocated to you runs on a different day each week and is scheduled to be in a different classroom each week. One of the elements present in your version of dyslexia is a problem with "time perceptions" which means that you have a distorted perception of time both in the immediate moment and in your longer term planning and organisation. Given this profile with your educational environment and timetabling, accessing the support that is offered becomes a challenge. It is clear that this would have an "adverse effect on ability to carry out normal day to day activities" (Equality Act, 2010). By focusing exclusively on the literacy aspect of dyslexia, the needs of this individual would not be met even with the protection of a Statement. The challenges of course will not disappear once out of the confines of the classroom. For adults with dyslexia who have these challenges with time perception, attending appointments on time, being able to estimate the time needed for travel or to complete a task could all potentially cause problems with gaining and keeping employment. These examples illustrate robustly why a wide ranging and collective understanding of the features of dyslexia is essential if it is to cease being a social issue with the subsequent impact on individual lives.

However, the provenance of that understanding is at the core of the controversies in relation to the question as to whether or not dyslexia exists. Elliott and Grigorenko (2014, p. 4) argue for "a rigorous scientific construct" and muster support in citing Brown and others (2011) that:

"Without an agreed-on definition [of dyslexia] that can be implemented reliably and validly, understanding the nature, causes and best treatments for reading disability is unlikely. Similarly, an agreed-on definition is essential for practice."

This view simply misses the point and demonstrates a lack of awareness of the complexity of dyslexia. The condition is not exclusively about reading whether that is in relation to decoding, comprehension or speed of processing (BDA, 2015). A more holistic and purposeful way of defining dyslexia starts by visualising it in three dimensions comprising separate but interlocking elements rather than a linear contained definable entity. Working extensively with dyslexics has shown that any element of learning may be compromised and create a hiatus in the learning process and each individual is likely to have a different profile of compromised elements which may well be contextually determined. Consequently for treatments or support, this needs to start with the individual. The puzzle remains however, as to why one individual, rather than another, is dyslexic and here neuroscience and genetics need to be considered.

In the past 20 years, understanding of the brain and how it functions has developed significantly and with this development has come recognition of how these new insights could be applied to education (CERI, 2008). There have been many challenges in the ways in which the new knowledge is applied to learning and in some cases an over simplistic interpretation of the science has led to misunderstandings and according to Howard-Jones (2014, p.1) "ineffective or unevaluated approaches to teaching in the classroom." This has been due in part to the complexity of neuroscience, which is in itself expressed in scientific language that may not be accessible to all. However, for an educator, having an understanding of why differences occur in the learning patterns of young children is tantalising. It implies a promise that if the causes are known, then interventions can be put in place which will make a difference and reduce or even eliminate the social consequences of learning difficulties. Neuroscience is though a "new" science, enabled, to a large extent, by developing technology which permits observation of brain functions but moving from the theory to practical interventions is far from straight forward. Howard-Jones (2014, p.3) cites the outcomes from the Santiago declaration in which 136 scientists acknowledged that "neuroscientific research, at this stage in its development, does not offer scientific guidelines for policy, practice, or parenting". Nevertheless, in spite of the plethora of neuromyths, which have been used to support learning support strategies, Howard-Jones (2014, p.1) maintains that an understanding of brain function holds possibilities for "influencing the outcomes" for those who are struggling with their learning".

Talcott (2014) has additionally identified further areas for investigation which will potentially illuminate aspects of dyslexia. For example, many practitioners working with children who have learning difficulties irrespective of whether or not dyslexia has been identified, will be aware of the complexity of pinpointing the individual needs of the child and will have recognised that there is a cross-over with other specific learning difficulties. This comorbidity factor is not new and Portwood (2004) has drawn comparisons between the features of specific learning difficulties such as dyspraxia, dyslexia and ADHD. Neuroscience is now recognising this as an area to explore and neuroscientists are building this comorbidity factor into their analysis (Talcott, 2014).

Brain differences between dyslexic and non-dyslexic groups are challenging to identify and to date research has failed to distinguish dyslexia from generalised reading difficulties (Elliott and Grigorenko, 2014). A model of a dyslexic brain has not been established. However, Breznitz (2008) refers to research which shows significant differences with speed of processing as measured via brain imagery between dyslexic and non-dyslexic groups. According to Breznitz (2008), word decoding, an essential skill in reading, occurs through the synthesis of different types of information which are processed in different parts of the brain. Where there is a lack of synchronisation and "a gap in the speed of processing (SOP)" (Breznitz, 2006, p. 12) then there are likely to be problems with word decoding. This is noted more frequently in the brains of dyslexics .but research does not currently offer supportive strategies to help those struggling with reading. Clearly the potential for neuroscience to contribute to resolving difficulties with learning to read is not yet close enough.

There are, however, other aspects of reading which have been identified as contributing to the profile of dyslexia. One such area is phonological processing. According to Guardiola (2001) some of the first researchers to explore this were Bradley and Bryant (1983) who made the link between recognising and categorising the individual sounds in words and efficient reading and word manipulation. This is now generally accepted as being a very common aspect in the dyslexic profile and one which presents exceptional challenges for English speakers. The richness and complexity of the English language, where 44 individual sounds are represented by only 26 letters accounts for some of these challenges. Later work by Rack, Snowling and Olson (1992) (cited by Guardiola, 2001) drew attention to the difficulties children with dyslexia tend to have with identifying rhyming words and matching sounds to their representative letters. Snowling (2012) has continued research in this area and has suggested that this pattern with learning can be instrumental in helping practitioners identify needs at an early age and the potential impact of this is explored later.

Whilst difficulties with the building blocks of reading and the process of reading itself have traditionally been linked with dyslexia and are clearly a major part of how dyslexia presents itself in individuals, it is only part of the picture. As the earlier definitions suggest, challenges with aspects of memory, short term, auditory and visual are also linked to the dyslexic profile. But caution needs to be applied in order to avoid suggesting that this is a simple issue or that it is manifested similarly across all profiles of dyslexia. Jeffries and Everatt (2004, p. 198) advise that from their research "a simple connection between type of learning difficulty and working memory component has not always been found".

Nevertheless, the ability to retain auditory or visual information long enough to process it is difficult for a significant number of dyslexics. There are individual disparities in working memory capabilities and these may be compounded by environmental factors such as distraction, or biological circumstances. Holmes (2012) makes the point that whilst variances might be expected between age groups, variances also exist within the same age group. Holmes (2012) observed that problems with the working memory are noted across a range of conditions such as ADHD, language difficulties and dyslexia, and are implicated in limited educational development. Within the classroom a poor working memory can lead to missed opportunities with learning and consequently poor progress.

These challenges persist through to adulthood, and essential life-skills, such as personal organisation, are compromised by a poor working memory. Skinner (2013, p. 87), exploring how women with dyslexia experienced motherhood, noted that "some tasks associated with 'good' mothering by the participants were perceived to be particularly difficult because of poor organisational skills, short-term memory and problems assimilating lots of different pieces of information". There are significant ramifications here for self-identity when being seen as a "good" mother is so important for self-esteem. This is explored in the next section.

The emotional and social costs of dyslexia

Shane Lynch, a member of the highly successful band "Boyzone" and recently identified dyslexic (Rawlings, 2012) described his feelings on travelling to an appointment for a dyslexia assessment *"I feel destructive, I feel evil, I feel reckless – why the f*** am I coming here if this is what it is doing to me"?* How could simply presenting oneself for assessment generate such intensity of feeling and overwhelming sense of despair from someone who is financially, creatively and personally successful? Irrespective of the feelings that the word "dyslexia" engenders, the condition is not in itself malevolent or cursed. 'Julie', one of the participants in Glazzard and Dale's (2013, p.31) study eloquently summarised the situation

> *"Dyslexia is not life threatening. It is not a disability. It is not a disease. Those who have it do not require huge amounts of resources to support them… Despite this, I believe that thousands of people have suffered similar experiences to me and that some children continue to suffer today".*

One very common manifestation of 'suffering' is stress and an understanding of the features of stress demonstrates why it is so clearly linked with the experiences of many of those with dyslexia. Miles (2004) acknowledges that the phenomenon of stress can have both positive and negative consequences: it can provide a valuable and motivating boost of cortisol which potentially enhances focus; it can also weaken the immune system, lead to fatigue and depression particularly where stress has an emotional basis and is long term and persistent. For those with dyslexia it is unfortunately more likely that they will experience the latter rather than the former stress particularly in the classroom context when failure is so common. The International Dyslexia Association (IDA, 2013) suggests that stress is positive when there is a sense of having some control over the situation and a belief that action will make a difference. The reality, however, for many with dyslexia, is that learning in school and indeed throughout life is challenging and they are faced daily with information that they struggle to make sense of or indeed have any influence over. Susan Hampshire, a successful actor, summarised this by saying *"As soon as I make a mistake I panic, and because I panic I make more mistakes"* (cited by Miles 2004, p. iv). She describes how her dyslexia impacts on driving and finding her way on unfamiliar roads and the frustration and stress that she describes is palpable – *"I was so distraught that I was screaming at the top of my voice"* (cited by Miles, 2004, p. vi). It is not difficult to recognise that in this scenario there is little that is positive in the stress that is being experienced.

Stress, at one time considered to be an apocryphal, fictional response to being very busy, has now (National Health Service, 2014) been identified as a real biological response to being overwhelmed either emotionally or mentally. This physical response initiates a complex chain of reactions which can be either instantaneous or longer term. From a simple perspective, when the body is under intense pressure it goes into the flight or fight mode in which hormones such as adrenaline and cortisol are released into the blood stream. This is a useful response if there is physical danger because blood is channelled from the cortex (the 'thinking' part of the brain) to the muscles – ready for flight or fight. However, when the stress is mentally induced such as in an exam situation or having to read out loud, it is less helpful as the cortex is needed for processing this information effectively. The saying "my mind went blank" sums up the outcome. In a physical situation the hormones are naturally dissipated through the action of the muscles, but when the stress is mental there is no dissipation of the hormones through physical exertion and the hormones remain in the body. Segerstrom and Miller (2004, p. 601) cite Elliot and Eisdorfer's (1982) taxonomy of stress in which they refer to "chronic stressors". These ongoing and persistent stressors "usually pervade a person's life, forcing him/her to restructure his/her identity or social roles". An additional feature of chronic stressors is an absence of stability in that the individual feels a lack of understanding of when – or if – the stressful situation will come to an end. Anyone who has worked with dyslexics or those who are dyslexic themselves will recognise this situation. This scenario in which chronic stress is ever present can then lead to longer term consequences such as loss of self-esteem and failure to engage effectively with learning.

Being in a constant state of stress related arousal with high levels of potent hormones can impact on the immune system (Segerstrom and Miller, 2004, p. 602). The situation gets even more complicated as research by Chetty et al. (2014) found that prolonged exposure to chronic stress can ultimately change the structure of the brain and potentially lead to mental illness. This is not to imply that all dyslexics will experience mental illness. Nevertheless, personal accounts of dyslexics confirm that for some, the day to day experiences endured don't contribute to a life well lived. One respondent to a request by Miles (2004, p. 135) to describe her experiences of stress and dyslexia said:

"I personally believe today that the overwhelming levels of anxiety created by the daily ignominies and embarrassments of being a dyslexic

functioning in society fuelled my abusing myself with prescribed medication and alcohol".

Additionally stress leads to exhaustion created by "elevated levels of arousal and information processing associated with the desire to understand and cope with the demands of an ongoing situation" (LePine, LePine, and Jackson, 2004, p. 884) - a situation which is experienced every hour of every day in classrooms and in the work place for many of those with dyslexia. Fawcett (2004, p. 156) considers that there are external and internal stressors for dyslexics and suggests that whilst it may be possible to reduce the external stressors through improving the learning situation and social awareness of dyslexia, the "internal stress of being dyslexic will prove more difficult to resolve". Riddick (2010, p. 100) cites a mother's comments on her son who was identified as dyslexic - *"he wanted to be dead. There was nothing for him. He wanted his tie so he could hang himself"*. If there was any doubt that dyslexia is a social issue, this mother's comments show that living with and supporting dyslexics profoundly affects families and significantly leads to levels of self-esteem where some feel that their life is not worth living.

Self-esteem is a much used phrase particularly in relation to academic achievement. It is related to the sense of value that an individual places on themselves. It is a complex concept which, like dyslexia, is subject to many influences and factors such as individual differences in personality and experiences. There is a link with low esteem and achievement although some research (Baumeister et al., 2003, cited by Swann et al., 2007) challenges the evidence for the predictive nature of self-esteem in terms of achievement. Nevertheless, Swann and others (2007, p. 93) maintain that if the caveat is accepted that there are many variables to be considered "self-views are meaningfully related to socially significant outcomes". This view is supported by Burden (2008) citing Hughes and Dawson (1995) whose research with dyslexic adults suggested that significant and persistent feelings of negative self-worth were a result of failure in the classroom. Challis (2013) acknowledges individual differences but asserts that a healthy self-esteem creates a situation in which negative experiences are not permanently disabling whereas with low self-esteem individuals find it difficult to cope with adverse experiences. The consequences of feeling unable to cope with life can then lead to depression, anxiety and ultimately more debilitating mental health issues.

Burden (2008) considers that how individuals view and value themselves (i.e. self-esteem) develops through childhood and at adolescence they will have developed a set of core constructs which will shape their life experiences. Their experiences may be such that emotional support or counselling is necessary to enable them to manage the effects of their dyslexia. However, these issues of stress and low self-esteem are not an inevitable outcome of dyslexia. Rather it is the way in which difference is perceived and managed, both by society and the individual, which results in the "suffering" and consequent life choices persisting into adulthood.

The social costs of dyslexia are as complex and varied as the condition itself and depend on many factors. One relates to employment issues for dyslexic adults and a second focuses on the association between dyslexia and crime. Reid (2005, cited in Reid, Came and Price, 2008), considered a significant range of occupations from the armed forces to zoo workers and came to the conclusion that none of these professions were beyond the capability of an individual with dyslexia. But, irrespective of the potential professional opportunities, this can only happen if the challenges evident in a dyslexic profile are appropriately supported. An effective, sympathetic and non-discriminatory response to supporting dyslexia as required by the Equality Act 2010 is in practice quite challenging. Dyslexia, like other specific learning difficulties, is essentially a hidden disability and for employers to take this into account on an individual basis they have to first be aware of the situation. Disclosure though is potentially fraught with difficulties. There is no legal requirement for disclosure. Morgan and Klein (2000, p. 118) noted that "Many people are reluctant to discuss their dyslexia for fear of prejudice or negative responses". Bryan (2012) makes the point that it is not always apparent as to how dyslexia may impact on a job and that disclosure may raise concerns where none exist. An additional factor is that if the individual decides not to disclose dyslexia and then subsequently has difficulties in the work place this may make it harder to gain the support that they need. Morgan and Klein (2000) suggest that the final decision is rarely taken following a rational summary of the issues but is more likely to be made on the basis of an individual's feelings about the job and their ability to cope.

There are few comprehensive studies of the impact of dyslexia on employment opportunities (Reid, Came and Price, 2008) and so it is difficult to gauge the social costs both for individuals and the national economy. Further compounding the issue is the fact that no two dyslexics are the same and each individual will have a unique profile of needs. Furthermore, different levels of resilience and self-belief will be contributory factors in how individuals respond to different employment demands. But there is significant anecdotal evidence (Bartlett and Moody, 2010) of the challenges faced by dyslexics in the search for employment and the potential wastage of talent can be surmised from these narratives. For some dyslexics this talent is redirected towards a life of crime.

Although an association between dyslexia and crime has been noted in the literature and is an area of continuing interest and research (Kirk and Reid, 2001), a correlation between crime and dyslexia is not indicative of any causal factors. There is no evidence that dyslexia and unlawful behaviours are genetically linked. It is reported though (Kirk and Reid, 2001) that between 30 and 50 per cent of those in prison have either literacy difficulties and/or dyslexia. Hewitt-Main (2012, p.6) when collecting narratives from prisoners concluded that "a life of crime, prison and serial re-offending" was too often a result of failure in the classroom – failure to teach and failure to learn – and failure in society to anticipate the needs of 10 per cent of the population.

Personal case studies attest to the failure of society to address the needs of dyslexics once they come within the judicial system. Julian Cox was committed to HM Prison Gartree in 1994 to serve a minimum of 20 years for a range of alleged offences, including murder. He was profoundly dyslexic but had "an IQ well above average" (Cox, 2001, p. 101). His testimony of his experiences, once in the legal system, illustrates how dyslexia compounds the failure to support individuals. He writes

> "During my Police interviews I was indeed in a state of shock, my depression was still evident during trial, this on its own would account for impaired thought processes which produces weaker communication skills. For a dyslexic this definitely isn't conducive for dyslexics often have these impediments to start with, so for me the situation was exacerbated" (Cox, 2001, p. 102).

This case led to the creation of a set of guidelines for the courts to enable dyslexics to more easily access the justice system and do themselves justice in the courtroom.

The number of dyslexics in the prison system remains disproportionally high. Kirk and Reid (2001) identified that 50% of 50 participants in a young offender's institution in Scotland had a dyslexic profile. This mirrors research by Hewitt-Main (2012) who interviewed over 2,000 prisoners and 53% were identified as being dyslexic. The social implications of this are overwhelming. Government statistics estimate that the cost to the country per year of keeping people in prison is £2,8 million (Ministry of Justice, 2014). Finding a way to reduce this cost would have huge implications for other demands on Government revenue. Two issues need to be addressed; one is to cut the number of offenders in the first instance and the second to reduce re-offending. The Dyslexia Institute

(2005, p. 4) reported that "80% of individuals leaving prison lack the skills for 96% of all jobs; half of all prisoners are at level 1 or below for reading". Nearly half of all male offenders had been excluded from school and one third had truanted. These statistics lead to questions about the experiences of some within the school environment. Clearly learning is influenced by many factors and dyslexia is only one.

Hewitt-Main's (2012) work with prisoners focused on learning and on their literacy skills. She developed a programme with literate prisoners to mentor others through the reading process. The results were "transformational" and with improved literacy skills the prisoners had, for the first time, extended career options. "They would always be dyslexic, but now they could achieve in their own ways" (Hewitt-Main, 2012, p. 8). In terms of sample size, this research was limited but the outcomes demonstrated the effectiveness of the intervention because, of the 17 offenders in the first cohort, only one was back in prison. Further research conceded that when compared with a group of dyslexic university students, the offenders' profiles were different in terms of cognitive and cultural resources and that the initial playing field was not equal. The conclusion, however, was that "The presence of a dyslexic pattern of strengths and weaknesses can be identified even amongst those who have other risk factors for educational failure and social exclusion." (Dyslexia Institute, 2005, p. 25). The recommendations from the DI report focused on preventative measures; specialist teaching in prison education, raising the awareness of dyslexia amongst those responsible for working with offenders and concentration on employability skills. Hewitt-Main's project, conducted seven years after the DI recommendations, demonstrated that this message had not been received. Her project was eventually terminated due to a lack of funds.

The role of schools and the wider community

Primary aged children in the UK spend on average 635 hours per year in school – less than 8% of their total time and yet this is the time when formal learning takes place and when children with dyslexia can learn what it is to fail. Schools can play a critical role in supporting the resilience and learning of children with dyslexia to ensure that their learning experience is transformative in the most positive way. Schools, however, are shaped by political agendas and hence susceptible to the vagaries of political parties. This is evident when looking at recent changes in relation to learning needs.

For the last 25 years education in the UK has been predicated on an ideology of inclusion. The UK was a signatory to the UNESCO Salamanca Statement (1994, p. viii) that expressed the principles that all children with their "unique characteristics" had a right to education and that education systems had to "take into account the wide diversity of these characteristics and needs". In the UK essential principles of the Salamanca Statement were incorporated into the 1996 Education Act. The Special Needs and Disability Act (SENDA) (2001) and the resulting revised Special Educational Needs Code of Practice (SEN CoP, 2002) translated the principles into practice. The SEN CoP gave practical guidance to schools on how to meet the legal requirements of SENDA and how to ensure that the needs of all children were identified and met. Dyslexia was categorised as a special educational need. The Code emphasised that different teaching strategies may be needed to develop the learning of these children and that the progress of all children was a whole school responsibility and teachers were teachers of all children.

This obligation of all teachers to be accountable for the full range of needs in a classroom rather than the practice in numerous schools of allocating those with additional needs to the Teaching Assistants, was underpinned by a "quality first" teaching approach (DCSF, 2008, p. 9). This enshrined the right of all children to have quality teaching as a starting point. Whilst being aware of the challenges inherent in meeting the individual needs of a class of young people, "quality first" teaching was not about differentiating by outcome (i.e. some will achieve all the lesson's outcomes and others may achieve writing the date on the top of the page). Quality first teaching was about "offering higher levels of support or extra challenge for those who need it, so that all pupils can access the learning" (DCSF, 2008, p. 9). The ideals here are irreproachable and in a perfect world this approach to teaching would embrace those with dyslexia. Unfortunately inclusion was only one of the topics on the Government's agenda for improving education. School league tables were introduced in 1994; Standard Assessment Tests (SATs) for children at seven, 11 and 14 were also introduced with all processes in place by 1998; and contextual value added scores (CVA) were taken into consideration from 2006. The agenda for inclusion and the scoring of schools in relation to the performance of their students were contradictory philosophies. Whilst schools where students are achieving well is an acceptable ideal, the reality of inclusion means that where there is a high percentage of need the average attainment of the students may be compromised. Even by taking into account CVA factors these conflicting agendas were not good news for dyslexics, whose learning may be out of synch with the majority.

In 2011 the Government published the Green Paper, Support and Aspiration, (DfE, 2011) and it appeared that inclusion was no longer on the agenda. Instead, the Paper focused on discussing the importance of early identification of need, parental choice and support, and the seamless support of individuals from early years through to adulthood. Labels such as School Action and School Action Plus categories would be replaced with one SEN category. These changes were finally introduced in the Children and Families Act 2014 and articulated in the Special Education Needs and Disability Code of Practice: 0 to 25 years (DfE, 2015, p. 92) which states that schools must "use their best endeavours to make sure that a child with SEN gets the support they need". Aspland (2014) questioned the exhortation for schools to "use their best endeavours" but acknowledged that "the proof will be in the pudding.   I have a feeling that there are going to be more than a few soggy bottomed ... puddings on the horizon". The changes in legislation and schools' responsibilities have yet to be fully evaluated in relation to support for those with additional learning needs.

In spite of the conflicting agenda regarding the role of schools in terms of achievement, the Government has continued to focus sporadically on literacy and dyslexia with the publication of two reports from Sir Jim Rose; the first focusing on teaching reading (Rose, 2006) and the second on dyslexia (Rose, 2009). The first report looked at the most effective ways to teach reading and concluded that the synthetic phonics approach was likely to have the highest degree of success for the majority of young people. What was particularly significant for those with dyslexia was that the use of context and comprehension as tools for decoding text was minimised. For many dyslexics, who struggle to make the sound to symbol connection, context is key and giving more of the same in terms of linking sound to symbol appears counter-intuitive for dyslexics. Also in the English language 38 of the 100 most frequently used words are irregular and have to be learned by sight recognition alone (Bald, 2007). Davis and Braun (2010) explained that for some dyslexics attempting to conceptualise a word that is not a noun created a blank screen in the mind. Non dyslexics in contrast, are more likely to see the word written out in their mind's eye. Synthetic phonics is not useful in this situation. The downgrading of comprehension as a tool for deconstructing text was another aspect of the report which was criticised by Wyse and Morgan (2007, p.41). They referred to the model of teaching reading advocated in the Rose Report as "prescriptive, rigid and limited". There were some positive elements in this report in that multi-sensory teaching which is a particularly effective strategy for dyslexics was advocated. Additionally, the Report reiterated that "quality first teaching" and monitoring by the senior management in schools was essential. Irrespective of criticism of the report, the synthetic phonics approach has been adopted in schools and is the focus of an end of Year One assessment. Initial results suggested that there was a 5% increase in those who are achieving the "expected standard", taking the percentage to 74% (DfE, 2014). Building on the evidence from Snowling (2012) regarding the link with phonological processing and literacy, this outcome suggests that there is still a substantial group of children who struggle to benefit from this revised "quality of teaching" even when phonics are taught in a focused way. An alternative explanation for their difficulties must be considered.

The second significant report compiled by Rose was *Identifying and Teaching Children and Young People with Dyslexia and Literacy Difficulties* (2009). In this report Rose summarised research into dyslexia, highlighted current effective strategies being used for support, and recommended ways forward. Most significantly Rose noted that it was not helpful to continually challenge the existence of the condition and that efforts should be focused on "building professional expertise in identifying dyslexia and developing effective ways to help learners overcome its effects" (Rose, 2009, p. 9). A series of far ranging recommendations were given which included the implementation of effective support programmes and training for teachers and support staff. However the Dyslexia Action Report (2012, p. 3) acknowledged that there were "still major challenges to address" and in July 2015 an All-Party Parliamentary Group on Dyslexia and other Specific Learning Difficulties was established to keep government appraised of the situation in schools and what statutory and non-statutory bodies are achieving in this field. One of the first tasks assigned to this group is to review the training in SEND and Specific Learning Difficulties which is to be given to teacher trainees. This review is anticipated to report in 2016 – however there is still debate as to the extent of SEND knowledge that should be mandatory in the training and in spite of the recommendations of Rose in 2009, there appears to be a lack of urgency to bring about change.

Summary

In summary, the evidence presented here supports the claim that dyslexia does matter and that it persists in presenting as a social issue. Clearly dyslexia is not a myth. It is the lived experience of millions of people and "face validity" (Kirk and Read, 2001, p. 79) is good enough to create identification processes and teaching programmes. Elliot's claim that dyslexia is a "meaningless label used by middle-class parents who fear their children are being branded stupid' and was a 'useless term" (Macrae, 2014) has no foundation as current research, supported by neuroscience demonstrates. Failure to identify and understand the nature of the condition and to then effectively scaffold learning opportunities has adverse consequences for individuals and society. Research (Rose, 2009) clearly shows that there is an understanding of the nature of dyslexia. The inconsistencies noted by Ott (2007) have been recognised and developing learning profiles is possible. Additionally, the evidence in the Rose Report (2009) highlights that effective support strategies for those with dyslexia exist. Personal experience of working with both young people and adults demonstrates that when these interventions are appropriately used and put in place in a timely manner, erosion of self-esteem and illiteracy are not inevitable consequences of dyslexia and the "deeply embedded fears" cited by Scurfield (2014) have the potential to be allayed. The issue is then clearly about the political will to create change rather than the issue of dyslexia itself. Resolving this will continue to challenge individuals and society.

Note

[1] Since 2015 Statements of SEN have been replaced by Education and Health Care Plans

Bibliography

Aspland, D. (2014). *SEN Code of Practice: what does this look like in schools?* Retrieved from: http://www.specialneedsjungle.com/code-practice-look-like-schools/

Bald, J. (2007).*Using phonics to teach reading and spelling*. London: Sage.

Bartlett, D. and Moody, S. (2010). *Dyslexia in the workplace,* (2nd Ed.). Retrieved from: http://site.ebrary.com/lib/portsmouth/reader.action? DocID=10577674&ppg=225.

Breznits, Z. (2006). *Fluency in reading: Synchronization of processes*. Mahwah, NJ: Lawrence Eribaum and Associates.

—. (2008). The Origin of dyslexia: the asynchrony phenomenon. In G. Reid, A. Fawcett, F. Manis and L. Siegel (Eds.), *The Sage handbook of dyslexia, (*pp.11-29). London: Sage.

British Broadcasting Corporation (BBC). (2009).*MP brands dyslexia as 'fiction'. Retrieved from:* http://news.bbc.co.uk/1/hi/england/manchester/ 7828121.stm

British Dyslexia Association & HM Young Offender Institution. (2005). *Practical solutions to identifying dyslexia in juvenile offenders.* Reading: British Dyslexia Association.

British Dyslexia Association (BDA). (n.d. a) *Dyslexia Research Information. Retrieved from:* http://www.bdadyslexia.org.uk/about-dyslexia/further-information/dyslexia-research-information-.html

British Dyslexia Association. (n.d.b). *Types of specific learning difficulty.* Retrieved from: http://www.bdadyslexia.org.uk/educator/what-are-specific-learning-difficulties

Brooks, G. (2002).*What works for children with literacy difficulties. Research Report (380).* London: HMSO. Retrieved from: http://dera.ioe.ac.uk/4662/1/RR380.pdf

Bryan, S. (2012, November 5). *Jobseekers with dyslexia: challenges and solutions.* Retrieved from: http://www.theguardian.com/careers/careers-blog/jobseekers-dyslexia-challenges-solutions

Burden, R. (2008). Dyslexia and self-concept. In G. Reid, A. Fawcett, F. Manis and L. Siegel (Eds.), *The Sage handbook of dyslexia* (pp.395-410). London: Sage.

Carroll, J. (2014). Phonological processing: is that all there is? In J. Carroll and Saunders K. (Eds.), *The dyslexia handbook* (pp. 95 -98). Bracknell: British Dyslexia Association.

Carroll, J. and Saunders, K. (Eds). (2014). *The dyslexia handbook.* Bracknell: British Dyslexia Association.

Centre for Educational Research and Innovation (CERI). (2008). *Understanding the brain: the birth of a learning science.* Paris: OECD. Retrieved from: http://www.oecd.org/site/educeri21st/40554190.pdf

Challis, S. (2013). *How to increase your self-esteem.* London: National Association for Mental Health (MIND). Retrieved from: http://www.mind.org.uk/information-support/types-   of-mental-health-problems/self-esteem/consequences-of-low-self-esteem/#.VTDXCiFViko

Chetty.S., Friedman, A., Taravosh-Lahn, K., Kirby, E., Mirescu, C., Guo, F. et al. (2014). Stress and glucocorticoids promote oligodendrogenesis in the adult hippocampus. *Molecular Psychiatry*, Vol.19 (12), pp.1275-1283. Retrieved from: http://dx.doi.org/10.1038/mp.2013.190.

Clark, C. and Dugdale, G. (2008).*Literacy changes lives: the role of literacy in offending behaviour.* London: National Literacy Trust. Retrieved from: http://www.literacytrust.org.uk/assets/0000/0422/Literacy_changes_lives__prisons.pdf

Cox, J. (2001).From inside prison. *Dyslexia,* Vol.7 (2), pp. 97-102. Retrieved from: http://dx.doi.org/10.1002/dys.189

Davis, R. and Braun, E. (2010). *The gift of dyslexia.* (Revised and expanded Ed.). New York: Perigee Books.

Department for Children, Schools and Families. (DCSF). (2008). *Personalised learning – a practical guide.* Annesley: DCSF Publications.

Department for Education. (2011). *Support and aspiration: a new approach to special educational needs and disability.* London: TSO.

—. (2014). *Phonic screening checks and national curriculum assessments at key stage 1 in England, 2014.* Retrieved from: https://www.gov.uk/government/uploads/system/uploads/attachment_data/file/356941/SFR34_2014_text.pdf

—. (2015). *Special Education Needs and Disability Code of Practice: 0 to 25 years.* Retrieved from: https://www.gov.uk/government/uploads/system/uploads/attachment_data/file/398815

Department for Education and Skills (DfES). (2002).*Special Educational Needs Code of Practice.* Annesley: DfES Publications.

—. (2002). *Special Educational Needs Code of Practice.* Annesley: DfES Publications.

—. (2004).*A framework for understanding dyslexia.* Annesley: DfES Publications.

Dyslexia Action. (2012).*Dyslexia still matters.* Retrieved from: http://www.dyslexiaaction.org.uk/files/dyslexiaaction/dyslexia_still_matters.pdf

Dyslexia Institute (DI). (2005).*The incidence of hidden disabilities in the prison population.* Egham: The Dyslexia Institute.

Dyslexia Research Institute. (2014).*Bright solutions for dyslexia.* Retrieved from: http://www.dyslexia-add.org/dyslexia.html

Dyslexia Research Trust. (n.d.). *About dyslexia.* Retrieved from: http://www.dyslexic.org.uk/about-dyslexia

Elliot, J. and Grigorenko, E. (2014). *The dyslexia debate.* New York: Cambridge University Press.

Fawcett, A. (2004). Individual case studies and recent research. In T. Miles (Ed.). *Dyslexia and stress.* (2nded. pp.156-187).London: Whurr Publishers Ltd.

Gilger, J. (2008). Some special issues concerning the genetics of dyslexia. In G. Reid, A. Fawcett, F. Manis and L. Siegel (Eds.) *The Sage Handbook of Dyslexia* (pp. 30-52). London: Sage.

Glazzard, J. and Dale, K. (2013). Trainee teachers with dyslexia: personal narratives of resilience. *Journal of research in special educational needs,* Vol.13 (1) pp. 26-37. Retrieved from: http://dx.doi.org/10.1111/j.1471-3802.2012.01254.x.

Guardiola, J. (2001).The evolution of research on dyslexia. *Anuario de Psycologia,* Vol. 32(1)*, pp* 3-30. Retrieved from: http://ibgwww.colorado.edu/~gayan/ch1.pdf

Hewitt-Main, J. (2012).*Dyslexia behind bars.* Benfleet: Mentoring 4U.

Holmes, J. (2012).Working memory and learning difficulties. *Dyslexia Review.* Retrieved from: http://www.mrc-cbu.cam.ac.uk/wp-content/uploads/2013/09/Working-memory-and-learning-diffculties.pdf

Howard-Jones, P. (2014).Neuroscience and education: myths and messages. *Nature Reviews Neuroscience*, Vol.15, pp.817-824. Retrieved from: http://dx.doi.org/10.1038/nrn3817

International Dyslexia Association (IDA). (2013). *Dyslexia-stress-anxiety connection.* Retrieved from: http://eida.org/the-dyslexia-stress-anxiety-connection

Jeffries, S. and Everatt, J. (2004).Working memory: its role in dyslexia and other specific learning difficulties. *Dyslexia*, Vol. 10(3*)*, pp.196-215. Retrieved from: http://dx.doi.org/10.1002/dys.278

Kirk, J. and Reid, G. (2001). An examination of the relationship between dyslexia and offending in young people and the implications for the training system. *Dyslexia*, Vol.7 (2), pp.77-84. Retrieved from: http://dx.doi.org10.1002/dys.184

Lepine, J., Lepine, M. and Jackson, C. (2004). Challenge and hindrance stress: relationships with exhaustion, motivation to learn, and learning performance. *Journal of Applied Psychology* Vol.89 (5), pp. 883-891. Retrieved from: http://dx.doi.org/10.1037/0021-9010.89.5.883

Macrae, F. (2014, February 26). Dyslexia is a 'meaningless label used by middle-class parents who fear their children are being branded stupid, professor claims. *Daily Mail*. Retrieved from: http://www.dailymail.co.uk/health/article-2567690/Dyslexia-meaningless-label-used-middle-class-parents-claims-Professor-Julian-Elliot.html

Miles, T. (Ed.). (2004). *Dyslexia and stress*. (2nd Ed.). London: Whurr Publishers.

Ministry of Justice. (2014). *Costs per place and costs per prisoner: national offender management service annual report and accounts 2013-14*. London: TSO. Retrieved from: https://www.gov.uk/government/uploads/system/uploads/attachment_data/file/367551/cost-per-place-and-prisoner-2013-14-summary.pdf

Moody, S. (2010). Dyslexia in the dock. In D. Bartlett and S. Moody, *Dyslexia in the workplace*, (2nded.), pp. 266-273. Retrieved from: http://site.ebrary.com/lib/portsmouth/reader.action?docID=10577674&ppg=225

Morgan, E. and Klein, C. (2000). *The dyslexic adult in a non-dyslexic world*. London: Whurr Publishers.

National Health Service (NHS). (2014).*Struggling with stress?* Retrieved from: http://www.nhs.uk/conditions/stress-anxiety-depression/pages/understanding-stress.aspx

Ott, P. (2007). *Teaching children with dyslexia: a practical guide*. (2nd Ed.). London: Routledge.

Portwood, M. (2004). Movement disorders in early childhood – an epidemic. *Dyspraxia Foundation Professional Journal*. Retrieved from: http://www.dyspraxiafoundation.org.uk/downloads/Professional_Journal_Issue_3.pdf

Rawlings, R. (Producer). (2012). *My Secret past* [Television series]. London: Channel 5.

Register of All-Party Parliamentary Groups. (2015). retrieved from: http://www.publications.parliament.uk/pa/cm/cmallparty/150730/dyslexia-and-other-specific-learning-difficulties.htm

Reid, G. (2008). *Definitions*. Retrieved from http://www.drgavinreid.com/free-resources/dyslexia

Reid, G., Came, F. and Price, L. (2008).Dyslexia: workplace issues. In G. Reid, A. Fawcett, F. Manis and L. Siegel (Eds.) *The Sage Handbook of Dyslexia*, (pp. 474-548).London: Sage.

Rice, M. (1999).Dyslexia and Crime. *Prison Report, 49,* pp.18-19.
Riddick, B. (2010). *Living with dyslexia.* (2nd ed.).Abingdon: Routledge.
Rose, J. (2006). *Independent review of the teaching of early reading.* Annesley: DfES.
—. (2009). *Identifying and teaching children and young people with dyslexia and literacy difficulties.* Annesley: DCSF publications.
Scurfield, M. (2014). *I could be anyone* (Revised Ed.). Manchester (New Hampshire): Monticello Publishing.
Segerstrom, S. and Miller, G. (2004). Psychological stress and the human immune system: a meta-analytic study of 30 years of inquiry. *Psychology Bulletin,* Vol.130 (4), pp.601-630. Retrieved from: http://dx.doi.org/10.1037/0033_2909.130.4.601
Skinner, T. (2013).Women's perceptions of how their dyslexia impacts on their mothering. *Disability and Society,* Vol. 28 (1), pp.81-95. Retrieved from: http://dx.doi.org/10.1080/09687599.2012.695526
Snowling, M. (2012). Early identification and interventions for dyslexia: a contemporary view. *Journal of research in special educational needs,* Vol.13 (1), pp. 7-14. Retrieved from: http://dx.doi.org/10.1111/j.1471-3802.2012.01262.x
Swann Jr., W., Chang-Scheider, C. and McClarty, K. (2007). Do people's self-views matter?' *American Psychologist,* Vol. 62(2), pp.84-94. Retrieved from: http://eds.b.ebscohost.com/ehost/pdfviewer/pdfviewer?vid=2&sid=e85978d8-c3c0-4183-9640-93e0d084e031%40sessionmgr114&hid=126
Talcott, J. (2014). Creating virtuous circles between the laboratory and the classroom: delivering the promise of educational research. In J. Carroll and K. Saunders. (Eds). *The dyslexia handbook,* (pp. 131-137). Bracknell: British Dyslexia Association.
The Dyslexia-SPLD Trust. (2013). *Dyslexia and literacy difficulties: policy and practice review.* Retrieved from: http://framework.thedyslexia-spldtrust.org.uk/
UNESCO. (1994). *The Salamanca statement and framework for action of special needs education.* Retrieved from: http://www.unesco.org/education/pdf/SALAMA_E.PDF
Warnock, M. (1978). *Report of the committee of enquiry into the education of handicapped children and young people.* London: HMSO.
Wyse, D. and Styles, M. (2007). Synthetic phonics and the teaching of reading: the debate surrounding England's Rose Report. *Literacy,* Vol.41 (1), pp.35-42. Retrieved from: http://dx.doi.org/10.1111/j.1467-9345.2007.00455.

CHAPTER EIGHT

SCHOOL-BASED MENTAL HEALTH LITERACY PROGRAMMES: A SYSTEMATIC REVIEW

PAUL GORCZYNSKI

Introduction

Childhood serves as a critical time for the physical, social, emotional, and cognitive development of an individual. Mental health problems that emerge between the ages of 4 and 18 years can be profoundly disruptive and affect the way individuals feel, think, and behave. Mental health problems can include stress, anxiety, depression, as well as other forms of mental illness, which are clinically diagnosed conditions that impact affective and cognitive functions as well as physical and social aspects of health (Belfer, 2008). These problems can affect one's ability to be productive, forge positive relationships and contribute meaningfully to society (Beddington et al., 2008). Research shows the prevalence of mental health problems amongst children in high-income countries ranging from 8 to 20 per cent (Belfer, 2008; Costello, Egger and Angold, 2005; Kieling et al., 2011). Identifying and treating mental health problems in childhood is vital to maximizing their academic potential and social, emotional, and cognitive development. Children spend a great deal of their formative years in schools, which is why they have been recommended as locations where mental health problems in children can be readily detected and addressed through careful screening procedures and interventions (Rutter et al., 1979; Wei, Kutcher and Szumilas, 2011; Wei and Kutcher, 2012). Teachers are also well positioned to play a major part in the promotion of good mental health and detection of mental health problems in children, provided they are professionally qualified to communicate their concerns to parents or carers. A major component of enhancing overall mental health in children is the delivery of programmes that enhance mental health literacy, where information is provided to help individuals: 1) better understand mental health problems and recognize their symptoms, 2) address stigmatizing attitudes, and 3) access necessary mental health resources (Wei et al., 2013). Previous research has shown that school-based mental health literacy programmes are still grappling with how best to deliver the necessary information to children (Wei et al., 2013). A major shortcoming of recent reviews of mental health literacy programmes is that they have not fully evaluated all three major components of mental health literacy for children across primary and secondary levels (Mellor, 2014; Schachter et al., 2008; Wei et al., 2013). The aim of this review of the literature is to address the gaps in knowledge and examine the effectiveness of primary and secondary level school-based mental health literacy programmes on mental health knowledge, attitudes, and help seeking behaviour in children from 4 to 18 years. Finally, the chapter offers advice as to how school-based mental health literacy programmes can be evaluated in a rigorous manner.

Method

This systematic review relied on similar methodologies employed by previous reviews conducted by Mellor (2014), Schachter and colleagues (2008), and Wei and colleagues (2013). Studies were included in the systematic reviews of the above researchers if they met the following criteria: 1) involved children between the ages of 4-18 years; 2) delivered mental health literacy programmes in school environments; 3) were written in English; and 4) included at least one of the following components; i) basic concepts of mental health knowledge from a biological, social, or psychological perspective; ii) resources or strategies to decrease stigmatizing behaviour toward mental health problems; and iii) resources or strategies to facilitate help seeking behaviour. No restrictions were placed on publication status or date, delivery format of intervention, geographic location, duration of intervention, evaluation method, or study design.

Results

A total of 47 studies were identified and included in this review. Most programmes, 21 in total, were evaluated using pre-experimental methods, meaning they were not compared against a control group. The remaining studies evaluated their programmes against control groups, however, only eight studies used more rigorous experimental methods where participants were randomly allocated to either experimental or control conditions. The majority of studies were conducted in the USA, Canada, Australia and the UK with others in Portugal Iceland Serbia, Nigeria, Germany, Greece, and Hong Kong. They were mainly conducted in secondary schools, rather than primary school settings. The participants were predominately female and aged between 8 and 18 years.

Most mental health literacy programmes focused on general mental health issues with only a small number concentrating on specific diagnoses, like anxiety, depression, and schizophrenia. All interventions varied in length, number of sessions, and delivery methods. Interventions lasted from 30-minutes to multiple hours, spanning single sessions to four-month curriculums. Delivery methods spanned the spectrum and included presentations, interactive learning opportunities, storytelling, theatre, puppets, music, videos, vignettes, art, Internet self-learning programmes, games, booklets, posters, visits from mental health teams, and personally meeting people living with mental illness. Interventions were delivered by teachers, healthcare professionals, and individuals living with mental illness. Nearly all studies addressed issues concerning mental health stigma. Over half of reviewed studies examined knowledge and symptomology, while a small number of studies provided information about improving help-seeking behaviours.

Mental Health Knowledge

Most studies that investigated mental illness knowledge reported significant increases in overall knowledge scores as a result of the intervention. Individuals were able to communicate greater knowledge of common illnesses such as stress, depression, anxiety, bi-polar disorder, and schizophrenia. They were also aware of key symptoms of mental illness, like low mood; sleeplessness; feelings of fear, panic, or uneasiness; mood swings; hallucinations; and delusions. In total, 26 studies investigated some aspect of mental health knowledge (Bella-Awusah et al., 2014; Campos et al., 2012, 2014; Chan. et al., 2009; Essler et al., 2006; Gestsdottir et al., 2010; Gudmundsdottir, 2002; Lake and Burgess, 1989; Lauria-Horner et al., 2004; Mcluckie et al., 2014; Naylor et al., 2009; Perry et al., 2014; Petchers et al., 1988; Pinfold et al., 2003, 2005; Pinto-Foltz et al., 2009, 2011; Rahman et al., 1998; Rickwood et al., 2004; Robinson et al., 2009; Skre et al., 2013; Stuart, 2006; Swartz et al., 2010; Ventieri et al., 2011; Watson et al., 2004; Wahl et al., 2011). Robinson and his colleagues (2009) were the only researchers to find no mental health knowledge improvements as a result of their intervention. Perry and colleagues (2014), in contrast, conducted a rigorous experimental study, amongst secondary school students, that illustrated the delivery of a refined mental health curriculum that improved overall mental health knowledge. Their study evaluated a classroom-based programme entitled *HeadStrong* that consisted of a booklet, slideshows, and various interactive activities. Trained teachers delivered the programme over a period of 5 to 8 weeks for a total of 10 hours that was embedded in Personal Development, Health and Physical Education (PDHPE) classes. The *HeadStrong* programme was organised into five modules that covered the following topics: 1) mood and mental well-being, 2) mood disorder, 3) reaching and helping others, 4) helping yourself, and 5) raising awareness about mental illnesses. Overall results for the programme showed significant changes in mental health knowledge that differed from control groups who received a standardised curriculum of PDHPE. A 6-month follow-up evaluation revealed that mental health knowledge decreased over time, suggesting that additional supplementary training may be required to maintain knowledge of various mental illnesses and their symptoms. This study illustrates the importance of proper teacher training in delivering these programmes and to incorporate them into an established curriculum.

Stigmatizing Attitudes:

The mental health literacy programmes that were evaluated mostly focused on addressing and changing negative attitudes toward mental illness. They were aimed at creating a more positive outlook on mental illness generally but also for those living with a mental illness diagnosis. Studies that investigated attitudes reported significant improvements in attitudes, understanding, and compassion towards those living with mental illness. The following references provide international examples - Battaglia et al., 1990; Bella-Awusah et al., 2014; Brewer et al., 2004; Campos et al., 2014; Chan et al., 2009; Conrad et al., 2009; Essler et al., 2006; Esters et al., 1998; Gestsdottir et al., 2010; Gudmundsdottir, 2002; Ke et al., 2015; Mcluckie et al., 2014; Morrison et al., 1979; Mound and Butterill, 1993; Naylor et al., 2009; Ng and Chan, 2002; O'Kearney et al., 2006; Pejvić-Milovancević et al., 2009; Perry et al., 2014; Petchers et al., 1988; Pinfold et al., 2003, 2005; Pinto-Foltz et al., 2009; Pitre et al., 2007; Rahman et al., 1998; Rickwood et al., 2004; Robinson et al., 2009; Saporito et al., 2013; Schell, 1999; Schulze et al., 2003; Shah, 2004; Skre et al., 2013; Spagnolo et al., 2008; Swartz et al., 2010; Tolomiczenko et al., 2001; Ventieri et al., 2011; Wahl et al., 2011; Watson et al., 2004)

Specific investigations were also conducted to examine willingness to disclose mental health status (Husek, 1965), use of derogatory language towards individuals with mental illness (Mount and Butterill, 1993), and willingness to interact with individuals living with mental illness (Chung and Chan, 2004).

Help Seeking Behaviour:

Overall, a total of 9 studies examined aspects of 'help-seeking behaviour. Most of these studies showed improvements in intentions to seek help for mental health problems, including accessing resources and talking to mental health professionals, teachers, friends, and others (Battaglia et al., 1990; Campos et al., 2014; Conrad et al., 2009; Gestsdottir et al., 2010; Rickwood et al., 2004; Robinson et al., 2009; Skre et al., 2013; Saporito et al., 2013). Campos and colleagues (2012) saw a significant increase in help-seeking behavioural intentions to seek help after the intervention, but Perry and colleagues' (2014) experimental study did not show any improvement in help-seeking behaviours despite improvements in knowledge and attitudes toward mental illness.

The UK case studies

There were seven studies that examined mental health literacy in primary and secondary schools in the UK. These studies were conducted between the years 1989 and 2006. Full study details, including programme and outcome specific information, can be found in Table 8.1 at the end of the chapter.

Lake and Burgess (1989) conducted a study that involved 18 students in years 12 and 13. The intervention involved six weekly 1.25-hour sessions delivered by a healthcare professional about mental illness, stress management, getting over disappointment, bereavement, and included different sections of the Mental Health Act. A questionnaire aimed to test knowledge about mental illness was administered before and after the programme. An increase in overall knowledge of mental illness and the professions involved in the Mental Health Act was detected.

Pinfold et al. (2003) examined 472 children in secondary schools who were aged 14 and 15 years. The study involved 345 girls and 127 boys. The intervention consisted of two one-hour educational mental health awareness workshops. The workshops involved videos and group discussions on mental health and illness that aimed to challenge stereotypical labels. Both mental health knowledge and attitudes towards mental illness were evaluated. Questionnaires were administered at baseline and one week after the programme was delivered. A cohort of 236 students was evaluated 6 months post intervention. A significant increase in knowledge about mental health was found after one week and after 6 months. There was also a significant improvement in attitudes towards mental health after one week and after 6 months.

Brewer et al. (2004) conducted a two-day music workshop that involved a band with 150 girls in year 10. All participants were 14 and 15 years of age. The first day of the workshop included presentations from service users where individuals shared their stories of dealing with mental illness. The second day of the workshop involved singing, songwriting, and teaching DJ skills that focused on mental health and recovery. Interviews on attitudes about mental health were conducted with participants after the workshops and revealed that attitudes towards mental illness had improved with participants being more understanding of those living with mental illness.

Shah (2004) examined an intervention in a primary school involving children aged between 5 and 11 in classes 1 through 6. Three 30-minute talks were given to three different age groups (5-7, 7-9, and 9-11). For each of the sessions, children were read a story involving characters with mental health problems; participated in drawing exercises; and engaged in group discussions. The researcher observed that some children held stigmatizing attitudes toward mental illness, which helped stimulate discussions on how to overcome such negative attitudes.

In another study, Pinfold et al. (2005) examined 2136 students aged between 14 and 16 years which involved schools in the UK and Canada. The intervention provided basic information about mental illness and addressed stigma over two one-hour sessions. The programme was co-facilitated by a person with direct experience of mental illness. Questionnaires examined knowledge recall, attitude change, and changes in social distance with those with mental illness. The questionnaires were administered several weeks before the study and after the programme. In both Canada and the UK, students significantly improved their knowledge of mental illness and their attitudes.

Essler et al. (2006) examined a theatre-based intervention in a secondary school with 104 students aged 13 and 14 years. The intervention consisted of two phases that were incorporated into a weekly citizenship class. Phase one involved a quiz, drama exercises, and games about mental health issues. Phase two focused on raising awareness of attitudes towards individuals with mental health problems. One month follow-up results showed that the intervention improved knowledge and attitude scores significantly.

Naylor et al. (2009) conducted an intervention involving 356 students between the ages of 14 and 15 years. The intervention consisted of six 50-minute class-based lessons on mental health issues. In a six month post-test, participants in the intervention group showed significant improvements in identifying mental health symptoms, showing awareness of why people are depressed, understanding why people are bullied, understanding why some people bully others, and were using fewer pejoratives.

Discussion

Overall, research on the effectiveness of mental health literacy programmes in primary and secondary schools shows that almost all studies demonstrate an intervention effect in enhancing mental health knowledge and improving negative attitudes toward mental illness. Mixed results, however, were found in encouraging children to seek support for mental health problems from teachers or mental health professionals, even after positive and significant changes were seen in mental health knowledge scores (Campos et al., 2012; Perry et al., 2014).

Most mental health literacy programmes were conducted in secondary schools and focused on mental illness in general and involved more female than male students. Programmes varied greatly in structure, length, delivery, and student interaction as well as methods of evaluation. Given programme and methodological heterogeneity it was not possible to determine either which mental health programme or their components were most effective in addressing mental health knowledge, attitudes, or help seeking behaviour. As a result of this heterogeneity, positive intervention findings must be viewed with extreme caution. The collective current research base does indicate that it is possible to implement mental health literacy programmes in primary and secondary schools and that they do afford some benefits with respect to mental health knowledge, improved attitudes toward mental illness and help seeking behaviour for mental health problems. However, more rigorous experimental research is needed to address this heterogeneity in programme design, delivery, and evaluation, to more fully understand their true impact. Studies must also address all aspects of mental health literacy, rather than focus on one or two components. To date only one experimental study has evaluated all three components of mental health literacy skills and has shown that positive changes in knowledge and attitudes do not necessarily translate into greater help seeking behaviours (Perry et al., 2014). Two pre-experimental (Campos et al., 2012, 2014) and three quasi-experimental studies (Gestsdottir et al., 2010; Rickwood et al., 2004; Skre et al., 2013) have evaluated all three components of mental health literacy. Like Perry et al. (2014), Campos et al. (2012) showed that improvements in mental health knowledge didn't necessarily translate into improved attitudes or help seeking behaviours.

To date, the trend shows that more experimental research is being conducted to help standardize mental health literacy programmes for children. In the last five years alone, there have been four randomized controlled trials, which account for half of all randomized controlled trials conducted in the last 55 years (Economou et al., 2011; Perry et al., 2014; Pinto-Foltz et al., 2011; Soporito et al., 2013). It is a positive and welcome sign that more researchers are beginning to conduct more rigorous school-based mental health literacy research. For school boards, this research is helping establish evidence-based curriculums that can be implemented in a systematic and cost effective manner. Experimental research helps to illustrate how curriculums can be structured; how many sessions are necessary to see changes in knowledge, attitudes, and help seeking behaviours; what resources are needed to run such programmes; and who is best positioned to deliver such curriculums. From the experimental research conducted so far, most studies have focused on improving knowledge and changing attitudes toward mental illness. These two areas of mental health literacy are important because students will be able to identify symptoms in themselves and others and address discriminatory behaviour. Ultimately, it is hoped that such knowledge and positive perspectives will lead to improved intentions to seek help, although more research is needed to examine this relationship.

The findings of this review are in line with previous reviews that have investigated mental health literacy programmes in schools (Kelly et al., 2007; Mellor, 2014; Schachter et al., 2008; Wei et al., 2013). Kelly and colleagues (2007) conducted a narrative review about early interventions for mental health disorders in youth that took place either in the community, in school settings, or individually. Their findings pointed to a small and methodologically poor research base where positive intervention effects could not be substantiated due to limited evidence and unreliable evaluation methods. Kelly and colleagues (2007) also emphasized a lack of standardization of mental health literacy programmes, which makes replication and implementation of such programmes in schools challenging. Their review recommended several steps that researchers and educators could take to strengthen the overall research base of mental health literacy programmes:

1) Conduct preliminary qualitative research to better understand audience information needs and preferences and the best methods of delivery. Dividing the audience into homogenous groups, by age, grade or gender, may help produce better-tailored messages and overall information content.
2) Establish a theoretical research base to design programmes in order to change health behaviours, like help seeking.
3) Ensure proper and rigorous programme evaluations are conducted to examine whether knowledge, attitudes, and behaviours are changing.

Since the publication of this review by Kelley et al. (2007), five experimental studies have been published, perhaps indicating that researchers have taken note of a need for more rigorous research. Unfortunately, all research since this review involves heterogeneous programmes and evaluation methods. It is interesting to note, no qualitative research involving further examinations of message and message delivery needs and preferences have been conducted, illustrating a major gap in programme design and implementation.

Schachter and colleagues (2008) conducted a systematic review of 40 school-based interventions, designed to eliminate or prevent mental health discrimination, aimed at children 18 years or younger. Their narrative synthesis revealed similar findings to Kelly and colleagues (2007) and found several major limitations which included interventions that prevented any conclusions to be made about the effectiveness of the programmes being delivered to children. Schachter and colleagues highlighted that mental health literacy programmes were predominately aimed at older children, and involved one-off and brief interventions with no on-going curriculum. The evaluation of the programmes was poor with unreliable measures conducted only immediately after the intervention was delivered. Overall, this review pointed to poor reporting of results, poor methodological design, high programme heterogeneity, inconsistent or null findings, and few experimental studies. As a result, Schachter and colleagues (2008) were unable to determine which interventions or intervention types were more effective than others and in what conditions or settings they should be used. These findings were similar to those found in a review conducted by Mellor (2014), who provided an update on anti-stigma programmes in schools. Together, both reviews recommend that programmes should be standardized, constructed as part of the existing curriculum, involve experiential activities in addition to cognitive learning strategies and be delivered at multiple points throughout the school year.

They should also be introduced early in primary school, and conducted in an on-going and sustainable manner where children in different years would be exposed to ever changing and more challenging material year after year.

Wei and colleagues (2013) also evaluated the effectiveness of school based mental health literacy programmes in secondary schools and colleges. They concluded that the field of mental health literacy is in its infancy and that greater steps need to be taken to address complex school environments. Their review provided a number of recommendations for future research, including:

1) Conducting observational and qualitative research to identify how interventions should be structured and modified for different school environments.
2) Organizing and executing rigorous randomized controlled trials with strategies in place to minimize methodological biases.
3) Collecting essential baseline characteristics, such as age, gender, race, social and economic status, mental health status of participants, previous contact of participants with individuals with mental health problems, and previous contact with mental health literacy programmes.
4) Standardizing the use of reliable and validated measures of mental health literacy outcomes.
5) Reporting on participant attrition.
6) Examining overall study and programme costs.

Overall, Wei and colleagues (2013) emphasize the need to establish strong research and information dissemination practices to help better construct mental health literacy programmes and better inform educators, school administrators, and policy makers about their strengths and limitations.

Implications for Researchers and Educators

The current knowledge base of school-based mental health literacy programmes suggest that greater efforts need to be taken to create standardized programmes that can be delivered as part of the curriculum. This presents many opportunities for diverse and participatory research collaborations, linking educators, mental health professionals, and researchers who specialize in multiple methods to create theoretically informed programmes, implement them in school environments, and evaluate them in rigorous ways.

One way of organizing such research is to structure future projects using the Medical Research Council Framework to develop and evaluate complex interventions (Craig et al., 2008). The MRC Framework has four specific elements that promote the development, feasibility and pilot testing, rigorous evaluation, and implementation and dissemination of health interventions.

In the development stage the current literature base is identified and important participatory input is gathered in order to develop an intervention that is theoretically sound. During this stage researchers, equipped with existing knowledge from systematic reviews, would work collaboratively with educators and school administrators. They would undertake observational and qualitative studies to better understand complex school environments and audience needs and, on the basis of those observations, design mental health literacy programmes that reflect the wishes and needs of children and other stakeholders. During this stage of the research process, it may be helpful to segment students into groups, either by age, gender, sexual identity, or year, to observe how programmes could be structured to reflect multiple viewpoints. Seeking input from families, educators, school administrators, and policy makers, is also essential in order to construct interventions that are both practical and feasible. For instance, in line with advice on mental health problems offered to school staff from the Department for Education (2015), it would be multiple stakeholders discuss how mental health literacy can be incorporated into Personal, Social, Health, and Economic (PSHE) education. Not only would such a discussion allow students, parents, and teachers to express their unique needs and wishes, but also provide an opportunity for researchers to present curriculum options and interventions that have been shown to be effective. Ultimately, results from this stage would help produce mental health literacy programmes that are theoretically sound, evidence based, and structured in a manner that addresses the needs of multiple audiences.

In the feasibility and pilot testing stage, programmes are evaluated in small samples to examine interest and acceptability, retention, delivery, and testing procedures. This feedback will assist in designing effective programmes. For example, PSHE programmes could be evaluated against schools delivering a different curriculum or compare groups, using reliable questionnaires, to ensure both students and teachers enjoy the curriculum and that it has an impact on core mental health literacy outcomes.

During the evaluation stage, cluster randomized trials can be implemented to determine intervention effectiveness, processes of behaviour change, and programme costs. For instance with PSHE education, a curriculum that has been structured with input from students, parents, and teachers and has been pilot tested successfully could be evaluated amongst participating schools in a catchment area. In this scenario, the programme could be implemented randomly in one school and tested against a control group in another school also selected randomly. Randomization and intervention assignment would be done using high standards (e.g., random number generators, using opaque sealed envelopes) in addition to blinding techniques that would mask participants knowing their allocation as well as study personnel collecting outcome assessments.

During the implementation and dissemination stage, programme results are presented and published and consultative feedback is pursued from multiple study stakeholders. Continual programme monitoring can also help provide valuable feedback on the long-term effects of the programme. Ultimately, input from stakeholders and long-term monitoring helps guide future intervention redevelopment and long-term sustainability. The MRC Framework promotes a systematic approach to research where continual evaluations allow programmes and evaluation methods to be modified and adjusted to reflect contemporary needs that are then fed into the redevelopment of the intervention. This Framework can potentially help structure a rigorous, sustainable research programme that allows close partnerships to be forged between researchers and educators. Currently, no studies included in this review showed any systematic approaches to designing, evaluating, and implementing a structured, theoretically driven mental health literacy programme aimed at children.

Conclusion

Health literacy for children is considered essential to the promotion and maintenance of overall health and wellbeing (Sanders et al. 2009). Although school-based mental health literacy programmes have shown much promise in improving mental health knowledge, attitudes toward mental illness, and help-seeking behaviours, much work remains to be done to fill gaps in programme design, delivery, and evaluation. Given programme and evaluation heterogeneity, no recommendations can be made as to what programme or programme components are most effective in improving mental health literacy outcomes. Greater effort needs to be made to structure long-term and sustainable programmes in a manner that addresses the needs of children and relevant stakeholders, and to evaluate such programmes in a systematic and rigorous manner. The future holds much opportunity for researchers, educators, school advisors, policy makers, and children to work together to structure school-based programmes to ultimately improve the mental health and wellbeing of all children.

A summary of what we know:
- There is a high prevalence of mental health problems in children, requiring school-based programmes to address mental health literacy in an effort to promote overall mental wellbeing in this population.
- Mental health literacy programmes have been delivered predominately in secondary schools with few programmes introduced at the primary level.
- Most mental health literacy programmes are delivered only once, as standalone interventions, with few follow-up evaluations, limiting our knowledge of the true impact of these programmes on mental health knowledge, attitudes, and help seeking behaviour.
- Mental health literacy programmes are extremely heterogeneous and vary in design and delivery.
- Research has shown that mental health literacy programmes have made a positive impact on mental health knowledge, attitudes about mental illness, and help seeking behaviour; however, the quality of this research varies and results must be treated with caution.
- UK based research is very limited and rigorous experimental research is needed.

A summary of what we need to know:
- How should mental health literacy programmes be structured, be integrated into the curriculum, and promote mental health knowledge, attitudes, and help seeking behaviours?
- What amount of mental health literacy is needed to impact mental health outcomes?
- What is the most optimal form of delivery for mental health literacy programmes?
- Who should deliver mental health literacy programmes?
- Which reliable and valid measures of mental health literacy outcomes should be used to evaluate programme efficiency and effectiveness?
- What are the costs of running school-based mental health literacy programmes?

Bibliography

Battaglia, J., Coverdale, J.H. and Bushong, C.P. (1990). Evaluation of a Mental Illness Awareness Week programme in public schools. *The American Journal of Psychiatry,* Vol. 147(3), pp. 324-329.

Beddington, J., Cooper, C.L., Field, J., Goswami, U., Huppert, F., Jenkins, R. (2008). The mental wealth of nations. *Nature, Vol. 455(7216),* pp.1057-1060.

Belfer, M.L. (2008). Child and adolescent mental disorders: the magnitude of the problem across the globe. *Journal of Child Psychology and Psychiatry, and Applied Disciplines,* Vol. 49(3), pp. 226-236.

Bella-Awusah, T., Adedokun, B., Dogra, N. and Omigbodun, O. (2014). The impact of a mental health teaching programmes on rural and urban secondary school students' perceptions of mental illness in southwest Nigeria. *Journal of Child and Adolescent Mental Health,* Vol. 26(3), pp. 207-215.

Brewer, P., Moore, K. and Reid, M. (2004). When Channel One met Year 10: using the arts to combat stigma. *A Life in the Day,* Vol.8 (4), pp. 4-8.

Campos, L., Dias, P. and Palha, F. (2014). Finding Space to Mental Health1- Promoting mental health in adolescents: Pilot study. *Education and Health,* Vol. 32(1), pp. 23-29.

Campos, L., Palha, F., Dias, P., Lima, V.S., Veiga, E., Costa. N. and Duarte, A. (2012). Mental health awareness intervention in schools. *Journal of Human Growth and Development, Vol. 22(2),* pp.259-266.

Chan, J.Y., Mak, W.W. and Law, L.S. (2009). Combining education and video-based contact to reduce stigma of mental illness: "The Same or Not the Same" anti-stigma programme for secondary schools in Hong Kong. *Social Science and Medicine,* Vol. 68(8), pp.1521-1526.

Chung, K. F. and Chan, J. H. (2004). Can a less pejorative Chinese translation for schizophrenia reduce stigma? A study of adolescents' attitudes toward people with schizophrenia. *Psychiatry and Clinical Neuroscience,* Vol. 58(5), pp. 507-515.

Conrad, I., Dietrich, S., Heider, D., Blume, A., Angermeyer, M.C. and Riedel-Heller, S. (2009). A school programme to promote mental health and reduce stigma – results of a pilot study. *Health Education,* Vol. 109(4), pp. 314-328.

Costello, E. J., Egger, H. and Angold, A. (2005). 10-year research update review: the epidemiology of child and adolescent psychiatric disorders: I. Methods and public health burden. *Journal of the American Academy of Child and Adolescent Psychiatry,* Vol. 44(10), pp. 972–986.

Craig, P., Dieppe, P., Macintyre, S., Michie, S., Nazareth, I. and Petticrew, M. (2008). Developing and evaluating complex interventions: the new Medical Research Council guidance. *BMJ,* Vol. 337. DOI: 10.1136/bmj.a1655

Department of Education. (2015). *Mental health and behaviour in schools: Departmental advice for school staff.* Retrieved from: https://www.gov.uk/government/uploads/system/uploads/attachment_data/file/ 416786/Mental_Health_and_Behaviour_-_Information_and_Tools_for_ Schools_240515.pdf

Department of Health. (2001). *Stop the stigma: a local action pack to stop the stigma surrounding mental health.* London: HMSO.

Economou, M., Louki, E., Peppou, L.E., Gramandani, C., Yotis, L. and Stefanis, C.N. (2011). Fighting psychiatric stigma in the classroom: The impact of an educational intervention on secondary school students' attitudes to schizophrenia. *International Journal of Social Psychiatry,* Vol. 58(5), pp. 544-551.

Essler, V., Arthur, A. and Stickley, T. (2006). Using a school-based intervention to challenge stigmatizing attitudes and promote mental health in teenagers. *Journal of Mental Health,* Vol. 15(2), pp. 243-250.

Esters, I.G., Cooker, P.G. and Ittenbach, R.F. (1998). Effects of a unit of instruction in mental health on rural adolescents' conceptions of mental illness and attitudes about seeking help. *Adolescence,* Vol. 33(130), pp. 469–76.

Gestsdottir, A.M. (2010). Evaluation of school-based mental health promotion for adolescents: Focus on knowledge, stigma, help-seeking behaviour and resources. Unpublished master's thesis. University of Iceland, Reykjavik, Iceland.

Greenwald, A.G., McGhee, D.E. and Schwartz, J.L.K. (1998). Measuring individual differences in implicit cognition: The implicit association test. *Journal of Personality and Social Psychology,* Vol. 74, pp. 1464–1480.

Gudmundsdottir, D.G. (2002). A study of adolescents' attitudes towards mental health: The Icelandic mental health promotion project. *Journal of mental health promotion,* Vol. 1, pp 32-35.

Husek, T.R. (1965). Persuasive impacts of early, late or no mention of a negative source. *Journal of Personality and Social Psychology, Vol. 2(1),* pp. 125-128.

Kelly, C.M., Jorm, A.F. and Wright, A. (2007). Improving mental health literacy as a strategy to facilitate early intervention for mental disorders. *MJA,* Vol. 187(7), S26-S30.

Ke, S., Lai, J., Sun, T., Yang, M.M.H., Ching Chieh Wang, J. and Austin, J. (2015). Healthy Young Minds: The Effects of a 1-hour Classroom Workshop on Mental Illness Stigma in High School Students. *Community Mental Health Journal,* Vol. 51(3), pp. 329-337.

Kieling, C., Baker-Henningham, H., Belfer, M., Conti, G., Ertem, I., Omigbodun, O., Rohde, L.A., Srinath, S., Ulkuer, N. and Rahman, A. (2011). Child and adolescent mental health worldwide: evidence for action. *Lancet,* Vol. 378 (9801), pp. 1515-25.

Kutcher, S. (2009). *The Canadian Mental Health Association: The mental health and high school curriculum: Understanding mental health and mental illness.* Halifax, NS: The Printing House Limited.

Lake, B. and Burgess, J.M. (1989). Mental health and mental illness: Educating six-formers. *British Journal of Occupational Therapy,* Vol. 52 (8), pp 301-304.

Lauria-Horner, B.A., Kutcher, S. and Brooks, S.J. (2004). The feasibility of a mental health curriculum in elementary school. *Canadian Journal of Psychiatry,* Vol. 49(3), pp. 208-201.

Mcluckie, A., Kutcher, S., Wei, Y., Weaver, C. (2014). Sustained improvements in students' mental health literacy with use of a mental health curriculum in

Canadian schools. *BMC Psychiatry,* Vol. 14, p 379. DOI: 10.1186/s12888-014-0379-4

Mellor, C. (2014). School-based interventions targeting stigma of mental illness: Systematic review. *The Psychiatric Bulletin,* Vol. 38(4), pp. 164-171.

Morrison, J. K., Becker, R.E. and Bourgeois, C.A. (1979). Decreasing adolescents' fear of mental patients by means of demythologizing. *Psychological Reports,* 44, pp. 855-859.

Mound, B. and Butterill, D. (1993). Beyond the Cuckoo's Nest: A high school education programme. *Psychosocial Rehabilitation Journal,* Vol. 16(3), pp. 146-150.

Naylor, P.B., Cowie, H.A., Walters, S.J., Talamelli, L. and Dawkins J. (2009). Impact of a mental health teaching programme on adolescents. *British Journal of Psychiatry,* Vol. 194(4), pp. 365-370.

Ng, P. and Chan, K. F. (2002). Attitudes towards people with mental illness. Effects of a training programme for secondary school students. *International Journal of Adolescent Medicine and Health,* Vol. 14(3), pp. 215-224.

O'Kearney, R., Gibson, M., Christensen, H., Griffiths, K.H. (2006). Effects of a cognitive-behavioural internet programme on depression, vulnerability to depression and stigma in adolescent males: a school-based controlled trial. *Cognitive Behaviour Therapy,* Vol. 35(1), pp. 43-54.

Pejović-Milovancević, M., Lecić-Tosevski, D., Tenjović, L., Popović-Deusić, S. and Draganić-Gajić, S. (2003). Changing attitudes of high school students towards peers with mental health problems. *Psychiatrica Danubina,* No. 21(2), pp. 213-219.

Perry, Y., Petrie, K., Buckley, H., Cavanagh, L., Clarke, D., Winslade, M., Christensen, H. (2014). Effects of a classroom-based educational resource on adolescent mental health literacy: a cluster randomized controlled trial. *Journal of Adolescence,* Vol. 37(7), pp. 1143-1151.

Petchers, M. K., Biegel, D. E. and Drescher, R. (1988). A video-based programme to educate high school students about serious mental illness. *Hospital and Community Psychiatry,* Vol. 39(10), pp.1102-1103.

Pinfold, V., Toulman, H., Thornicroft, G., Huxley, P., Farmer, P. and Graham, T. (2003). Reducing psychiatric stigma and discrimination: evaluation of educational interventions in UK secondary schools. *British Journal of Psychiatry,* Vol.182, pp. 342–346.

Pinfold, V., Stuart, H., Thornicroft, G., Arboleda-Florez, J. (2005). Working with young people: The impact of mental health awareness programmes in schools in the UK and Canada. *World Psychiatry,* No. 4(1), pp. 48-52.

Pinto-Foltz, M.D., Logsdon, M.C. and Myers, J.A. (2011). Feasibility, acceptability and initial efficacy of a knowledge-contact programme to reduce mental illness stigma and improve mental health literacy in adolescents. *Social Science and Medicine,* Vol. 72(12), pp.2011-2019.

Pinto-Foltz, M.D. (2009). School-based intervention to reduce stigma toward mental disorders and improve mental health literacy in female adolescents. (Unpublished Doctoral Dissertation). University of Louisville, Louisville, Kentucky.

Pitre, N., Stewart, S., Adams, S., Bedard, T., Landry, S. (2007). The use of puppets with elementary school children in reducing stigmatizing attitudes towards mental illness. *Journal of Mental Health,* Vol. 16(3), pp. 415-429.

Rahman, A., Mubbashar, M. H., Gater, R. and Goldberg, D. (1998). Randomised trial of impact of school mental-health programmes in rural Rawalpindi, Pakistan. *The Lancet,* No. 352(9133), pp 1022-1025.

Rickwood, D., Cavanagh, S., Curtis, L., Sakrouge, R. (2004). Educating Young People about Mental Health and Mental Illness: Evaluating a School-Based Programme. *The International Journal of Mental Health Promotion,* No. 6(4), pp. 23-32.

Robinson, J., Gook, S., Pan Yeun, H., Hughes, A., Dodd, S., Bapat, S., Schwass, W., McGorry, P. and Young, A. (2009). Depression Education and Identification in Schools: An Australian-based Study. *School Mental Health,* No.2, pp. 13-22.

Royal College of Psychiatrists. (1998). *Mental Illness and Stigma, Module 217.* London: ONS.

Sanders, L. M., Federico, S., Klass, P., Abrams, M. A. and Dreyers, B. (2009). Literacy and child health: A systematic review. *JAMA Pediatrics,* Vol. 163(2), pp. 131-140.

Saporito, J.M., Ryan, C. and Teachman, B.A. (2013). Reducing stigma toward seeking mental health treatment among adolescents. *Stigma Research and Action,* 1(2), pp. 9-21.

Schachter, H.M., Girardi, A., Ly, M., Lacroix, D., Lumb, A., B. Van Berkom, J. and Gill, R. (2008). Effects of school-based interventions on mental health stigmatization: a systematic review. *Child and Adolescent Psychiatry and Mental Health,* 2(18). DOI: 10.1186/1753-2000-2-18

Schell, L.N. (1999). Preadolescents' attitudes toward mental illness. (Unpublished doctoral dissertation). Texas Women's University, Denton, Texas, USA.

Schulze, B., Richter-Werling, M., Matschinger, H. and Angermeyer, M.C. (2003). Crazy? So what! Effects of a school project on students' attitudes towards people with schizophrenia. *Acta Psychiatrica Scandinavica,* Vol. 107(2), pp.142–150.

Shah, N. (2004). Changing minds at the earliest opportunity. *Psychiatric Bulletin,* No.28, pp. 213-215.

Skre, I., Friborg, O., Breivik, C., Johnsen, L.I., Arnesen, Y. and Wang CE. (2013). A school intervention for mental health literacy in adolescents: effects of a non-randomized cluster controlled trial. *BMC Public Health,* Vol.13, p.873. DOI: 10.1186/1471-2458-13-873

Spagnolo, A.B., Murphy, A.A. and Librera, L.A. (2008). Reducing stigma by meeting and learning from people with mental illness. *Psychiatric Rehabilitation Journal,* No. 31(3), pp.186-193.

Stuart, H. (2006). Reaching out to high school youth: The effectiveness of a video-based antistigma programme. *Canadian Journal of Psychiatry,* No. 51(10), pp. 647-653.

Swartz, K.L., Kastelic, E.A., Hess, S.G., Cox, T.S., Gonzales, L.C., Mink, S.P. and DePaulo Jr., J.R. (2010). The Effectiveness of a School-Based Adolescent

Depression Education Programme. *Health Education and Behavior,* Vol. 37(1), pp.11-22.

Tolomiczenko, G.S., Goering, P.N. and Durbin, J.F. (2001). Educating the public about mental illness and homelessness: a cautionary note. *Canadian Journal of Psychiatry,* No. 46(3), pp. 253-257.

Ventieri, D., Clarke, D.M. and Hay, M. (2011). The Effects of a School-Based Educational Intervention on Pre-adolescents' Knowledge of and Attitudes towards Mental Illness. *Advances in School Mental Health Promotion,* No.4 (3), pp.5-17.

Watson, A.C., Otey, E., Westbrook, A.L., Gardner, A.L., Lamb, T. A., Corrigan, R.W. and Fenton, W.S. (2004). Changing middle schoolers' attitudes about mental illness through education. *Schizophrenia Bulletin,* No. 30(3), pp. 563–572.

Wei, Y., Hayden, J., Kutcher, S., Zygmunt, A. and McGrath, P. (2013). The Effectiveness of School Mental Health Literacy Programmes to Address Knowledge, Attitudes, and Help-Seeking among Youth. *Early Intervention in Psychiatry,* No.7 (2), pp.109-121.

Wei, Y., Kutcher, S. and Szumilas, M. (2011). Comprehensive school mental health: an integrated 'School-Based Pathway to Care' model for Canadian secondary schools. *McGill Journal of Education,* No.46 (2), pp.213–230.

Wei, Y. and Kutcher, S. (2012). International school mental health: global approaches, global challenges, and global opportunities. *Child and Adolescent Psychiatric Clinics of North America,* No. 21(1), pp.11–27.

Wahl, O.F., Susin, J., Kaplan, L., Lax, A. and Zatina, D. (2011). Changing Knowledge and Attitudes with a Middle School Mental Health Education Curriculum. *Stigma Research in Action,* 1(1), pp.44-53.

World Psychiatric Association. (2000). *The WPA Programme to Reduce Stigma and Discrimination because of Schizophrenia, Volumes 1-5.* Geneva, Switzerland: WPA.

Table 8.1. UK School based Mental Health Literacy Programmes

Study	Sample Size, Sex, Age	Primary or secondary level	Study Design	Intervention	Assessments Mental Health Literacy (Knowledge, Attitudes, Help Seeking)	Outcome of Mental Health Literacy (Knowledge, Attitudes, Help Seeking)
Brewer et al., 2004	N=150; 150F; Age Range = 14-15 years	Secondary; Grade 10	Pre-experimental; One-Shot Case Study	Intervention: Two-day workshop. The first day included presentations from service users. The second day involved the Channel One band and included singing and songwriting, DJ Skills, and mental health and media workshops.	Attitudes: Interviews with some participants. Administered after the workshops.	Attitudes: Attitudes toward individuals with mental illness improved. Participants were more understanding toward those living with mental illness.

School-based Mental Health Literacy Programmes

Essler et al., 2006	N=104; Age Range = 13-14 years	Secondary	Pre-experimental; One-Group Pretest, Post-test	Intervention: Part of a weekly citizenship class. Two phase theatre intervention. Phase one involved a quiz, drama exercises, and games about mental health issues. Phase two focused on raising awareness of attitudes towards individuals with mental health issues.	Knowledge and Attitudes: Mindout for Mental Health quiz (Department of Health, 2001). Administered before and one-month after the intervention.	Knowledge and Attitudes: Knowledge and attitudes scores increased significantly at follow-up (p=0.015).
Lake and Burgess, 1989	N=18	Secondary, Grades 12-13	Pre-experimental; One-Group Pretest-Post-test	Intervention: Six weekly 1.25-hour sessions delivered by a healthcare professional about mental illness, stress management, disappointment, bereavement, and the Mental Health Act.	Knowledge: Questionnaires aimed to assess knowledge about mental illness. Administered before and after the sessions.	Knowledge: Increase in overall knowledge of mental illness and professions involved in the mental health act.

Naylor et al., 2009	N=356; 188M 168F; Age Range = 14-15 years	Secondary	Quasi-experimental; Pretest-Post-test Control Group Design; Intervention 149, Control 207	Intervention: Six 50-minute lessons on mental health issues delivered in class. Control: Able to take the lessons after the intervention.	Knowledge and Attitudes: Mental Health Questionnaire. Adapted from the Attitudes to Mental Health and Knowledge of Mental Health Issues questionnaires (Royal College of Psychiatrists, 1998). Administered one week before and six months after the sessions.	Knowledge and Attitudes: At post-test, participants in the intervention showed significant improvements in identifying more mental health problems (p=0.01), showing awareness of why people are depressed (p=0.03), understanding why people are bullied (p=0.013), understanding why some people bully others (p=0.08), and using fewer pejoratives (p=0.0001)

School-based Mental Health Literacy Programmes

Pinfold et al., 2003	N=472; 127M, 345F; Age range = 14-15 years	Secondary, Grade 10	Pre-experimental; Single group, Pre-test-Post-test Design	Intervention: Two 1-hr educational mental health awareness workshops. Workshops consisted of videos and discussions on mental health and illness and challenging stereotypical labels.	Knowledge and Attitudes: Questionnaires based on World Psychiatric Association's anti-stigma schools project in Canada (World Psychiatric Association, 2000). Included statements about knowledge and attitude towards mental illness. Administered before and 1-week after the programme. Participants in one school were given 6-month evaluations (N=236).	Knowledge: Significant improvement in mental health knowledge at 1-week post-programme (p<0.0001) and 6-months evaluations (p<0.05). Attitudes: Significant improvements in attitudes towards individuals with mental illness at 1-week post-programme (p<0.0001) and 6-month evaluations (p<0.001).

| Pinfold et al., 2005 | N= 2136; 956M, 1180F; Age Range = 14-16 years | Secondary, Grades | Pre-experimental; Two separate studies, One-Group Pretest-Post-test Design | Intervention: Programmes provided basic information about mental illness and addressed stigma. Programme co-facilitated by an individual with direct experience with mental illness. UK programme was delivered over two 1-hr sessions. Canadian programme delivered in one session. | Knowledge and Attitudes: Questionnaires focused on factual recall, attitude change, and changes in social distance.

Canada: Administered several weeks before and immediately after the programme.

UK: Administered before and 1-week after the programme. | Knowledge: Both UK and Canadian students significantly improved their knowledge of mental illness (p<0.001).

Attitudes: Both UK and Canadian students significantly improved their attitudes toward mental illness (p<0.001). |

School-based Mental Health Literacy Programmes

Shah, 2004	Age Range = 5-11 years	Primary, Grades 1-6	Pre-experimental; One-Shot Case Study	Intervention: Three talks for three different age groups (5-7, 7-9, 9-11 years). Talks were 20-30 minutes in length. Children were read a story and participated in drawing and discussion exercises.	Attitudes: Observations after talks.	Attitudes: Some older participants expressed stigmatizing attitudes and these attitudes were discussed.

PART 3

CHAPTER NINE

BULLYING AND DISCRIMINATION IN HIGHER EDUCATION

HELEN COWIE

Introduction

Over the past 25 years, a substantial body of research has investigated bullying (and more recently cyberbullying) among school children on the one hand and among adults in the workplace on the other. However, only a very small number of studies address aspects of bullying in higher education, despite the fact that a series of National Union of Students (NUS) Reports highlight the problem, with disturbing case study accounts of long-term damage to self-esteem, academic achievement, and emotional well-being experienced by some students.

This chapter invites the reader to consider the major theme of the book– that education leads to the development not only of *personal* but also of *social* qualities, with equality and inclusion being key factors in achieving these qualities. Unfortunately, bullying and discrimination are regular features of campus life with certain groups of students being particularly vulnerable to attack. The chapter begins by considering the current literature about bullying/cyberbullying amongst university students with particular emphasis on gender issues and on discrimination on the grounds of sexual orientation. It then explores what we know about the individual nature of bullying as well as the contexts where it flourishes. Next we look at some proposed solutions to the problem at the levels of the individual, the class/seminar group, the campus community, and the university as an institution. At a practical level, the chapter discusses implications, to include the role of student unions, the role of the university health and counselling services, and the need for stronger anti-bullying and anti-harassment policies. Finally, in harmony with the aim of the book, there is a discussion of equality and inclusion in the context of higher education.

The primary issue

At the time of writing, a disturbing report appeared in the Guardian (Ellis-Petersen, 2014, p. 4) The men's Rugby Club at the London School of Economics (LSE) had distributed a leaflet at the fresher's fair that described women as "mingers", "trollops" and "slags" and women who play sports as "beastlike". The leaflet also stated that "outright homosexual debauchery" would not be tolerated. Although the club issued an apology after outraged complaints from students, no single individual member accepted responsibility for actually writing the leaflet. Consequently, an enquiry was set up and the club was disbanded for the rest of the academic year. If this were an isolated case, it would be shocking enough. However, a series of reports commissioned by NUS has revealed a disturbing trend, broadly defined as 'lad culture', that is widespread across the university sector. Lad culture (as identified by Jackson, Dempster and Pollard, 2014), rooted in misogyny and homophobia, can scaffold sexual violence and normalise it. "Laddishness" has been described as:

> "… a "pack" mentality evident in activities such as sport and heavy alcohol consumption and "banter" which was often sexist, misogynist and homophobic. It was also thought to be sexualized and to involve the objectification of women and at its extremes rape supportive attitudes and sexual harassment and violence". (Phipps and Young, 2013, p. 53).

As Pearce (2016), currently the President of NUS (at the time of writing this chapter) writes, the NUS report (Phipps and Young, 2013) into women students' experiences of lad culture in higher education demonstrated just how pervasive laddism and the behaviour that goes with it is on our campuses. NUS researchers Phipps and Young (2013) found that 1 in 7 respondents had experienced a serious physical or sexual assault during their time as a student, with fellow students as the majority of perpetrators. 1Twelve per cent had been stalked and 68% had been a victim of some form of sexual harassment. Disturbingly, only 4% reported the assault to the university authorities and 10% to the police. The women students reported being exposed on a daily basis to sexist, misogynistic, and homophobic comments, commonly termed "banter". Here is an example from one young woman:

> "Some close friends from our feminist society have been violently verbally attacked by a group of lads while having a drink at the student union bar for simply being from the feminist society" (Phipps and Young, 2013, p. 44).

Bullies will often dismiss such concerns and label those who challenge their behaviour as "kill-joys" or "prudes". They tend to describe what they do as simply "banter" or "a bit of harmless fun". Such attitudes minimize the significant impact on how safe women students feel on campus and deny the fact that such a sexist stance can all too often spill over into sexual harassment and humiliation. Young people who spontaneously defend the victim are to be found in all social groups. However, it must be remembered that even at university level these individuals remain a minority and are easily overruled by the majority. As one student in the NUS study reported:

> "[It's a] culture in which misogyny and sexism is seen as cool or masculine. A lot of it revolving around sexist jokes and banter so that the sexism is trivialized so that people who challenge it are made to seem like kill-joys or people with no sense of humour" (Phipps and Young, 2013, p. 36).

The role-play study by Myers and Cowie (2013) in which students enacted the roles of bully, victim and bystander indicated no demonstration of altruism in the bystander group until they were required to reach a resolution of the problem, at which point some recognition of the psychological distress to the victim became apparent. The findings from this study were that the students in the role of "bystanders" tended to blame the bullied students and showed little inclination to intervene, either to support that individual or to challenge the bully The "victims" reported that they felt isolated and marginalized by the perceived indifference or hostility of their peers. The "bullies" showed no understanding of the emotional damage inflicted on their targets and dismissed their behaviour as "only a joke". The role play demonstrated the power of the group in undermining the victim and in affirming the popularity and power of the bully.

In confirmation, Phipps and Young (2013) found that individuals who challenged bullying behaviour reported that they were often at the receiving end of pressure to conform to the oppressive behaviour or risk social exclusion and other forms of psychological bullying or even physical violence.

The impact of bullying at university

Cowie et al. (2013), in an overview of the issue, report that bullying at university takes many forms and includes such behaviour as spreading nasty rumours on the grounds of age, race, sex, disability, sexual orientation and religion or belief; ridiculing or demeaning someone; social exclusion; unwelcome sexual advances; posting embarrassing material online; threatening someone, either directly or anonymously online. The recent emergence of cyberbullying as a new form of bullying (see Aricak, 2016; Myers and Cowie, 2013; Sourander et al., 2010) also indicates distress amongst university students. Schenk and Fremouw (2012) found that college student victims of cyberbullying scored higher than matched controls on measures of depression, anxiety, phobic anxiety, and paranoia. In the context of cyberbullying at university level, Bennett et al. (2011) found evidence of hostility, humiliation, exclusion, and intrusiveness by means of electronic victimization in friendship and dating relationships. Giovazolias and Malikiosi-Loizos (2016) in a survey of 464 undergraduates from six Greek universities (mean age 21.27 years) found that the most frequent bullying behaviours were indirect, to include social exclusion, rumour spreading and name calling. Lappalainen et al. (2011) surveyed 2805 Finnish university students and found that around 5% reported being bullied either by a fellow student or by a member of staff.

Greatly concerned about the issue, NUS commissioned research into the experiences of lesbian, gay, bisexual and transgender (LGBT) students at university (NUS, 2014). The findings are similarly disturbing. One in five LGB+ students and one in three transsexual students experienced at least one form of bullying or harassment on their campus, with far-reaching effects on their academic progress and their emotional health and well-being. Those students who had experienced homophobic or transphobic harassment were two to three times more likely to consider leaving their course than other students. As Rivers (2016) indicates, for LGBT students, university can be a terrifying place where they fear "coming out" because of the risk of ridicule, humiliation and even physical attack. Many LGBT students hide their sexual orientation and feel obliged to make changes in their lives in order to avoid harassment, for example, by staying away from LGBT clubs or pretending to have a romantic partner of the opposite sex. Valentine, Wood, and Plummer (2009), in a survey of 2,704 LGBT students, 781 support staff and 720 academic staff, found a similar picture. LGB students reported negative treatment by fellow students (46.8%) and by staff (8.9%). For transgender students the situation was worse, with 50% reporting negative treatment from fellow students and 19.4% from academic staff.

Should universities take action?

Universities, like all organisations, are bound by the Equality Act of 2010 to ensure equality of opportunity and to provide protection to those in their care from all forms of discrimination. However, although anti-bullying policies do exist in some universities; reports from students indicate a widespread belief that universities in practice offer very little support. Kenworthy (2010) carried out an online survey of 452 United States university students inviting those who had experienced cyberbullying to respond. In this sample, the majority of victims did not report it to anyone and only 14% indicated that their formal complaints had resulted in disciplinary action against the perpetrator. Some students considered the phenomenon to be simply a prank rather than a crime, indicating widespread misunderstanding of the ethical, moral, and legal implications.

Furthermore, it is essential to recognize the complexity of bullying as well as the interactions amongst such factors as social class, culture, gender, ethnicity, and sexual orientation. As Zhang, Osberg and Phipps (2014) argue in the context of schools, bullying has many facets with wide variation in its impact on students and, therefore, potentially different implications for policy and practice. By focusing purely on individual bullies and victims, the wider social context in which bullying occurs is overlooked; most importantly the roles and responsibilities of the majority who are witnesses, reinforcers and assistants to bullying are not taken into account (Salmivalli, Lagerspetz et al., 1996).

Clearly we need to understand bullying in different contexts - individual, year group, social group, and institutional level - within the university if we are to develop effective interventions and policies. The lack of research into the nature and incidence of bullying and the piecemeal approach to dealing with the problem means that this is an aspect of student life that is neglected. One argument that Coleyshaw (2012) proposes is that the university environment may resist such investigations since this could be counterproductive in terms of recruiting new students and promoting a positive image of university life. So it is safer to pathologise bullying and view it as an individual problem, not an organisational one. Coleyshaw (2012) argues that there needs to be more focus on universities as organisations if we are serious about tackling the issue of bullying and discrimination.

Insights can be gained from the extensive literature on workplace bullying, especially where the focus is often on the role of the organisational environment as a powerful determinant of the quality of interpersonal relationships at work. For example, some investigators propose that competitive work environments, hierarchical workplace norms and strong power differentials can create a context where bullying is tolerated or even encouraged as a management tool. Coyne (2016), for example, argues that unclear or tokenistic policies that are not properly implemented with any conviction can further promote an environment where bullying is likely to occur. He proposes that it is necessary to take action at different levels – at *organizational* level, by actively promoting a culture of dignity and respect; at *group* level, by changing norms and values; at *individual* level, by providing counselling and peer support for vulnerable students; he also recommends training for staff to be more skilled at detecting abusive interpersonal relationships when they occur in class or informally on campus.

Conclusion

As has been argued in this chapter, at institutional level, there need to be strong policies in place to address the problem. Perhaps university authorities have hesitated to tackle the issue of student-on-student bullying since they view the students on the campus as independent adults rather than young people in need of support. Tutors and lecturers need to be trained to be alert to this issue and to have knowledge about how to deal with it directly when it occurs, for example, during a lecture or seminar. They also need to know how and when to refer the situation on to relevant support agencies, either within the university (for example, to the student counselling service) or outside it (for example, to the police). Universities also need to be much more proactive in creating a community where dignity is valued, where diversity is accepted and where inclusion is visibly promoted. In such a community, discrimination, both overt and covert, is always challenged. Evidence from schools shows us how essential it is to have systems in place to provide a framework within which the organization demonstrates its commitment to the prevention of bullying and the provision of interventions to support the victims (Ttofi and Farrington, 2011). Furthermore, a policy consistent across universities needs to be designed and implemented along the lines of whole school policies adopted across the school sector. Universities would benefit by taking account of these procedures rather than leaving the issue to be resolved piecemeal as appears to be the case at present. In fact, as Sullivan (2016) recommends, each university's administration and management should be actively committed on an on-going basis to the issue of bullying among staff and students. This would involve planning and clarifying the university's philosophy with regard to the rights and expectations of both staff and students and then, after a process of consultation, developing policies and programmes that would be regularly monitored and evaluated.

Students' Unions have a key role to play and, in fact, have already been pioneering in commissioning reports and research into the phenomenon of bullying and discrimination on campus. They are in a unique position of being able to offer interventions, such as peer support, that have already been shown to be effective in school contexts with younger students. They can also continue their active promotion of the positive recognition of minority groups. Sullivan (2016) discusses the potential power that student unions possess that could be utilized to challenge inaction on the part of the authorities and to demand that a much clearer stance should be adopted. They could also continue to challenge the reactionary and prejudiced attitudes on the part of some members of the student body itself. So, he argues, the students themselves have the power to make it clear to the authorities that it would be irresponsible to ignore this serious problem and against the best interests of the university as a community and as a learning institution in the broadest sense.

Student health services and counselling centres are places where staff must be alert to the impact of bullying on the emotional health and well-being not only of the targets of bullying but also of the perpetrators. Luca (2016), from the perspective of a university counsellor, points out that the victims of sexual bullying often fear to tell anyone through shame and guilt about what happened to them. Many studies of school and workplace bullying document the catastrophic impact that bullying can have on the mental health of those involved. There are many negative consequences of bullying, including long-term psychological problems, like chronic anxiety, depressive symptoms, suicidal ideation, and suicide attempts on the part of victims. Perpetrators have also been found to be at heightened risk of anxiety, depression, psychosomatic symptoms, and eating disorders, as well as anti-social behaviour. So it is of paramount importance that university authorities take action to protect the students in their care from such risks to their emotional health and well-being and their capacity to study.

Universities also need to be considerably more proactive in demonstrating their commitment to inclusion, the promotion of tolerance and the celebration of diversity. The presence of bullying and discrimination on campus undermines the role of universities as places where ideas are explored through dialogue and debate, not violence and discrimination. Policies and interventions provide an essential framework for addressing the issue. But ultimately the university should also be a place where values are openly explored and where difference is a matter for celebration not shame. As Phipps and Young (2013) conclude, the corporatization of Higher Education is on the rise with its typical valuing of individualism and competitiveness. Not only can this promote "laddish" values, it can also act as a powerful deterrent for apparently "vulnerable" students to seek help when they experience social and emotional difficulties. University authorities should never lose sight of the role of learning in developing personal and social qualities in students, many of whom will be the future leaders in their workplaces and in their communities.

Bibliography

Aricak, T. (2016). The Relationship between Mental Health and Bullying. In H., Cowie and C-A., Myers (Eds.), *Bullying among University Students.* (pp. 76-90), London: Routledge.

Bennett, D., Guran, Ramos and Margolin et al. (2011). College Students' Electronic Victimization in Friendships and Dating Relationships: Anticipated Distress and Associations with Risky Behaviors. *Violence and Victims Vol. 26,* pp. 410-429.

Coleyshaw, E. (2012). The Power of Paradigms: a Discussion of the Absence of Bullying Research in the Context of University Student Experience. *Research in (Eds.) Post-Compulsory Education, Vol.*15, pp.377-386.

Cowie, H., Bauman, Coyne, Myers, Porhola, Almeida et al., (2013). Cyberbullying amongst University Students: an Emergent Cause for Concern? In P.K., Smith and G., Steffgei (Eds.) *Cyberbullying through the New Media,* (pp. 165-177), London: Psychology Press.

Coyne, Iain. (2016). Commentary: What Universities can learn from Workplace Bullying Research. In H., Cowie and C-A., Myers (Eds.), *Bullying among University Students.* (pp. 203-206), London: Routledge.

Ellis-Petersen, H. (2014). Season Over for LSE Rugby Club as Sexist Leaflet Angers Students. *The Guardian*, p.4.

Giovazolias, T and Malikiosi-Loizos, M. (2016). Bullying at Greek Universities: an Empirical Study. In H.Cowie and C-A Myers (Eds.), *Bullying among University Students.* (pp. 110-126), London: Routledge.

Jackson, C., Dempster and Pollard. (2014). They Just Don't Seem to Really Care, They Just Think it Cool to Sit There and Talk: Laddism in University Teaching-learning Contexts. *Educational Review* Vol. 9, pp. 1-15.

Kenworthy, A. (2010). One Goal, One Community: Moving Beyond Bullying and Empowering for Life, Bond University Centre for Applied Research in Learning, Engagement, Andragogy and Pedagogy.

Lappalainen, C. et al. (2011). Bullying Among University Students – Does it Exist? *Finnish Journal of Youth Research,* Vol. 29, pp. 64-80.

Luca, M. (2016). The Role of the Therapist in Helping University Students Who Have Been Bullied: a Case Study of Sexual Bullying. In H.Cowie and C-A.

Myers (Eds.), *Bullying among University Students.* (pp. 145-156), London: Routledge.

Myers, C-A. and Cowie, H. (2013). University Students-Views on Bullying from the Perspective of Different Participant Roles. *Pastoral Care in Education,* Vol. 31, pp. 251-267.

National Union of Students. (2014). *Education Beyond the Straight and Narrow; LGBT Students' Experience in Higher Education.* London: National Union of Students.

Pearce, T. (2016). The Undergraduate Student Experience. In H. Cowie and C-A. Myers (Eds.) Bullying among University Students. (pp. 17-20), London: Routledge.

Phipps, A. and Young, I. (2013). *That's What She Said: Women Students' Experiences of 'Lad Culture' in Higher Education.* London: National Union of Students.

Rivers, Ian. (2016). Homophobic and transphobic bullying in universities. In H. Cowie and C-A. Myers (Eds.), *Bullying among University Students.* (pp. 48-60), London: Routledge.

Salmivalli, C., Lagerspetz, Biorkqvist, Osterman and Kaukia. (1996). Bullying as a Group Process: Participant Roles and their Relations to Social Status within the Group. *Aggressive Behavior*, Vol. 22, pp. 1-15.

Schenk, A. and Fremouw, W. (2012). Prevalence, Psychological Impact, and Coping of Cyberbully Victims among College Students. *Journal of School Violence,* Vol.1, pp.21-37.

Sourander, A., Brunstein, Klomek, Ikomen, Lindroos, Luntamo, Koskelainen, Ristkari and Helnenius et al. (2010). Psychosocial Risk Factors Associated with Cyberbullying among Adolescents. *Archives of General Psychiatry,* Vol. 67, pp: 720-728.

Sullivan, K. (2016). Commentary: Bullying Among University Students: Awakening and Harnessing the Sleeping Dragon of Student Power. In H., Cowie and C-A., Myers (Eds.), *Bullying among University Students.* (pp. 193-202), London: Routledge.

Ttofi, M. and Farrington, D. (2011). Effectiveness of School-based Programs to Reduce Bullying: a Systematic and Meta-analytic Review. *Journal of Experimental Criminology,* Vol.7, pp.27-56.

Valentine, G. Wood and Plummer. (2009). *The Experience of Lesbian, Gay, Bisexual and Trans Staff and Students in Higher Education.* London: Equality Challenge Unit.

Zhang, L., Osberg and Phipps. (2014). Is all bullying the same. *Archives of Public Health*, Vol.72, pp.1-8.

CHAPTER TEN

DIVERSITY AND RACE IN A HIGHER EDUCATION CONTEXT

SUKH HAMILTON AND TANYA RIORDAN

Introduction

Bomber (2007, p. 54) states that:

> "Social development refers to the development of interaction between individuals and the surrounding human world, including relationships with others and also the social skills needed to fit into our culture and society"

This reference to "our culture and society" evokes notions of those on the "inside" and those on the "outside", or to put it another way: how society constructs "otherness", which in turn highlights why the topic of diversity and minority ethnic students is a social issue. This chapter seeks to address the issue of diversity within a higher education context with specific reference to black and minority ethnic students. It examines past and present situations. The labels of 'Black and Minority Ethnic' (BME) or 'Black, Asian and Minority Ethnic' (BAME) are used to describe people of non-white descent who are resident in the UK. The term "International" when describing students, is a reference to those who have come to the UK specifically to participate in the educational system. Thus these two groups have differing needs and experiences. The chapter explores what those might be. Much of the content is based on a case study of the School of Education of a University which provides courses for full and part-time undergraduate and postgraduate students from diverse backgrounds. Many of these courses have developed in partnership with a range of external educational organisations to ensure students meet the requirements for professional careers. A course with a work based element and which has an annual cohort of 150 students is presented to highlight the methods of attracting and retaining students, from a range of backgrounds, cultures and nationalities in order to develop sound inclusive practice and pedagogy.

Diversity within a Higher Education context

In 1998 the Department for Education and Employment (DFEE) announced that the education profession as a whole should reflect the society in which we live, by assembling a workforce that both recruits and brings diverse strengths and qualities from all groups. Since then there have been attempts, through a variety of government initiatives, to raise attainment and improve access to higher education (HE) for students from BME backgrounds. Historically, recruitment to HE courses and in particular post graduate teacher training courses has been a challenge. There is a particular issue with recruitment and more significantly retention. Many BME students are late applicants or do not hold the required qualifications (Rampton, 1981; Swann, 1985; CRE, 1986; Wilkins and Lall, 2011). Basit (2012) reveals a range of variables which contribute to these disparities including "term time working, parental income and education, English as an additional language, and previous institution attended" (p.176). A particular challenge facing universities is the clustering of BME students on some degrees and their low numbers on others. For example, there are low numbers of students from BME backgrounds who apply to degree courses in the arts, humanities and social sciences. The Higher Education Funding Council for England's (HEFCE) (2015) data also indicates only minor fluctuations in numbers entering HE since 2006. The issue is not just one of accessing HE, but also which universities are attended. Bhopal (2015) states that, in comparison to white students, students of BME heritage are less likely to attend prominent universities. The Elevations Trust Network (2012) highlights that a particular London based university has more black students than the combined total at the 20 Russell group universities. Bhopal (2015) also notes that people from BME groups are more likely to attend universities that have students who mirror their own ethnic and social backgrounds. This highlights the real need to feel part of the establishment, rather than feeling different.

The Equality Acts of 2006 and 2010, which replaced the Race Relations Amendment Act (RRAA) 2000 and the Disability Discrimination Act 2005 respectively, stressed a need for all institutions, including universities, to promote equality. Kimura (2013) cites Ahmed et al. (2006) and Ahmed (2012) who voice that in order to stress their progressiveness, social inclusiveness, (international) excellence and ability to provide diverse social and cultural experiences, many universities have stated their 'commitment' to promote equality and diversity under the auspices of these acts. Kimura (2013) further points out that diversity among student cohorts in many universities is much greater than before. So there is a responsibility on universities to enable interaction between those from different strands of society be it "social class, ethnicity, age and previous educational background" (p.2), in order to not only "achieve a socially just and culturally diverse society" (p.2), but also to extend students' perspectives.

Stevenson (2012), using figures from the Equity Challenge Unit (ECU) (2011), stresses that whilst BME students statistically have increased their presence in HE, there is still a disparity in both retention and degree attainment. Degree attainment is measured by the number of first and upper second class degrees awarded. The figures for these classifications are: 73.2% of white students compared to 57.1% of BME students and out of the 57.1%, only 38.1% were Black students. This indicates that even within the BME figures, there is disparity because black students are doing much worse than other minority ethnic students. In isolation these figures do not cause alarm, however when it becomes apparent that all of these students arrive with similar entry level tariffs, questions do arise. Stevenson (2012) highlights research by Broecke and Nicholls (2007) for the DfES which stressed that even after looking at prior influencing factors such as: "attainment, subject of study, age, gender, disability, deprivation, type of HE institution attended, type of Level 3 qualifications, mode of study, term-time accommodation and ethnicity" (p.3) there was still an impact on degree attainment if the student was from a minority ethnic background. This research was confirmed further by HEFCE in 2010. There has been much discussion (Richardson, 2008; Berry and Loke, 2011; Singh, 2011) about issues that may be responsible for this disparity but Stevenson (2012) suggests the attainment gap cannot be simplistically rationalised. She highlights a multitude of factors- structural, organisational, attitudinal, cultural and financial, which all play a part but the consensus is that poor learning and teaching practices, including course design, the curriculum, assessment and tutor expectations, may all have an impact. Singh (2011) additionally cites segregation, misidentification of ability and pre-judgements based on linguistic competence also as important factors.

Berry and Loke (2011) advocate a number of changes that may enable Higher Educations institutions (HEIs) to address this attainment divide. They draw on research funded by the Higher Educational Academy (HEA) and ECU based in 15 HEIs, which suggests that having a co-authored curriculum, which is intercultural in flavour, will allow for more students to feel as if they belong and have a voice. This in essence means a more diverse, rather than white-centred curriculum that looks to position all students as co-constructors of their learning.

"Race" as an ideology and outcomes for minority ethnic students

Notions of race emerged at the point in history where white Europeans went out and colonized large areas of the globe (Wade, 2014). Wade argues it is also the point at which euro-centrism was born since societal order became based on what was deemed to be 'civilised' (and Christian) within a European framework. What/who was 'savage' was outside of European societies, which were projected as being superior. This notion ultimately fed into doctrines about human evolution. Wade's (2014) argument about the sub-textual change in the context of the word "race" and the notion that it no longer denoted what it did 50, 100, or 500 years ago, is particularly interesting as it has implications beyond simple labelling. It is also about the relationship between the idea of "race" and the manifestation of racism itself. The Lacanian notion of "the gaze" and how people position themselves in relation to what they see and what they identify with is discussed by Bhopal and Meyers (2008) with particular reference to race and ideology. They argue that the dominant elements of society see subjects within a particular framework and this "gaze" is then used to construct the identity of those subjects. They further stress that it is the means by which boundaries are created and reinforced for people which ultimately dictates how they function within society.

Dovidio, Gaertner and Kawakami (2010) note that racism has three elements which can be summarised as: first, a culturally shared belief that people can be categorised according to shared "race" based characteristics; second, that those characteristics then determine hierarchies and positioning with regards to the human race; and third, that racism is not simply negative attitudes and dogmas but also about power that translates into unequal outcomes. Dovidio et al. (2010) further argue that racism is maintained through a range of culturally accepted "social norms, policies, and laws" (p.312). This is further developed by Garner (2010) who stresses that society is flooded with ways of stating that "race" is a *natural* facet of cultural norms. This was an argument first developed by Hatcher (1995) who noted that racism was not simply imprinted upon passive recipients, he cited Miles (1989) who stressed that ideologies are often constructed and reshaped by people in order to make sense of and act within, the circumstances they find themselves in. This ultimately feeds back into the notion of the "gaze". Berman and Paradies (2010, p. 216) specify that racism is most commonly understood to be a "combination of prejudice and power", while Bonilla-Silva (1997) deems racism to be: "a social system involving ethno-racial categories and some form of hierarchy that produces disparities in life chances between ethno-racial groups" (p.216). The fact that racism creates difference and hierarchies and so ultimately impacts on life chances and also on how individuals define themselves, is central to the topic of understanding ethnic minorities' achievement and disadvantage.

Modern racism is multi-layered. Basit et al. (2007) stress that it can be overt, covert, deliberate, inadvertent, individual, institutional, acknowledged or disregarded. Poteat and Spanierman (2012) argue that it has evolved and no longer involves strong, blatant expressions, but rather a more subtle form of prejudice. They further state that by not acknowledging that racism is still evident in contemporary society is, in itself, a subtle form of racism because this denial negates the experiences of those who actually bear the brunt of expressions of racism. However, this is a common sentiment and one where there is a belief that society has moved on from racism which has evolved like any other concept (Modood, 2010).

The distinction between ethnicity and race is more unclear. Jessop and Williams (2009) state that ethnicity is constructed on a shared identity based on history, cultural background, religion and language. For Wade (2014) the terms themselves are unimportant but it is more about what they represent, and that is the notion of otherness, and ultimately about "insiders" and "outsiders". The labels, or ethnicity categories of white European, Asian and Black, are deeply embedded within colonial history and, within that, the policy of dividing and conquering. This policy continues to the present day, where the notion of what Bhatt (2012) refers to as "good" minorities as opposed to "bad" minorities, is evident in the popular media with Muslims being portrayed negatively and Hindus and Sikhs commended for their ability to integrate into mainstream British society. This viewpoint is also evident within educational establishments. Archer and Francis (2005) found that teachers were pre-judging minority ethnic students which actually indicated elements of "unwitting" racism. Much research over the last 20 years (Wright, 1987; Mirza, 1992; Sewell, 1995; Basit, 1997; Shain, 2003; Miah, 2015) indicates constant lower expectations for ethnic minorities. The issue of typecasting and stereotyping is also an area of concern. This is highlighted by Brah (1994) who states that lower expectations are held for South Asian girls who are seen as being oppressed and victims of their heritage. Connolly (1998) and

Mac and Ghaill (1988) suggest that non- Muslim Asian boys are seen as docile and well behaved but also achievers; while Muslim boys are perceived to be "fundamentalist" but also low-achievers (Miah, 2015). Baggley and Hussain (2007) disclose, from their interviewees, prevalent negative assumptions about Islam and Muslims within teaching contexts, especially issues about the relationship between Islam and "the West". Furthermore, they stress that some of their interviewees mentioned quite explicit comments or actions from some academic staff that questioned their academic ability because of their cultural heritage. The idea that all non-white students are singular homogeneous cultural groups who, in turn, have a typical engagement with education is very harmful. This assumption based on stereotyped conceptualisations that Knowles and Ridley (2005) refer to as a "one size fits all" approach, is detrimental to a young person's wellbeing as well as being both simplistic and patronising.

Elton-Chalcraft (2009, p. 12) cites research in which educators declared that they did not discriminate between young people, and that they "saw" all young people as the "same" irrespective of what colour they were. This "colour blind" approach is, in essence, a form of racism as there is a denial of the student's cultural heritage. According to Blandford (2011) professionals working within education need to understand the multi-faceted nature of personal identity and also the complexity of each layer of that identity amongst the students they work with. Hence, each person from different ethnic, socio-cultural and socio-economic groups may belong to a number of social groups, as well as having different cultures, cultural practices and beliefs and social identities. This wealth of heritage, of the students, represents specific strengths, experiences and valid histories. This practice is supported by Cole and Stuart (2005) who, through interviews with BME students, found that they wanted the opportunity to celebrate their identities and also to talk openly about their ethnicity.

BME and International students:
learner needs and experiences

Berry and Loke (2011) highlight that a common source of confusion for many academics is the difference between international and UK-domiciled BME students. This failure to distinguish between these two categories means that students who may identify themselves as British are often put into the same taxonomy as those who are simply here as "visitors" involved in the learning forums. Another common issue it that of misidentification. Some students are automatically assumed to be 'immigrants' because they wear the hijab, or a turban. Stevenson (2012) echoes this point when drawing on her research in which some staff in HE doggedly misidentify BME students as: having language difficulties; being insufficiently prepared for learning as a result of differences between the UK and other overseas schooling systems; and also that the students experience a sort of "culture shock" because they are studying in a "new" country.

The Macdonald Report (1989) which was seminal in regards to raising awareness of racism highlighted the need for an appropriate mechanism for tackling racism within an educational context. The report was extremely critical of systems which were well intended but which inadvertently fed both prejudice and resentment. Basit et al. (2007, p. 295) highlight that the report also attacked the stereotyping of ethnic groups, as well as assumptions about attitudes, needs and values. Yet 20 years after the report was published, Read, Archer, and Leathwood (2003) question the extent to which ethnic minorities feel they fit into academia. They state that minority students often group along ethnicity lines in order to increase their own sense of belonging. Earlier research by Eimers and Pike (1997) suggests that this cultural grouping and lack of "academic integration" carried more "negative consequences" for the students from ethnic minorities rather than those from a majority background. In simple terms, there is more likely a comment to be made about how BME students stick together, than about how white students stick together. This also ties in with research from Basit et al. (2007) that found minority ethnic students felt they were, on occasion, more likely to get negative criticism than their majority ethnic peers. They further argued that the Macdonald Report was a clear example of how policies need to be accepted and affirmed by communities in order to be implemented, rather than simply imposed.

Case study of a University based Initial Teacher Education Course

This section of the chapter demonstrates how an awareness of issues surrounding the inclusion of students from diverse backgrounds influenced the design and management of a university based Postgraduate Certificate in Education (PGCE) programme. Strategies were designed to support the recruitment, retention and success of students from a range of different cultural and linguistic backgrounds .The course as a whole, year on year comprises 150 students of which approximately seven percent are from BME backgrounds, some of whom self-identify as British. These have been born and brought up in the UK but have a minority ethnic heritage, while other students are international students who are recent arrivals to the UK from another country.

The background to this case study is in part the role of the Office for Standards in Education (Ofsted) which carries out external inspections of teacher training courses. Such inspections were carried out in the case study university in 2007 and 2011 when special attention was given to the key question "To what extent does the provision promote equality of opportunity, value diversity and eliminate harassment and unlawful discrimination?" (Ofsted Framework for Inspection, 2011). The course leaders introduced a survey at the beginning and end of the course 10 years ago to produce evidence for OFSTED of how they were seeking to accommodate the needs of all their students. Those annual surveys, as well as interviews with BME students, provided the data for this chapter.

Surveys are undertaken at the beginning and end of each course and evaluation forms are collated and analysed. Semi structured interviews were first undertaken when the earlier surveys sought to discover what additional support would be beneficial to students and if the students' strengths and contributions had been positively exploited. Based on the answers, modifications were made to the course. One improvement was employing a BME support tutor, a second was amending selection questions at recruitment interviews, and a third was providing specific mentor training. Exit interviews continue to be a feature of the course. The last OFSTED review (2012) examined the surveys to assess the effect of changes introduced and whether the current strategies were meeting the expectations of the students and the aims of the course leadership team.

Increasing BME students recruitment to the PGCE Course

Increasing recruitment to the course was done through a variety of mechanisms. Primarily the language used in advertising the course was reframed to highlight the positive impact cultural diversity brings and also the inclusivity of the HE setting itself, which stresses a commitment to equality of opportunity through effective support. The advertisements were placed in specialist journals which targeted diverse sections of the community. The evidence is that this strategy has had a limited impact because interviews with students revealed little or no knowledge of such journals or of the advertisements within them. The course was also promoted in a range of community settings and recruitment talks were held in local community. Both International and BME students were given guidance on form filling and opportunities for interview practice. A support tutor was present at all the talks, offering advice on interview techniques and guidance on producing written applications. It was also noted that international students need a substantial amount of time to acclimatise and understand the systems in place. The numbers recruited continues to be satisfactory although it is difficult to measure the effect of these changes.

Retention

Two thirds of the students' time on the course is spent in schools and problems arise pertaining to their work-based placements. A variety of studies have identified these problems as: not enough baseline data on schools' attitudes or approaches to diversity training for staff (John, 2010); universities being over sensitive about placing students in work placements where they are likely to encounter racial harassment (Carrington et al., 2000); understanding the importance of diversity in settings that are predominantly white (Rollock, 2009) or where countering racism is not high on the schools' Senior Management's agenda (Cole and Stuart, 2005); lack of a shared ethos and the promotion of fundamental principles across the partnership of University and schools (Wilkins and Lall, 2011); insufficient, positive targeted BME induction sessions for newly qualified teachers (NQTs) (ibid); and the need for better training of mentors (Basit et al., 2006). These issues need to be addressed in order to find a way forward for students to be better supported whilst on work-based placements. Wilkins and Lall's study (2011) shows that there is a need for a strong partnership between workplace settings and the HEI in order to provide a clear framework promoting equality and dealing with racism.

In order to retain numbers it is important that problematic areas, as identified by the students both within the university and also in their work placements, are swiftly dealt with. One of the key aspects of student success rate is to pre-empt potential obstacles and to initiate an early intervention programme (Basit et al., 2006). The latter seeks to address these issues promptly in order to fully integrate students in their academic environment by reducing the disadvantages (Eimers and Pike, 1997). In the case study programme all students have their written and spoken English tested at interview and pre course tasks are sent out to individuals. Students with English as an additional language (EAL) are required to attend a specifically designed course to improve their academic English. As well as focusing on academic writing, the English for Academic Purposes (EAP) course also teaches students how to: understand the language of teenagers; deal with awkward questions; develop strategies for "saying what you mean" without being confrontational; and practise the language of "persuasion" e.g. using cautious language and "hedging". According to research conducted by McNamara and Basit (2004), problems of language not only pertain to minority ethnic groups, so all students on the PGCE are invited to attend the EAP course should they require additional support with academic writing. Many mature, non BME students take up this opportunity. Student evaluations at the end of the course report how the support allows for a better student experience and one that demystifies the process especially for non- native speakers of English and those unfamiliar with the English HE system.

A further strategy undertaken by the Department was to appoint a BME support tutor. The tutor is both local and from an ethnic minority heritage. This is an approach advocated by Wilkins and Lall (2011) who urge providers to prioritise diversity amongst university departmental teams. The BME support tutor's role is multifaceted. She advises the team on a range of issues which include an understanding of different cultural norms and expectations. Student responses to the course's end of year evaluations (2012/2013/2014) suggested that those of either BME heritage or who are international students have common issues regarding stereotyping. This correlates with Basit et al. (2006) who suggest that students have raised concerns about their work placements regarding stereotypical qualities and unrealistic expectations of their own ability to support others from both international and BME backgrounds. The BME support tutor gives introductory lectures to students and also to work-based mentors and offers additional seminars on valuing diversity as well as continuous online support. As a person who has English as an additional language, the BME support tutor is also able to advise international students on strategies for those who struggle to understand regional accents or "slang". Evidence from Basit et al. (2006) research shows that students often face problems with their mentors due to the latter's lack of training in ethnic minority matters. Thus, mentors, working in partnership with the university, are provided with training which consists of awareness-raising of the course support structure; of legislation and responsibilities; and of support strategies for students, based on a video of a past student's experiences. In addition, a guidance toolkit or handbook, is given to each mentor to include background information on a variety of religions and cultures, with some suggested strategies for improving inclusion and diversity within schools. Further assistance is provided on the "good practice in mentoring" website, which contains a section on guidance for supporting BME and international students. Regular surveys are given to mentors of trainee teachers' pre and post the training to establish their personal confidence and experiences when dealing with students from a BME background. True or False responses are requested to statements such as:

I am knowledgeable in the school's procedures for dealing with racist incidents

I am confident in my knowledge of the problems faced by BME trainees.

Mentors' responses to the surveys post training indicate a greater awareness and understanding of the impact of diversity on their practice and on their schools as opposed to those completed pre training. .

Ongoing University based support

Each year support seminars for students are scheduled in addition to the normal timetable. The purpose of these seminars is to give access to topics that are not covered elsewhere. These include: developing an understanding of the culture of English education; strategies for dealing with behaviours and racist comments; applying for jobs and preparing for interviews; as well as shared experiences and frequently asked questions. Seminars encourage students to identify their heritage in a supportive environment and to identify their strengths and areas for development. Evaluations year on year, show these sessions to be "invaluable, interesting and helpful". The sessions are made available to all students, irrespective of their background, and all students are actively encouraged to attend.

Whilst in work placements, regular support is provided for all students who are experiencing problems For BME students these problems may range from racist abuse to language barriers. This support takes place in a variety of ways: one to one, online or via email. There is no doubt that BEM students suffer from xenophobic and, at times, racist comments. Cole and Stuart's research (2005) confirms similar experiences in other organisations. There is awareness by the university-based tutors that there needs to be sensitivity shown to the reluctance of some students to report incidents which they may feel undermine their academic and professional development (Wilkins and Lall, 2011).

Conclusions and recommendations

When developing and equally valuing, "diversity" and "race" within an HE context, a consideration of how to increase meaningful participation from a diverse cohort should be deliberated in the first instance. This has to be within the remit of best practice. This means that, rather than using material that denotes a diverse campus with policies that are carefully filed away, HEIs need to ensure that the material used truly reflects their institution and that all policies are actively applied. This also means it is not enough simply measuring data to state what the makeup is, institutions need to look at their holistic community and put measures in place to ensure that there is diversity at every level from cleaners to senior management and across the range of degrees.

In addition to reflecting society as a whole, universities need to engage with micro systems that allow for a more level playing field for all students. This must permeate all policies and practices starting with admission through to support whilst undertaking the degree. The subtle nuances within present day racism create differences and hierarchies, which in turn impact on life chances and on how individuals define themselves and are pivotal to understanding ethnic minorities' achievement and disadvantage. The fundamental difference in learner needs and experiences between international students and those from a BME background, including those with EAL, must stop being an area of ignorance for all involved in HEIs but especially for those who come into contact with these students.

This chapter has examined and described some good practice. It highlights the need to attract and retain students from a range of backgrounds and to enhance all learners' experiences. It illustrated that sensitivity to students' histories and experiences can be a useful way of enabling an inclusive ethos to flourish. It can also stress to the students the value the establishment places on the notions of equality and diversity. The case study used here illustrated a number of support mechanisms such as the benefits of the EAP course, which is signposted to all students but particularly those who need to learn the language of HE. A pre-emptive usage of this type of course meant fewer failures in students' first essays and a noticeable improvement in all required skills. Students commenting on EAP stated that they had gained confidence in approaching their studies and their work placements. Some students opted to join generic EAP classes, despite their heavy commitments and workload in the second semester. It was also observed that there were higher percentages of positive evaluations and most importantly, fewer withdrawals from the course after participating in the EAP sessions.

Until HEIs acknowledge that in order to attract and retain students, from a range of backgrounds, cultures and nationalities will have to be mutually accepted and respected or progress will continue to be slow. The

UK has been a forerunner in the concept of diversity and integrating minorities but there is more to be done. HEIs are but a microcosm of society and their challenge is not whether this can be done, but more importantly how soon and how well it can be achieved.

Bibliography

Archer, L. and Francis, B. (2005). "They never go off the rails like other ethnic groups": teachers' constructions of British Chinese pupils' gender identities and approaches to learning. *British Journal of Sociology of Education*, Vol.26 (2), pp. 165 – 182.

Baggley, P. and Hussain, Y. (2007). *The Role of Higher Education in Providing Opportunities for South Asian Women*. Abingdon: The Joseph Rowntree Foundation.

Basit, T. (1997). *Eastern values, Western milieu: identities and aspirations of adolescent British Muslim girls*. Aldershot: Ashgate.

Basit, T.N. (2012). 'I've never known someone like me go to university': Class, ethnicity and access to higher education. In T.N. Basit and S. Tomlinson (Eds.) *Social Inclusion and Higher Education*. Bristol: Policy.

Basit, T.N., Roberts, L., McNamara, O., Carrington, B., Maguire, M. and Woodrow, D. (2006). Did they jump or were they pushed? Reasons why minority ethnic trainees withdraw from initial teacher training courses. *British Educational Research Journal,* Vol.32 (3), pp. 387-410.

Basit, T.N., McNamara, O., Roberts, L., Carrington, B., Maguire, M. and Woodrow, D. (2007). The Bar is Slightly Higher: the perception of racism in teacher education. *Cambridge Journal of Education*, Vol.37 (2), pp. 279- 298.

Berman, G. and Paradies, Y. (2010). Racism, disadvantage and multiculturalism: towards effective anti-racist praxis. *Ethnic and Racial Studies*, Vol. 33(2), pp. 214-232.

Berry, J. and Loke, G. (2011). *Improving the Degree Attainment of Black Minority Ethnic Students*. York: ECU/HEA.

Bhatt, C. (2012). Secularism and Conflicts about Rights (pp.6-9). In N. Yuval-Davis and Philip Marfleet (Eds.) *Secularism, Racism and the Politics of Belonging*. Retrieved from: http://www.runnymedetrust.org/uploads/publications/pdfs/Secularism%20RacismAndThePoliticsOfBelonging-2012.pdf

Bhopal, K. (2015). Race, identity and support in initial teacher training. *British Journal of Educational Studies* (pp1-15). DOI:10.1080/00071005.2015.1005045

Bhopal, K and Meyers, M. (2008). *Insiders, outsiders and others*. Retrieved from: http://eds.a.ebscohost.com/eds/ebookviewer/ebook/ZTAwMHR3d19fNDAwNDUzX19BTg2?sid=6c6e4ece-e4a7-43c7-bf2c-ae6b26c07106@sessionmgr4003&vid=5&format=EB&rid=5

Blandford, V. (2011). Foreign language education: Preparing for diversity. In R. Heilbronn and J. Yandell (Eds.) *Critical Practice in Teacher Education. A study of professional learning* (pp.90-101). London: Institute of Education, University of London.

Bomber, L. (2007). *Inside I'm Hurting*. Duffield: Worth Publishing.

Bonilla-Silva, E. (1997). Rethinking Racism: Toward a Structural Interpretation. *American Sociological Review*, Vol. 62(3), pp. 465-480.

Brah, A. (1994). 'Race' and 'culture' in the gendering of labour markets: South Asian young Muslim women and the labour market. In H. Afshah and M. Maynard (Eds.) *The dynamics of' race' and gender: some feminist interventions*. London: Taylor and Francis.

Broecke, S. and Nicholls, T. (2007). *Ethnicity and Degree Attainment*. London: Department for Education and Skills.

Carrington, B., Bonnett, A., Nayak, A., Skelton, C., Smith, F., Tomlin, R., Short, G. and Demaine, J. (2000). The Recruitment of Teachers from Minority Ethnic Groups. *International Studies in Sociology of Education*, Vol.10 (1), pp., 3-22.

Cole, M. and Stuart, J.S. (2005). 'Do you ride on elephants' and 'never tell them you're German': the experiences of British Asian and black and overseas student teachers in South-east England. *British Educational Research Journal*, Vol. 31 (3), pp.349-366.

Connolly, P. (1998). *Racism, gender identities and young children: social relations in a multi-ethnic inner-city primary school*. London: Routledge.

CRE. (1986). *Teaching English as a Second Language: Report of a Formal Investigation in Calderdale Local Education Authority*. London: Commission for Racial Equality.

Dovidio, J.F., Gaertner, S.L. and Kawakami, K. (2010). Racism in J.F. Dovidio, M., Hewstone, P., Glick and V.M. Esses (Eds.), *Handbook of prejudice, stereotyping, and discrimination* (pp.312-327). London: Sage.

Department for Education and Employment. (1998). Green Paper: *Teachers: meeting the challenge of change*. London: HMSO.

Eimers, M.T. and Pike, G.R. (1997). Minority and non-minority adjustment to college: Differences or similarities? *Research in Higher Education*, Vol. 38 (1), pp.77–97.

Elevations Trust Network. (2012). *Race to the Top: The Experience of Black Students in Higher Education*. London: Bow Group.

Elton-Chalcraft, S. (2009). *'It's Not Just About Black and White, Miss'*. Stafford: Trentham.

Hatcher, R. (1995). Racisms and children's cultures. In M. Griffiths, and B. Troyna (Eds.) *Antiracism, Culture and Social Justice in Education* (pp.97-114).

Garner, S. (2010). Racisms, an introduction. SAGE Publications Ltd: Birmingham.

HEFCE. (2015). *Time series of undergraduates in higher education subjects*. Retrieved from: http://www.hefce.ac.uk/analysis/supplydemand/ug

Jessop, T. and Williams, A. (2009). Equivocal tales about identity, racism and the curriculum. *Teaching in Higher Education*, Vol.14 (1), pp.95-110.

John, J. (2010). Discussion paper for Steering Committee of South East BME Project titled: 'Outline of Potential Project Strands Emerging from Discussions with South East Providers'.

Kimura, M. (2013). Non-performativity of university and subjectification of students: the question of equality and diversity in UK universities. *British Journal of Sociology of Education,* Vol. 34 (4) pp.523-540. DOI: 10.1080/01425692.2013.777207

Knowles, E. and Ridley, W. (2005). *Another Spanner in the Works.* Stoke on Trent: Trentham.

Mac and Ghaill, M. (1988). *Young, gifted and black.* Milton Keynes: Open University Press.

MacDonald Report. (1989). *Murder in the Playground. Report of the MacDonald Inquiry into Racism and Racial Violence in Manchester Schools.* London: Longsight Press.

McNamara, O. and Basit, T.N. (2004). Equal opportunities or affirmative action? The induction of minority ethnic teachers. *Journal of Education for Teaching: International research and pedagogy,* Vol. 30 (2), pp.97-115.

Miah, S. (2015). *Muslims, Schooling & the question of self-segregation.* Basingstoke: Palgrave -Macmillan.

Mirza, H.S. (1992). *Young, Female and Black.* London: Routledge.

Modood, T. (2010). Still Not Easy Being British, struggles for multicultural citizenship. Stoke on Trent: Trentham.

Ofsted. (2007). *University of Portsmouth. A secondary initial teacher training short inspection report.* London: Ofsted.

—. (2011). *University of Portsmouth. Initial Teacher Education Inspection Report.* London Ofsted.

Poteat, V.P. and Spanierman, L.B. (2012). Modern Racism Attitudes among White Students: The Role of Dominance and Authoritarianism and the Mediating Effects of Racial Colour-Blindness. *The Journal of Social Psychology,* Vol.152 (6), pp. 758–774.

Rampton, A. (1981). *The Rampton Report, West Indian Children in our Schools. Interim report of the Committee of Inquiry into the Education of Children from Ethnic Minority Groups.* London: TSO.

Read, B., L. Archer and C. Leathwood. (2003). Challenging culture: Student conceptions of belonging and isolation at a post-1992 university. *Studies in Higher Education,* Vol. 28 (3), pp: 261–77.

Richardson, J.T.E. (2008), *Degree attainment, ethnicity and gender: a literature review.* Retrieved from: http://www.heacademy.ac.uk/assets/documents/research/J_Richardson_literatu re_review_Jan08.pdf

Rollock, N. (2009). *NQT 'Achieving Race Equality in Schools', training programme Final Report.* London: The Runnymede Trust.

Sewell, T. (1995). 'A phallic response to schooling: Black masculinity and race in an inner-city comprehensive'. In M. Griffiths and B. Troyna (Eds.) *Antiracism, Culture and Social Justice in Education,* Stoke-on-Trent: Trentham.

Shain, F. (2003). *The schooling and identity of Asian girls.* Stoke on Trent: Trentham Books.

Singh, G. (2011). *Black and minority ethnic (BME) students' participation in higher education: improving retention and success. A synthesis of research evidence.* York: HEA.

Stevenson, J. (2012). *Black and minority ethnic student degree retention and attainment.* Retrieved from:
   https://www.heacademy.ac.uk/sites/default/files/bme_summit_final_report.pdf

Swann, Lord. (1985). *The Swann Report. Education for All. Report of the Committee of Enquiry into the Education of Children from Ethnic Minority Groups.* London: HMSO.

Wade, P. (2014). Race, Ethnicity, and Technologies of Belonging. *Science, Technology, and Human Values*, Vol.39 (4), pp. 587-596.

Wilkins, C. and Lall, R. (2011). 'You've got to be tough and I'm trying': Black and minority ethnic student teachers' experiences of initial teacher education. *Race, Ethnicity and Education,* Vol.14 (3), pp.365-386.

Wright. (1987). 'Black students - white teachers'. In Troyna, B. (Ed.). *Racial Inequality in Education.* London: Hutchinson.

CHAPTER ELEVEN

SOCIAL BARRIERS TO WIDENING PARTICIPATION IN HIGHER EDUCATION

JO WATSON

Introduction

Few would argue with the observation that higher education (HE) in the UK is currently navigating turbulent times, but significant and far-reaching changes have been a feature of the field for a number of years. The 1963 Robbins Higher Education Report was produced at a time when only approximately five percent of young people entered HE (Willets, 2013). A central principle of the Robbins Report was that 'courses of HE should be available for all those who are qualified by ability and attainment to pursue them and who wish to do so'. Building on that principle, expanding admission figures were subsequently given renewed impetus by the publication of the 1997 Dearing Report and the widening participation agenda that followed. The deficit model adopted by the Dearing Report suggested that the failure of students from less privileged socio-economic groups to access HE was based on poor qualifications, low aspirations and flawed educational decision-making (Maringe and Fuller, 2006). Its recommendations placed an emphasis on the raising of aspirations and achievement, and resolving issues associated with applications and admissions to HE (Greenbank, 2006). The Dearing Report became the starting point for a succession of policies and performance indicators and was later followed by declaration of the then Labour government's ambition to increase participation in HE towards 50 percent of those aged 18 to 30 by 2010 (DfES, 2003). Although considerable progress towards this ambition has been made, it is not equally reflected in all parts of the field, particularly within the most selective universities.

The most recent report into HE, the Browne Report of 2010, laid the groundwork for the current model of substantially increased repayable tuition loans (BIS, 2010) and an increasingly marketised field featuring greater competition between increasingly diverse institutions and, ostensibly, more student choice. The transfer of public funding from institutional teaching grants to student loans for fees, which have almost universally escalated to a £9000 cap, has shifted the financial burden to students. While universities retain the autonomy, enshrined in law, to decide who to admit and on what basis, Student Numbers Controls, which were lifted for the 2015/16 academic year, have hitherto limited access to student loans to fund fees, and potentially encouraged universities to be more selective (Bravenboer, 2012). The practices of the post-Browne HE landscape, therefore, sit uncomfortably with the espoused on-going commitment to supporting social mobility through widening participation and fair access (Milburn, 2012; Bowl, 2013).

This chapter draws on empirical research to illustrate the challenges to social inclusion in HE. First, it considers the HE landscape in terms of the successes of and ongoing challenges to widening participation. It then briefly introduces the theoretical perspectives of social theorist Pierre Bourdieu, which provides a framework for the subsequent exploration of some of the social barriers to widening participation in HE and how they might be addressed.

Widening participation in HE?

Despite significant increases in the proportion of students securing the necessary qualifications to enter and the number actually participating in HE, under-representation of those from less privileged social backgrounds has been highlighted as an enduring problem (Reay, David and Ball, 2005). More recently, the Universities and Colleges Admissions Service (UCAS) has reported substantial proportional increases in the entry rates of students from disadvantaged backgrounds (UCAS, 2013). Although disadvantaged 18 year olds were 40 – 60% more likely to enter HE in 2012 than they were in 2004, entry rates for 18 year olds in advantaged areas remained three to four times higher than for those in disadvantaged areas (UCAS, 2012). What is equally evident is that entry and participation across the stratified field of UK HE continues to be unevenly distributed (UCAS, 2012; 2013). Entry rates to higher tariff institutions are typically six to nine times greater for those from advantaged than those from disadvantaged areas, a larger difference than that noted for entry to all institutions (UCAS, 2013). These figures highlight the persistent imbalance in the opportunities provided by the HE sector to students from different backgrounds.

For many students, simply securing a place at university is an achievement in itself (Clegg, Bradley and Smith, 2006), but widening participation involves a great deal more than admissions processes and policies or "opening the door" that bit wider. All systems of education are premised on theories regarding who and what knowledge is for, how people learn and the value of specific forms of knowledge and practice for both individuals and society (Amsler and Bolsmann, 2012). There is no doubt that HE potentially has much to offer, but non-traditional entrants, who may be unfamiliar with 'the system,' can encounter a variety of challenges that influence their experiences, performance and retention. Literature suggests that these students are likely to be poorly prepared to study in HE (May and Bousted, 2004; Sambell and Hubbard, 2004) and that they may require and seek more guidance (Leathwood and O'Connell, 2003). These finding illustrate the potential for feelings of frustration and isolation amongst students who may not "fit" the expectations that universities have of them (Briggs, Clarke and Hall, 2013). Recognition of the complexity of the issues involved in these circumstances has witnessed a movement away from deficit model explanations towards greater recognition of the role played by institutions themselves (Sambell and Hubbard, 2004; Burke, 2005; Greenbank, 2006). Limited attention has been given to the culture and practices of HE in the UK where, as UCAS figures reveal, the operationalization of widening participation is not shared equally between all institutions, with the bulk occurring in lower status institutions. It is in the higher status institutions that the dominant culture and long-established traditions and practices hold most firmly and remain oriented towards traditional white, middle-class student populations who possess the economic, social and cultural capital most valued by the field of HE (Archer, 2007).

Introducing Bourdieu's theory of practice

The work of Pierre Bourdieu offers a theoretical framework that is useful in conceptualising the experiences of students entering the social world that is HE. Bourdieu's theory of practice focuses on the way that the routine behaviour of individuals is largely determined by the history and structure of their existing social environment, and how their actions within their taken-for-granted social world unintentionally contribute to maintaining its existing patterns. He highlights that individual behaviour is organised and produced neither entirely consciously nor entirely unconsciously, and that, beginning in childhood, it is linked to continuous learning about the usual patterns of social action and interaction within a particular environment. Bourdieu uses a metaphor based on a "feel for the game" which highlights the possibility of a degree of what is sometimes less than conscious strategizing and illustrates that social interactions represent a mixture of constraint and freedom (Jenkins, 1992; Grenfell and James, 1998).

Emerging from Bourdieu's work are some core theoretical concepts that are particularly useful for guiding the analysis of the issues underlying and influencing given social situations, such as entry to HE. 'Habitus' describes the system of durable and transposable dispositions and perspectives through which an individual perceives, judges and behaves within and thinks about the world (Bourdieu, 1990). It represents all of the unconscious patterns of being and perceiving that an individual acquires as a result of lengthy exposure to particular social conditions. Habitus is structured by the patterns of the social forces that produce it and is simultaneously structuring in the way that it shapes an individual's behaviours, perceptions and expectations (Wacquant, 1998). It is not fixed or inert, but dynamic and changeable, reflecting the influence of the social context in which an individual is immersed (Jenkins, 1992; Grenfell, 2004). While it embodies a degree of fluidity, which allows some adjustment in response to shifting social contexts and experiences, the habitus acquired in the early years of childhood remains essentially durable and stable because it establishes individual dispositions which tend to default to a range of largely unconscious responses to external stimuli (Grenfell, 2004).

"Fields" represent the bounded social spaces or arenas of life (such as HE) which form distinct social worlds and include unique, established and taken-for-granted practices that are imposed, often implicitly, on those wishing to enter or remain within them. While habitus informs an individual's actions or practice from within according to their established dispositions, perspectives and ways of being, the field in which they operate structures practice from without by circumscribing the range of possible and acceptable actions and behaviour available to individuals operating within it (Wacquant, 1998; Grenfell, 2004). In this way, there is a dynamic, reciprocal relationship between "field" and "habitus": a field is only realised by the expression of the habitus of those within it (particularly the most dominant members of the field), and individual habitus is based on the expression of the field. They might be thought of as two sides of the same coin, with neither independently determining social action (Wacquant, 1998). It is congruence or the "fit" between field and habitus that establishes the "legitimate" thought and action of individuals operating within a particular social space, and as Bourdieu explains, "when habitus encounters a social world of which it is the product, it is like a "fish in water": it does not feel the weight of the water, and it takes the world for granted" (Bourdieu and Wacquant, 1992).

The third of Bourdieu's key thinking tools is "capital", which refers to those resources that hold symbolic value within a particular field and therefore come to act as a form of currency symbolising the position of an individual within the social hierarchy of the field. Bourdieu classified capital into three primary forms: economic capital - referring to material and financial assets, cultural capital - incorporating scarce symbolic goods, skills and titles along with embodied dispositions such as accent, clothing and behaviour, and social capital - reflecting the resources accrued through membership of social groups and networks. The significance of capital resides in its capacity to influence social positions and trajectories within a field as a result of its volume and composition (Wacquant, 1998). Notably, as discussed below, some individuals will have capital relevant to a new field they enter (such as HE) as a result of their established habitus and the similarity of the new field to the social context from which they originate. This affords them an advantage over others whose habitus and social provenance is less congruent with the new field (Grenfell and James, 1998).

Individual fields each have their own particular "logic of practice" or "game", the governing principles of which reflect the interests of the field's most powerful or dominant groups, and entry into a field requires at least implicit acceptance of the "rules of the game" (Grenfell, 2007). These rules, or the patterns and conventions which define the ordinary functioning of the field, are not explicit or codified (Bourdieu and Wacquant, 1992), and "orthodox" and acceptable ways of doing and being within a field are largely implicit (the fish just knows how to swim). Similarly, the rules and principles of the game are not consciously held in the heads of individuals operating within the social field (the fish does not think about how it knows how to swim), but become partially internalised, shaping thoughts and actions to profit from, or succeed within, the field according to the capitals valued by it (Grenfell and James, 1998; Grenfell, 2007).

Drawing on research evidence

Bourdieu's theory of practice provided the theoretical framework guiding the analysis of the empirical data drawn upon in this chapter which emerged from a three-year longitudinal case study centred on an undergraduate programme in an allied health discipline in one UK' research intensive university. The case study provided a vehicle for exploring the experiences of students with non-traditional academic backgrounds studying in HE, with a particular focus on exploring how students' learning experiences were influenced by the culture, practices and nuances of the environment they had entered. Full details of the research are reported elsewhere (Watson et al., 2009; Watson, 2013a, b) and will not be reiterated here beyond briefly outlining its two primary elements.

Thirteen volunteer participants were drawn from a single cohort as they prepared to commence their studies. Data were collected via initial focus groups exploring pre-entry educational experiences and expectations of studying in HE; reflective diaries recording educational experiences that participants considered significant or meaningful, and one-to-one semi-structured interviews conducted towards the end of participants' first and third years of study, which focused on exploring their learning experiences. Demographic data and background information regarding patterns of education and employment within families was also collected. Documentation produced by the institution, school and department (e.g. mission statements, strategies, policies, regulations, validation documents, programme specifications, timetables, module profiles and assessment criteria) were analysed as representations of the case study site and to offer insight into the pervading culture, values and assumptions of that social field (Bogdan and Biklen, 2007).

A further arm of the study involved the analysis of the progression routes and exit awards of 239 students, drawn from four consecutive cohorts enrolled at the case study site, which provided further context to understanding student experiences. Binary logistic regressions focused on the successive outcomes, or dependent variables, of passing at National Qualification Framework Level 4, Level 5 and Level 6 and finally the award of a "good' (upper second or first class) honours degree. Following appropriate management of the raw data (Field, 2009), the predictor, or independent, variables used in the analysis were maturity at entry, gender, entry qualifications and socio-economic background.

Patterns of progression and achievement

Table 11.1 provides a summary of the full regression analysis, highlighting the significant predictors of outcome in each of the models representing points of progression and achievement through the programme: passing Level 4, Level 5 and Level 6, and the award of a 'good' (upper second or first class) honours degree. Predictors that did not reach statistical significance (including maturity at entry and backgrounds from the middle socio-economic groups) are not included. Academic background (whether traditional A-level routes or non-traditional routes such as Access or BTEC qualifications or Advanced Vocational Certificates in Education) was not influential at any stage. However, the analysis revealed a consistent pattern of male gender and backgrounds from amongst the lower socio-economic groups acting as significant predictors of poorer outcomes at each level of analysis. Each of these predictor variables had a significant influence at each level of the analysis even when the effect of the other was held constant. Male gender was the stronger predictor of a poor outcome at Level 4, while a background from the lower socio-economic groups was the stronger predictor of poor outcomes in all other models.

Table 11.1: Significant predictors of progression through the programme

Level of Analysis	B (Std Error)	Significance	95% Confidence Interval for Odds Ratio		
			Lower CI	Odds Ratio	Upper CI
Pass at Level 4 $R^2 = .09$ (Cox & Snell), .18 (Nagelkerke). Model X^2 (4) = 18.27, p = .001					
Constant [a]	-2.90 (0.44)	.000	.	.06	.
Gender (male)	1.77 (0.58)	.002**	1.88	5.84	18.15
SEB (lower groups)	1.56 (0.54)	.004**	1.66	4.78	13.77
Pass at Level 5 $R^2 = .09$ (Cox & Snell), .17 (Nagelkerke). Model X^2 (4) = 18.61, p = .001					
Constant [a]	-2.86 (0.43)	.000	.	0.06	.
Gender (male)	1.65 (0.58)	.004**	1.69	5.22	16.11
SEB (lower groups)	1.67 (0.53)	.002**	1.88	5.32	15.06
Pass at Level 6 $R^2 = .11$ (Cox & Snell), .19 (Nagelkerke). Model X^2 (4) = 21.64, p < .001					
Constant [a]	-2.72 (0.41)	.000	.	0.07	.
Gender (male)	1.72 (0.56)	.002**	1.85	5.58	16.82
SEB (lower groups)	1.74 (0.51)	.001***	2.11	5.71	15.47
'Good' Degree $R^2 = .08$ (Cox & Snell), .12 (Nagelkerke). Model X^2 (3) = 15.63, p = .001					
Constant [a]	-1.65 (0.28)	.000	.	0.19	.
Gender (male)	1.30 (0.51)	.011*	1.34	3.67	10.04
SEB (lower groups)	1.22 (0.41)	.003**	1.53	3.39	7.50

a: constant or baseline model in which all predictor variables are omitted and it is assumed that all cases fall into the outcome category with the highest frequency (i.e. 'yes' in all levels of analysis in Table 11.5); * p < .05; ** p < .005; *** p = .001

For the purposes of providing context for the discussion that follows, the key area to focus on is socio-economic background (SEB) as a predictor. The related figures in Table 11.1 can be summarised in the following observations:

1) The odds of a student from the lower socio-economic groups failing to pass Level 4 are *approaching five times higher* than for a student from a higher socio-economic group.
2) The odds of a student from the lower socio-economic groups failing to pass Level 5 are *more than five times higher* than for a student from a higher socio-economic group.
3) The odds of a student from the lower socio-economic groups failing to pass Level 6 are *more than five and a half times higher* than for a student from a higher socio-economic group.
4) The odds of a student from the lower socio-economic groups failing secure a good honours degree are *more than three times higher* than for a student from a higher socio-economic group.

Capital that counts in HE

The research was undertaken in a school of allied health professions in a research intensive university. Like all social fields, this "microcosm" of the field of HE has a logic of practice that privileges that field's most dominant inhabitants; in this case, the white middle classes. What is it about the practices of the field that generate such odds against the success of students from less privileged social backgrounds? Figure 11.1 offers a model or conceptual framework illustrating the key forms of capital highlighted by the qualitative data as underpinning a "feel for the game", or the successful engagement with the logic of practice of the field under consideration. As will be illustrated in the learner stories and discussion that follows, the individual experiences of participants in this research reflected their variable configurations and stocks of academic, linguistic, social and professionally-oriented capital and the role of a balanced and mixed portfolio of these types of capital.

Figure 11.1: Key forms of capital valued by the field

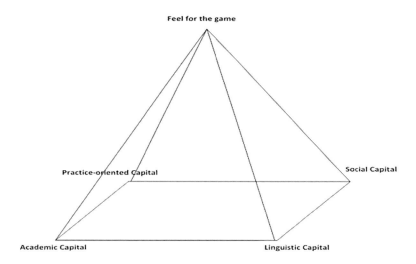

Before examining these forms of valued capital in more detail, their influence is exemplified in two illustrative summaries describing how two different individuals experienced the game in the field of HE they entered.

George: A 'fish in water'

George left school at 17 with a single A-level qualification. She moved from the mainland to a UK island when she married. Prior to starting a family and with a Higher National Diploma (HND) qualification, she worked in the hospitality industry. She realised that she'd chosen the wrong career, but it took time to identify what she really wanted to do. In the interim, she started a family and left full-time employment to work in various jobs which she described as *"just crap really"* [first interview]. In the end, she concluded: *"I've got to do it. Bite the bullet. [...] it was now or never"* [focus group], and with educational opportunities on the island limited, George completed an A-level through correspondence in just seven months while caring for a toddler and a new baby. The family relocated to the mainland so she could enter university, aged 33. George's father had been an engineer and her mother a teacher, and although going to university *"wasn't really mentioned"* [focus group], there was a wall of graduation photos in her grandmother's house that she, her cousins and her brother "aspired to" [family education/employment map], and upon which all ultimately achieved representation.

Fitting in with the HE field was a strong theme throughout George's data. Unlike some participants, she'd moved to a position of greater congruence between her established habitus and the pervading field than was previously the case. George said:

"For me it was brilliant because I'd been bringing up kids and working part-time for three years, so my friends were very much housewives with kids. All they used to talk about was shopping and housework and my brain just felt like it was seeping out of my ears! So to finally come and be around people who had a bit more to say for themselves [laughing] was brilliant. It's like meeting a load of like-minded people" [first interview].

Despite the competing demands on her time, George was thriving in many respects. Naturally, she needed to learn new skills and develop capital relevant to the new field, but her established habitus was much more closely aligned with it than was the case for some other participants. This congruence, her natural "feel for the game" and the clarity for her of the (explicitly stated) "rules of the game" was clearly illustrated when, early in her programme, she discussed the requirements of the assessments she had encountered. She said: *"these people who say it wasn't laid out correctly for them and people who failed saying "oh, we weren't told what to do"… and I'm going, well, we were. It's right there, you know!"* [First interview].

A striking feature of George's data was that she seemed to be very capital conscious (although it was described in her terms as being "strategic") and she took active steps to accrue and deploy to her advantage various forms of capital. Social capital played a particularly significant role and was often alluded to. In her first interview, George commented: *"learning in groups, that's definitely the key. We use a lot of study groups and we find so long as you've got like-minded people and they're on the same wave length …"* The concept of "like-minded people" was repeated throughout George's data and she was clearly discriminating about who she worked with. She said: *"I think I need to be a little 'cold' and strategic and find people with good understanding of subjects and people on similar wavelengths"* [reflective diary]. George's approach had the effect of ensuring that she developed high value social capital that afforded the greatest benefit.

Language, however, was scarcely mentioned in George's data. Viewed alongside her clarity about the "rules of the game", the fact that language was apparently unremarkable and did not warrant discussion suggests that

George naturally possessed a repertoire of linguistic capital appropriate to the field. While she was excited by extending and developing her academic skills and achieving academically (and thereby accruing academic capital), when she felt that theoretical learning wasn't directly relevant to her future professional practice, she disengaged and had the confidence to adopt a very strategic approach. In relation to one such area of the curriculum she said:

> *"When it came to the assessment, I literally did the bare minimum to scrape through and knew that I had. [Laughs] I just didn't enjoy that one. I kind of just thought, "What's the point of this?" really. I could see the point, but not the point of having so many lectures on it, especially when I thought we could be doing so much more in other areas"* [second interview].

George's data suggest that her efforts were focused on the development of capital that would benefit her as a future professional, and it was again clear that she was strategic and proactive in this regard. She clearly attributed the development of professionally-oriented skills and understanding (or capital) to both the academic and practice contexts of the programme but she wasn't averse to challenging either field, which may be related to the apparent confidence she had in her position within both. The overwhelming themes emerging from George's data were of fitting in and of gathering capital – most often very strategically. George was very much a "fish in water" from the outset and remained so throughout her engagement with the field. She was awarded a first class honours degree and even before graduating, she was contemplating a Masters' degree.

Betty: 'Growing' and 'changing'

Betty was one of the participants whose established habitus was **least** congruent with the new field. She self-identified as "extremely working-class" [first interview] and highlighted that university was never mentioned by her parents when she was growing up. Betty left school when she was 15 and before entering university she had a varied employment history in a wide range of skilled and semi-skilled roles which included working as a clerk, barmaid and manager, receptionist, driver, cleaner and care-support worker. During the focus group, Betty described living as the single parent of her daughter on a council estate for a number of years. In her early 20s, she studied for a National Vocational Qualification (NVQ) before working as a beauty therapist despite knowing even then that she really wanted to be an allied health professional. Having completed an Access course the previous year, Betty eventually commenced her undergraduate studies at the age of 34, weeks after marrying her self-employed mechanic husband.

Personal development was always part of Betty's project, but she clearly valued her established identity and was quick to emphasise that her overarching aim wasn't to *change*, but to grow. She said: "I'm *not going to become somebody that I'm not. You know … I want to remain quite grounded and I don't want to lose myself along the way"* [first interview]. The strength of Betty's assertion, which came at the end of her first year, hinted at resistance to the often unspoken demands that individual habitus align harmoniously with the expectations of the field, which in this case, as Burke (2005) suggests, were to become more middle-class. There is, however, also evidence of some insecurity about her position within the field. Discussing her reaction to an academic's comment highlighting the dominance of the middle classes in HE, Betty said: "*Maybe that was my own insecurities. It made me feel a little bit 'Well, does she think that people like me shouldn't be here?'"* [First interview].

Betty was ambitious to do well and in her first interview spoke of having "adapted to what's expected of [her]". A notable feature of her dataset was its power to illustrate the role and value of linguistic capital in the field, and to highlight the impact of having limited stocks of the particular form of language that was valued. Speaking during her first interview she said:

> "*I remember a lot of note-taking … the thing that sticks in my mind is this, writing down words. I didn't have a clue what they were; I just wrote them down [laughing] not just medical words just normal … language. Sometimes some of the words that we used, I was thinking, I don't know. I haven't got a clue what that means, so I'll write that down and I'll look it up when I get home "…'*

The development of language skills (and through them, linguistic capital) was an ongoing and active undertaking for Betty which she differentiated from the need to develop discipline-specific language, saying:

> "*On placement, I tend to do it with medical terms, which I think everybody does; you know … but in university, it just can be a word. One of the girls, she's great for telling me words. We'll sit and have a chat and I'll go, 'Whatever are you talking about?' [Laughs] She's great at explaining and just giving me a definition of words … [I'd say]"OK; and how would you use that in a sentence?" [Laughs]'* [second interview]

Betty felt that her life experiences prior to entering the field were "invaluable" [second interview]. Her effective communication and inter-personal skills stood as an example of (in this case, professionally-oriented) capital born out of her existing habitus that was valuable within the new field. Betty's increasing reflexivity enabled her to maximise her learning on placement, and through it to gather additional professionally-oriented capital; she said:

> *"I think you gather pieces of people really ... Even if it was a negative experience it made me think 'Well, that's not how I think. That shouldn't have been done"* [second interview].

Betty's data also exemplify the role of social capital. As we've seen, she actively used social networks (or the social capital accrued from them) to help her progress and gather capital within the field (such as learning new words and how to use them correctly) but, unlike George, she was unwilling and unable to dedicate herself entirely to the social network that she became associated with. Betty felt that her personal preferences in this regard, together with the physical distances and practicalities of her life, limited her opportunities to access support. She said:

> *"sometimes you really do value the social network, but there have been quite a few times where I've felt quite isolated ... Because I'm away; I'm in a different town. I haven't got people around me with a similar sort of experience or even who have gone through Uni themselves ... And: 'I think because I sort of almost wasn't in that little clique, when you are sort of struggling a little bit with your academic work, you think 'I could have done with that', you know, just to sort of bounce ideas off"* [second interview]

There was always some tension or conflict associated with Betty's distinction between change and growth, and with her ambitions within the field and her aversion to letting go of her established identity. In her first interview she observed:

> *"I think you grow because you want to adapt to the society that you're in as well...I don't want to just pass my degree or pass my exams, I want to do well in them. So ... I've had to sort of change my language, change my terminology and just fit in here at university."*

This shift in habitus to meet the expectations of the new field generated tensions and was incompatible with that expected within her home environment. By the end of her first year, Betty was aware of the impact on her family and said:

'... It's quite funny actually, because my husband looks at me sometimes and says: What was that you just said? I haven't a clue what you're on about there!" [Laughs] *And I'll come out with a word and [my daughter] will just look at me and then just walk off [laughs].'* [First interview]

The language that Betty had begun to adopt to fit into the field of HE was met with scepticism and incomprehension by players in her usual field in an apparent reversal of her own initial experiences in HE. The lack of congruence between Betty's existing social environment and the HE field, her desire to keep her established identity intact, and what she described as her "really limited" [second interview] social network meant that Betty experienced HE from the margins of the field. She was nevertheless able to adapt her habitus to more closely align with the expectations of the field and to develop a balanced portfolio of capital relevant to it and therefore beat the odds that the quantitative arm of the research suggested were against her. Betty went on to graduate having already been offered professional employment in social care [second interview].

Having illustrated the impact on individual experiences of operating within a given field of HE with varying portfolios of the capital valued by that field, the discussion now turns to examining how each of those capitals might be understood and how they underpin a "feel for the game" or the successful engagement with the logic of practice operating within the field.

Academic Capital

The term 'academic capital' is used by Bourdieu (1988) with reference to academic staff and specifically in relation to having graduated from an elite institution, the age at which a highly selective French national examination was passed (Grenfell, 2007) and with regard to the development of intellectual artefacts such as 'lectures, textbooks, dictionaries, encyclopaedias, etc.' (Bourdieu, 1988: 98). He used the different language of "educational capital" to refer to the options studied or grade awarded in the baccalaureate (Bourdieu, 1988: 168). Intellectual cultural capital of this nature is clearly of relevance to higher education in the UK. In the model presented in Figure 11.1, the term academic capital is used to reflect those legitimated forms of academic skills and knowledge profitable to students within the field, which ultimately translate into academic attainment and award, and therefore a higher value cultural capital in the form of academic and professional qualifications.

The foundations of academic capital lie in the academic skills, knowledge and approaches that students bring with them to the field of

HE. The more closely aligned the logic of practice of their previous educational and broader social environments with the field of higher education, the stronger their academic capital on entry to the new field, the firmer the foundations upon which it builds, and the greater the potential for the development of a strong portfolio as it strengthens and accumulates throughout a student's engagement with the field. Academic capital embodies a range of factors including legitimated disciplinary and related knowledge, orthodox approaches to searching for, accessing, critically appraising and synthesising knowledge sources, and to justifying and substantiating ideas and arguments. It also encompasses adherence to referencing and citation conventions and a legitimated style and delivery of oral presentation and written work, including the structure and tone of academic writing. The marking criteria developed by academic staff as dominant players in the field provide some insight into the characteristics of academic capital but, holding true to the largely symbolic nature of cultural capital, much remains implicit. Those, like George, who hold strong portfolios of academic capital know and readily recognise what is required of them. Those who have limited stocks of academic capital struggle to appreciate what is required. Despite what is at times considerable effort to do and be what is demanded, and the 'goal-posts' remain obscured.

Linguistic Capital

Bourdieu understood language as much more than an unproblematic instrument of communication. He observes that:

> "it provides, together with a richer or poorer vocabulary, a more or less complex system of categories, so that the capacity to decipher and manipulate complex structures, whether logical or aesthetic, depends partly on the complexity of the language transmitted by the family" (Bourdieu and Passeron 1977: 73).

Each individual develops a repertoire of language reflecting that used within, and the logic of practice of, the social field in which they are immersed, with the early familial social field having a strong primary influence. Language is a medium of cultural transmission (Grenfell 2007), and the way that it is used and understood varies across society. It can therefore be understood as a specific form of cultural capital, called linguistic capital (Bourdieu, 1991), the form or style of which potentially differs greatly between social contexts or fields (Grenfell, 1998).

Linguistic capital can be understood to encompass various aspects of the form and content of language valued within the field, including, for example grammar, linguistic repertoire, forms of phraseology, and tone and mode of written and verbal expression or expressive style (Bourdieu and Passeron, 1977; Bourdieu, 1991). In HE, there is an important relationship, and potential for conversion, between linguistic and academic capital. Illustrating the impact of linguistic capital on the efficiency of verbal or written communication in an educational setting (Bourdieu and Passeron 1977), linguistic capital influences the accessibility of a whole range of learning activities, particularly when that used by staff, who represent more dominant voices within the field, is markedly different from that held by individual students. Linguistic capital plays an important role in the interpretation of learning outcomes, marking criteria and feedback, is critical to the capacity to present knowledge and understanding in a form expected and legitimated by the field, and to the ability to think using language and therefore to manipulate, question and develop concepts and ideas.

The impact of linguistic capital is vividly illustrated in Betty's narrative. It highlights the differences in the forms of language that can be found between social environments, and the barrier that language can present to accessing information and demonstrating knowledge in situations where the linguistic repertoire possessed lacks congruence with the logic of practice of the field in which an individual is operating.

Social Capital

Betty's narrative also exemplifies the value of social capital in helping her to remedy her "deficient holdings" of appropriate linguistic capital. Bourdieu describes social capital as:

> "the sum of the resources, actual or virtual, that accrue to an individual or group by virtue of possessing a durable network of more or less institutionalized relationships of mutual acquaintance and recognition" (Bourdieu and Wacquant 1992).

In the context of HE, social capital may originate from the field within which an individual is studying, or more broadly from across their entire social network. The value of the latter in terms of their experience within HE will very much depend on whether those with whom an individual is socially linked possess the capital valued by the field of HE. Similarly, when drawn from networks developed within the HE field, social capital has the potential to confer benefits to an individual in a number of ways including, for example, access to collaborative study groups, peer-review of draft submissions, the sharing of resources and skills, and access to what can be all-important practical and emotional support that is grounded in a genuine appreciation of the challenges encountered. Reflecting what Bourdieu (2006) describes as its "multiplier effect", social capital can serve as a powerful medium assisting the development of a feel for the game and to facilitate the acquisition of linguistic and academic capital in particular.

It is important to note that social networks, and the social capital derived from them, are not all equally profitable. Reflecting what Grenfell (2007) describes as a degree of social solidarity, those networks developed amongst students who are positioned on the margins of the field do not afford the same capital value as those networks including students who fit more comfortably within the field. Social capital depends not only on the size of the network of connections an individual has access to, but also on the portfolio of capital held by each of those with whom the individual is connected (Bourdieu, 2006). Betty's ability to develop her language skills was dependent on those of a peer who was situated more comfortably within the field and who possessed linguistic capital more congruent with the logic of practice of the field.

Professionally-oriented Capital

Cultural capital is an overarching concept that reflects the logic of practice of a field as it is translated into 'physical and cognitive propensities expressed in dispositions to act in particular kinds of ways' (Moore, 2008) Amongst a range of other things, it incorporates knowledge and skills (Bourdieu, 1991) and in the context the empirical research drawn upon in this chapter, professionally-oriented capital is recognised as a valued form of cultural capital incorporating those aspects of students' skills and knowledge particularly focused on the practical, enacted aspects of professional healthcare practice. Professionally-oriented capital is related to academic capital, and while each has the potential to enhance the other, they are independently identifiable, although are best conceived of as overlapping somewhat.

Examples of professionally-oriented capital include the depth and breadth of knowledge appropriate to and legitimated by the professional practice context, a suitably professional disposition and appearance, enactment of the legitimated core values and skills underpinning professional practice, and proficient execution of the professional role and associated personal management. In parallel with academic capital, professionally-oriented capital develops throughout students' engagement with the field and its most profitable form are partially characterised within marking criteria. Although emerging from an investigation focussing on a particular healthcare discipline, the concept of professionally-oriented capital has relevance for other vocationally oriented programmes of study undertaken in the field of HE, within which it can prove equally as profitable as academic capital. Professionally-oriented capital also translates into attainment, primarily but not exclusively in relation to practice-based assessments. It too has the potential to be transposed into higher value cultural capital via academic and professional qualifications, and is likely to continue to be of value and to confer benefit to graduates making the transition from the field of HE into the field of professional practice. With her sights firmly set on a career as a healthcare professional, and with that social arena her ultimate aim, Betty's focus was always positioning herself to assimilate into this field more so than the field of HE, although she was required to succeed in the latter in order to gain access to the former.

A feel for "the game"

Bourdieu's (1990) theory of practice explains that a 'feel for the game' implicit within a social field provides a sense of meaning and emerges from experience of inhabiting that field and of the structures within which "the game" is played. In describing the feel for the game developed by a native member of a field, he uses the analogy of a child learning simultaneously to speak her mother tongue and to think in that language as a result of being exposed to and surrounded by it. Bourdieu proposes that non-natives who enter a field cannot achieve an equivalent state consciously or through will alone, only through a slow process of co-option or initiation. Those who enter the field of HE from a previous social context that lacks congruence with it are therefore highly likely to encounter challenges in understanding what is going on around them and how they are expected to be, behave and think in this new environment.

It is, of course, inherently difficult to render the implicit explicit, but the research evidence drawn upon in this chapter makes it possible to illustrate that the established practices, expectations and requirements of the field of HE, or the "rules of the game", include, for example, how to behave, take responsibility for and manage learning, access and utilise support appropriately, and present knowledge and understanding in the required or legitimated manner. Only some aspects of these and other legitimated or orthodox ways of being are made explicit to a greater or lesser extent via learning outcomes, marking criteria, academic and programme regulations, verbal and written guidance and support. Reflecting observations made within the literature that the onus falls to students entering HE to adapt to its established culture and practices (Burke, 2005; Briggs et al., 2013), conforming to the 'rules of the game' is pivotal to attaining a legitimate position and succeeding within the field, which is why a "feel for the game" is positioned at the apex of the pyramidal model in Figure 11.1.

In order to secure a legitimate position within the field, students need to have or develop a sufficient appreciation of the underpinning logic of practice and demonstrate and/or accumulate capital valued by the field. Habitus can and does shift to varying degrees, but it is slow to do so because, as Maton (2008) highlights, "our dispositions are not blown around easily on the tides of change in the social worlds we inhabit". A lack of congruence of habitus with the field of HE can, at times, generate reflexivity as a result of dissonance, leading to agentic deliberations and the development of new aspects of the self (Reay, 2004). It is also true, however, that this sort of incongruence may result in students being positioned on the margins of the field at best. In either case, gathering capital valued by the field is crucial, and it is in this regard that inclusive pedagogies have such a vital role to play.

To the extent that it is possible to do so, educators need to demystify and make the rules of the game more explicit. They need to be more aware of and reflective about their own and institutional practices and how much of a barrier taken-for-granted assumptions and expectations can be when they have never been encountered before. Letting students in on the nature of the game rather than assuming that failure to grasp expectations and requirements is illustrative of individual (or even collective) deficits is pivotal, as is actively supporting the development of the requisite capital. Inclusive, collaborative pedagogic practices embedded throughout programmes can facilitate this aim while capitalising on the richness of experiences and perspectives offered by diverse cohorts.

Although derived from a particular disciplinary context, the concepts of linguistic, academic and social capital are readily translatable. However, the logic of practice operating within different disciplines and fields will naturally define the specific nuances particularly of academic and linguistic capital. With a considerable range of professional or vocationally oriented disciplines within HE and increasing emphasis on graduate employability more generally, the relevance of the concept of professionally-oriented capital across the sector seems only likely to increase. There are a range of strategies that can be employed to support the development of these forms of capital, including, planning and supporting educational activities that facilitate the development of social networks; reflecting on language used, and, rather than avoiding unusual or complex terms, explaining them naturally and discursively as part of the discussion that follows; facilitating collective 'think aloud' problem solving and reasoning activities with opportunities to collaboratively build and develop the underpinning logic and rationale; unpacking assessment tasks on a similar basis; actively and knowingly role-modelling. That said, without a corresponding shift in habitus to more closely align with the expectations of the field, the development of capital is likely to be minimal or to go unrealised as capital is symbolic in nature – symbolic of an affinity with the field.

Concluding thoughts

There is more to widening participation in HE than expanding admissions. Inviting diverse student groups into the field and signing up to institutional Access Agreements is a start, but it is certainly not enough if the central tenet of widening participation – increased engagement by students from under-represented social groups – is to be achieved. Archer (2007) cautions against mistaking greater diversity amongst student entering HE for greater equality within the system, and raises pertinent questions about the ethics of focusing on recruitment of diverse entrants without giving equal consideration to their experiences within the system.

There is an additional need to be cautious about developing a narrow view in which success is equated with participation in, or more precisely, graduation from, HE. The desirability of participation does not hold universally, even amongst those with the qualifications necessary to gain access, and it is a gross injustice to pathologise those who elect not to do so. Even amongst students from under-represented groups who do respond to the message that HE is now a viable next step for the many, not just the elite few, "success" needs to be understood in context and recognised as a potentially highly personalised concept defined, for example, according to individual starting points and goals. It is a concept that expands beyond completion or even academic award, incorporating the capital that students are able to accrue and the degree to which that capital holds its value and is transposable into other fields, including graduate employment. Capital is, after all, profitable in terms of its practical consequences rather than in and of itself (Grenfell and James, 1998).

The trajectories of students entering HE under the auspices of the widening participation agenda; the extent to which they are able to establish a legitimate position within the field; and whether these positions were enhanced, static or undermined as they progress through their studies will reflect their ability to develop a feel for the game and, where necessary, adapt their habitus, together with their ability to accrue or extend portfolios of the forms of capital valued by the field. The conceptual framework presented in Figure 11.1 identifies capital valued in and underpinning the logic of practice in a specific sub-field of HE, and the interplay between academic, linguistic, social and professionally-oriented capitals demonstrates the capacity for capital to beget capital. Augmented by inclusive pedagogies that facilitate productive engagement with the logic of practice of the field, the model potentially provides a tool to guide curriculum development, to support efforts to facilitate social inclusion and enable students from diverse backgrounds, and to enhance student experiences and achievements across the board.

Bibliography

Amsler, S. and Bolsmann, C. (2012). University ranking as social exclusion. *British Journal of Sociology of Education*, Vol.33 (2), pp. 283-301.

Archer, L. (2007). Diversity, equality and higher education: a critical reflection on the ab/uses of equity discourse within widening participation. *Teaching in Higher Education*, Vol.12 (5-6), pp.635-653.

Bogdan, R.C. and Biklen, S.K. (2007). *Qualitative research for education: An introduction to theory and methods,* 5th Edition. Boston: Pearson.

Bourdieu, P. (1988). *Homo academicus.* Oxford: Polity Press.

—. (1990). *The logic of practice.* Cambridge: Polity Press.

—. (1991). *Language and symbolic power.* Cambridge: Polity Press.

—. (2006). The forms of capital. In H. Lauder, P. Brown, J. Dillabough and A. H. Halsey *Education, globalisation and social change.* Oxford: Oxford University Press.

Bourdieu, P. and Passeron, J-C. (1977). *Reproduction in education, society and culture.* London: Sage.

Bourdieu, P. and Wacquant, L.J.D. (1992). *An invitation to reflexive sociology.* Cambridge: Polity Press.

Bowl, M. (2013). Discourses of 'fair access' in English higher education: What do institutional statements tell us about university stratification and market positioning? *Widening Participation and Lifelong Learning*, Vol.15 (4), pp. 7-25.

Bravenboer, D. (2012). The official discourse of fair access to higher education. *Widening Participation and Lifelong Learning*, Vol. 14(3), pp.120-140.

Briggs, A., Clark, J. and Hall, I. (2013). Building bridges: understanding student transition to university. *Quality in Higher Education*, Vol.18 (1), pp.3-21.

Browne, J. (2010). *Securing a sustainable future for higher education. An independent review of higher education funding and student finance.* London: Department of Business, Innovation and Skills.

Burke, P.J. (2005). Access and widening participation. *British Journal of Sociology in Education,* Vol.26 (4), pp. 555-562.

Clegg, S., Bradley, S. and Smith, K. (2006). 'I've had to swallow my pride': Help seeking and self-esteem. *Higher Education Research and Development,* Vol.25 (2), pp. 101-113.

Dearing Report. (1997). *Higher education in the learning society.* London: HMSO.

Department of Business, Innovation and Skills. (2010). Higher Ambition: *The future of universities in a knowledge economy.* London: HMSO.

Department for Education and Skills. (2003). *The future of higher education.* London: TSO.

Field, A. (2009). *Discovering statistics using SPSS.* London: Sage.

Greenbank, P. (2006). Institutional widening participation policy in higher education: Dealing with the 'issue of social class'. *Widening Participation and Lifelong Learning,* Vol.8 (1), pp. 27-36.

Grenfell, M. (1998). Language and the classroom. In M. Grenfell and D. James *Bourdieu and Education* pp.72-88: *Acts of practical theory.* Abingdon: Routledge Falmer.

—. (2004). *Pierre Bourdieu: Agent provocateur.* London: Continuum.

—. (2007). *Pierre Bourdieu: Education and training.* London, Continuum.

Grenfell, M. and James, D. (1998). *Bourdieu and Education: Acts of practical theory.* Abingdon: Routledge Falmer.

Jenkins, R. (1992). *Pierre Bourdieu.* London, Routledge.

Leathwood, C. and O'Connell, P. (2003). 'It's a struggle': The construction of the 'new student' in higher education. *Journal of Education Policy,* Vol. 18(6), pp: 597-615.

Maton, K. (2008). Habitus. In Michael Grenfell (Ed.) *Pierre Bourdieu: Key Concepts,* pp. 49-65. Stocksfield: Acumen Publishing.

Maringe, F. and Fuller, A. (2006). *Widening participation in higher education: A policy overview.* School of Education, University of Southampton.

May, S. and Bousted, M. (2004). Investigation of student retention through an analysis of the first-year experience of students at Kingston University. *Widening Participation and Lifelong Learning,* Vol.6 (2), pp. 42-48.

Milburn, A. (2012). *University challenge: How higher education can advance social mobility. A progress report by the independent reviewer on social mobility and child poverty.* London: Cabinet Office.

Moore, R. (2008). Capital in M. Grenfell *Pierre Bourdieu: Key concepts.* Stocksfield: Acumen.

Reay, D. (2004). 'It's all becoming a habitus': Beyond the habitual use of habitus in educational research. *British Journal of Sociology of Education,* Vol. 25(4), pp. 431-444.

Reay, D., David, M.E. and Ball, S. (2005). *Degrees of choice: Social class, race and gender in higher education.* Stoke on Trent: Trentham Books.

Robbins Report. (1963). Higher Education. London: HMSO.

Sambell, K. and Hubbard, A. (2004). The role of formative 'low-stakes' assessment in supporting non-traditional students' retention and progression in higher education: Student perspectives. *Widening Participation and Lifelong Learning*, Vol.6 (2), pp.: 25-36.

UCAS. (2012). *End of cycle report* 2012. Cheltenham: UCAS.

—. (2013). 2013 *Application cycle: End of cycle report*. Cheltenham: UCAS.

Wacquant, L. (1998). Pierre Bourdieu. In R. Stones *Key sociological thinkers*. Basingstoke, Palgrave.

Watson, J., Nind, M., Humphries, D. and Borthwick, A. (2009). Strange new world: Applying a Bourdieuian lens to understanding early student experiences in higher education. *British Journal of Sociology of Education,* Vol. 30 (6), pp.665-681.

—. (2013a). Profitable portfolios: Capital that counts in higher education. *British Journal of Sociology of Education,* Vol.34 (3), pp 412-430.

—. (2013b). Progression routes and attainment in occupational therapy education: The impact of background characteristics. *British Journal of Occupational Therapy,* Vol.76 (12), pp. 520-527.

Willets, D. (2013). *Robbins revisited: Bigger and better higher education.* Westminster: Social Marketing Foundation.

CHAPTER TWELVE

REFLECTIVE PRACTICE IN TEACHER EDUCATION

CHARLOTTE MEIERDIRK

Introduction

Reflective practice is acknowledged to be a characteristic of all professions. There are, however, many theoretical perceptions and definitions of what it is and so it is not surprising that professions interpret its meaning in different ways. This chapter first explores the concept and its various manifestations before examining its role in the training of professional teachers.

Different interpretations of reflective practice

Finlay (2008) argues there are three approaches to reflective practice and these exist on a continuum ranging from reflection, through critical reflection to reflexivity (Fig. 12.1). The first stage on the continuum, reflection, is a technical approach to reflective practice and includes the action of reflecting or looking back upon the work being done to assess its effectiveness and improve the performance if necessary. A more holistic interpretation encourages critical reflection which involves looking at the role of power within the social fields the professionals find themselves in (Schon, 1987; Bourdieu, 1990). There are also advocates of reflexivity; the third stage of Finlay's model, which Loughran (2006) defines as "personal reflection" and the "turning of the lens" on oneself to reflect on the professional's changing identity.

Figure 12.1: Reflective practice continuum

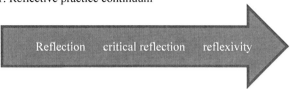

(Adapted from Finlay, 2008, p. ix)

Reflection can be broken down into five different types (Fig 12.2). The first three types were identified by Schon (1995), one of the earliest and most authoritative writers on the subject. He distinguished between "knowing in action", "reflection in action", and "reflection on action". A fourth and fifth type were added by Ghaye (2010), which are "reflection for action" and "reflection with action". "Knowing in action" describes the instant response to an occurrence. That response will change as the professional becomes more knowledgeable and experienced. Eraut (1994) refers to this as "tacit knowledge" or the knowledge gained through experience that dictates how a professional behaves and responds. "Knowing in action" then is the unconscious practice that occurs when a person's acts are based on prior experience. The person does not actively reflect on the event but uses "tacit knowledge" before engaging in action. Tacit knowledge is the knowledge a person has built up from different experiences they have had. As the novice moves to becoming a professional their tacit knowledge increases and influences their actions but unconsciously.

Figure 12.2: Types of technical reflection

- Knowing in Action
- Reflection in Action
- Reflection on Action
- Reflection for Action
- Reflection with Action

"Reflection in action" is undertaken "on the spot"; it is a conscious reaction to what is occurring at the time, rather than an instant response using tacit knowledge. An example of this type of reflection would be a professional reflecting and acting in response to a situation that occurred in the workplace. Schon's (1991) third type of reflection, "reflection on action," occurs after the event and is a continual process of review and improvement. Schon (1987, p. 40) developed a three stage model for "reflection on action" including providing student teachers with technical training; helping them to think like a professional; and enabling the trainee to develop a new form of understanding and action. Here, the practitioner is encouraged to use "reflection on action" by continuously reflecting on a problem to generate new knowledge and then use the new knowledge to solve the problem. According to Schon (1987) this cyclical process improves the performance of the professional in their field. Ghaye's "reflection for action" is when the reflections are taken forward to the next situation and applied and "reflection with action" is when the reflections are discussed with a third party. In the case of the student teacher this may be their school mentor (2010).

Zeichner and Liston (1996, p. 1) believe that a practitioner has not engaged in reflective practice unless they have questioned the context in which they are operating and their own individual beliefs. This "critical reflection" encourages reflection on the practitioner's past experiences, ideological beliefs, and the social context in which they are operating. This type of reflection moves away from the technical reflective practice advocated by Schon (1987) and offers a more holistic approach. The process of critical reflective practice involves a questioning of the norms of the organisation and emancipates the practitioner from the social constraints, within the complex social environment, and practices that are "taken for granted".

The third form of reflective practice is reflexivity, which is the process of constantly updating and reconstructing identities in the face of a fast changing world (Sweetman, 2003). Archer (2007, p. 94) emphasises the importance of reflexivity in navigating our way through the world, and defines it as "the regular exercise of the mental ability, shared by all normal people, to consider themselves in relation to their social context and vice versa". Finlay's model encompasses all three types of refection but implies a linear relationship which the author will challenge.

The use of reflective practice in teacher education

Reflective practice is a well-established feature of the teaching profession and plays an important role in teacher education and training. Researchers confirm its presence and using the theoretical frameworks outlined above explore the practice in developing professionalism among graduate teachers. Reflective practice is interpreted differently by teacher educators but there is agreement that it is the "process of learning through and from experience towards greater insights of self or practice" (Finlay, 2008, p.

1).This 'process of learning' is the basis for all interpretations of the term, and whatever form it takes the reflective practitioner should learn and grow from engaging with it. Reflective practice within teacher education enables the student teacher to learn and critique teaching practice (Meierdirk, 2016). Contention amongst researchers and educators occurs, however, when discussing what it is exactly the student should be learning when engaging in reflective practice.

Much of the research on reflective practice in initial teacher education (ITE) focuses on its use "with others". Parkinson (2009) and Freese (1999) both use "reflection with practice" by investigating the use of reflecting in pairs and with the student teacher's mentor. Harford (2008) not only investigates student teachers' reflecting on their own teaching ability (reflecting in practice) but includes the practice of reflecting with others about their practice. Harford's (2008) action research project investigates the use of reflective practice, centring on student teachers' videoing as they reflect in a group. The student teachers use videoing as an analytical tool to help them engage in Ghaye's (2010) "reflection on action" and "reflection with action". Reflection with others occurs on most ITE courses as the student teacher's lesson is often discussed and reflected upon with the subject or university tutor. Harford's study takes "reflection with practice" further by involving other student teachers in the reflection process. The students chose two video clips, of themselves teaching, which they showed to a small group of student teachers who discussed and reflected on observations and improvements. The findings from Harford's (2008) study highlight the positive nature of engaging in peer reflection. At first the student teachers were reluctant to be critical about other student teacher's video clips, but with time they became more critical and analytical. This study shows the importance of peer-based learning and reflection with others including peers on the course and the university tutor.

Freese's (1999) research focused on "reflection-with-practice" and the importance of learning from an experienced "other" and the role of the subject mentor. After an observation the student teacher engaged in retrospective reflective practice with the tutor. Freese found a number of advantages of engaging in retrospective reflective practice with the school mentor:

> "Debriefing using the reflective framework helps the pre-service teacher become more aware of the complexities of teaching, to go beyond the technical aspects of teaching and focus on student learning as well as teacher decision making" (p.899).

The student teacher gained a greater insight into their own teaching by engaging in "reflection with others" and this improved their awareness of the pupils' learning as well as the teacher's planning.

Not all the research into the reflective practice of student teachers is limited to "reflection with practice". Parkinson's (2009) research investigates the misconceptions student teachers have about education and schooling. He advocates a need for the student teacher to deconstruct their own beliefs, by questioning the epistemologies and knowledge they have constructed over their lifetime. By following a pupil the student teachers reflected on areas of educational concern and reconstructed their preconceptions about education. Parkinson refers to the student teacher's gained knowledge and experience as eco-epistemology and uses Horn and Wilburn's (2005) interpretation of the term as "on-going maintenance of growth". It is the student's prior experiences that are reflected upon in their preconceptions, and these change as the student teachers "articulate their worlds". This interpretation is very similar, if not identical, to Bourdieu's (1977) concept of habitus. A student teacher's habitus is influenced by their experiences of the social worlds they previously and presently belong to. The difference between Bourdieu's "habitus" and Parkinson's "gained knowledge" is that Bourdieu believes habitus can influence the social and so it is a two way rather than a one way process. This interpretation of reflective practice goes beyond Schon's (1987) technical approach of evaluation as there is reflection on the student teacher's own beliefs and identity, which is reflexivity.

When a student teacher starts their teacher education they will have preconceptions of what a teacher is and the role of learning in the classroom. This knowledge is built up over years of participating in different social arenas and experiencing different events. Even before the training course begins, students will have preconceptions about the profession of teaching, and these will be questioned and critiqued during their training until new knowledge is formed (Dang 2013). This deconstruction of preconceptions is important for the student teacher, as it provides them with an opportunity to reflect on their own beliefs.

It is clear from this brief survey of the literature that reflective practice is an essential element of ITE and that it takes the form of multiple practices. A more detailed study undertaken by the author is reported on below.

Reflective practice in practice

The author embarked upon a research project into student teacher's use of reflective practice during a Post Graduate Certificate in Education (PGCE) programme. The aim and objectives are set down in Table 12.1. In order to meet this aim the concept of reflective practice was explored through a study of the literature and Finlay's (2008) continuum was used as the research framework

Table 12.1 Aims and Objectives of the Study

Aim:	To investigate the role of reflective practice during the PGCE year
Objectives:	1. To explore the concept of reflective practice
	2. To explore the impact of reflective practice on the PGCE student
	3. To investigate the PGCE student's changing identity
	4. To investigate the impact of the social environment on the PGCE student

The context of the research was a university based PGCE programme in secondary education which recruited 100 students each year distributed across eight subject groups. All students attended taught units in the university at the beginning and end of the programme and all had two placements in local schools or further education colleges. One placement was in Phase1 and the second in Phases 2 and 3 (See Figure 12.3). All students were introduced to reflective practice at the beginning of the programme and required to complete reflective practice sheets during their placements. Their university tutor made observation visits to both placements and in each placement the student teacher also had a subject mentor who met with them for tutorials on a weekly basis.

Six students from the Business Studies group volunteered for the in depth case study. There were three women and three men; three were married, one was in a stable partnership and two were single; four had children; and their ages ranged from 24 to 49 years. The data collection methods used were semi-structured interviews and analysis of the reflective practice sheets. Over 100 reflective practice sheets with over 1,000 reflective comments were coded and analysed covering each of the three phases of the PGCE programme (Figure 12.3).

Figure 12.3: Phases of the PGCE year

Phase 1 (Placement 1)	Oct – Dec
Phase 2 (Placement 2)	Jan – April
Phase 3 (Placement 2)	April – June

The interviews were spread across six months from January to June. They were semi-structured to allow for flexibility but key questions were asked of all students. The January interviews focused on what education meant to the students; how many roles they thought they played; what had surprised them in their first placement; what kind of teacher they wanted to be; what they thought reflective practice was; and what it was designed to discover? The February interviews repeated some of the questions above to detect changes but pursued additional questions including: is there anything stopping you from being the teacher you want to be? Do you think you have changed as a person since undertaking the course? The March interviews repeated again the questions relating to identity but also sought information on the two placements and how, if at all, they differed? A deeper question about how the students had engaged in reflective practice was also asked. The final interviews in June asked students to reflect on how they thought reflective practice had changed their teaching, were they now able to be the teacher they wanted to be?, how their views of teaching and education had changed?; how they had changed as individuals; and did they think they were now a good teacher?

Critical discourse analysis (Fairclough, 1995) was used with a priori coding to categorise the interview data, to make connections and discover patterns in the students' narratives. The content of the reflective practice sheets was also analysed using in vivo coding into five categories - classroom activities, lesson planning, pupil behaviour, performance and teacher-self-identity. An analysis of the sheets revealed how the students assessed their strengths and weaknesses and how these changed across the three phases and the different placements.

Results and analysis

During the PGCE year student teachers continually reflected on their lessons. As they engaged in reflection they evaluated their lessons and set new targets against which to judge their progress (See Figure 12.3). This process continues throughout the year as all student teachers need to meet the teaching standards set down by the government. However, the way reflection developed was different for individual students. For example, one student in the case study was familiar with reflecting from years in industry and found he was reflecting "in his head" early on and he chose not to record his thoughts as his knowledge quickly became tacit. This did not occur with the other student teachers until after Phase 3, although one student still felt the need to write his reflections down:

> "...actually reflective, on what I do and write, you know, you are committing that to, writing. I think it's been really useful and there's certainly, you know the, especially the circular stuff has been really useful in identifying what I've done."

The student cited above was the lowest graded student teacher at the end of the programme and there is a possible link here between the ability of the student teacher and how far their reflections have progressed from being "fully thought out" strategies on paper to ones that occur quickly in the mind. According to the case study respondents there was a need to reflect quickly because there was so much pressure on them. The evidence suggests that reflective cycles are much quicker once the student gains experience and knowledge resulting in a spiral of reflection. This spiral of reflection does not occur within a vacuum but a complex set of social fields, and competing social structures.

Finlay's (2008) model of reflective practice, as stated above, was originally used as the analytical framework for the study with its continuum of reflection, critical reflection and reflexivity illustrating a linear movement. The research findings, however, challenged that model in a number of ways. First, evidence suggested that reflective practice is not in fact a linear progression. In Finlay's model the student teacher starts off engaging in reflection as illustrated in Figure 12.1. They then move on to critical reflection and finally to reflexivity. This progression was not borne out by the study's empirical findings. The evidence demonstrates that student teachers engage in reflection throughout the training year. The form the reflection takes changes but the students carry on reflecting upon their lessons, in all five forms identified by Schon (1995) and Ghaye (2010) up to the end of their second placement.

Critical reflection and the act of reflecting on external structures happened early on in some cases. It was triggered for example when an "event" occurred that caused the student teacher to question those external forces. This could occur at any stage in the training programme. Such "events" took the form of a disagreement with the subject mentor's preferred pedagogy or a disagreement with the school's management policy on dress codes. All students began to question the requirements set down by OFSTED during their first placement. It was clear that the student teachers questioned these external forces when they conflicted with their own values or perceptions of education and the role of the teacher. Critical reflection also occurred when the student teachers came up against agents, such as subject mentors, that were trying to determine their practice which they themselves disagreed with. In some instances this occurred early on in the programme, sometimes in the second placemen but in one case not at all.

Figure 12.4: The reflective cycle

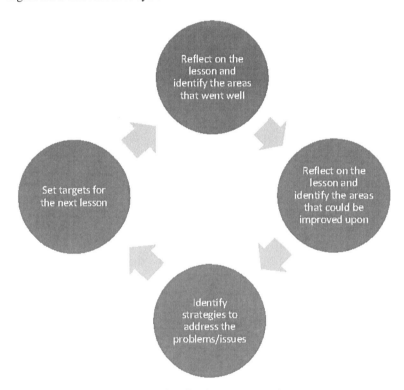

See centrefold for this image in colour

When there was a "clash" of ideas about pedagogy, teaching styles and the teacher's role this triggered the student teacher to engage in reflexivity.

The students did not continually question their own identity but did so when confronted with a situation that challenged their teaching. This is illustrated by a narrative from a student in the Phase 3 interview. The student struggled between her preconception of the teacher's role and her first placement school's perception of a teacher's "institutional identity" (Gee, 2000). In the narrative below (lines 6-23), there is a belief that teachers should behave in a certain way. The student sees herself as a caring teacher, who does not want to shout and raise her voice, but this is in conflict with the institutional identity of the school in her first placement. This clash of identity continued throughout the student's time in that school placement. She never accepted this institutional identity and, although she tried hard to please her mentor, this expectant role clashed with her own strong beliefs. However in her second placement the institutional identity was closer to her own teacher identity.

Figure: 12.5 Student's clash of identity

1   **I:** Do you think anything has stopped you throughout the 2   year teaching the way you wanted to teach? Being the 3   teacher you want to be? 4   **P** I think I feel more like the teacher I want to be now than I 5   did say four months ago. I think that I realised that the kind 6   of teacher I am is more suited to a college And I think when 7   I was at school I knew that, that I felt very constrained, 8   almost strangled by the teaching there and how I had to be 9   because I'm not, I just don't care about lots of stuff. That 10 sounds really awful but I'm not a disciplinarian, I care about 11 the important things , as I see them, and I don't feel I could 12 be bothered with uniforms and with, you know, telling 13 people not to have an earring, or you've got nail varnish on, 14 you know these things to me are miniscule and unimportant 15 and it's the main boundary rules that you know I use. And so 16 I think those things when I was at school stopped me being 17 what I wanted to be, I felt very constrained about how 18 everything had to be. I also prefer the longer lessons because 19 I feel you can really go into depth I found when you only 20 have an hour lesson or a 55 minute lesson you can't go into 21 the depth you can, even just an hour-and-a-half you can do 22 so much more and you can allow the students to really start 23 working and getting onto tasks and actually do a proper 24 activity and I like that.

Reflexivity then occurs in a social field which may itself have a desired teaching identity. This "institutional identity", for example how a school believes a teacher should behave and act, will be projected onto the student teacher and become part of a reflexive process as they decide how much of the institutional identity they subsume (Gee, 2000). This process is not just reflexive but also critically reflective. Both of these reflective practices can happen simultaneously, as opposed to Finlay's (2008) sequential continuum. Finlay's model also fails to give a reason for their occurrence, when in fact critical reflection and reflexivity both appear to occur after a conflict of ideologies with another agent. The findings in this research pointed to reflection, critical reflection and reflexivity sometimes occurring simultaneously and often being more of a fused process than linear and sequential.

The interview analysis found there were a number of key factors that impacted on the student teacher. One was power relationships. Power is not interpreted here just as "top down and hierarchical", although this type of power was present, but as strategic power that exists in day to day interactions (Foucault, 1980). These day to day interactions with other teachers and mentors sometimes presented moments of conflict when ideologies clashed. Due to the greater experience of some teachers in the placement schools and therefore more social capital, students tended to surrender to their (other teachers) dominant beliefs. In this study social capital was interpreted as "resources based on connections and group membership" (Bourdieu, 1990, p. 3–4). Reflexivity is an important part of ITE, because of the need to reflect on these complex social pressures.

When the student teachers were placed in an educational establishment they became agents of numerous 'fields of play' (Bourdieu, 1977). Bourdieu interprets the 'field' as a "space of conflict or competition" (cited in Winkle-Wagner, 2010, p. 8). The 'fields' are the various social and institutional arenas in which people express and reproduce their cultural competences and knowledge. There are no general rules within a field; each field has its own rules that determine the conditions of entry or exclusion. Hence, one's own social capital may be very useful in one field but meaningless in another. In the extract below of a Phase 3 interview the student reflects on the teaching environment. Her initial belief about the role of the teacher changed over the PGCE year. She was surprised by the 'target driven culture that existed in schools. In the interview (Figure 12.6, line 5) she speaks about how she found teachers more egotistical than she initially thought, she also found a performance culture that she believed only existed in the business environment and thirdly she was surprised that the teaching profession was not as supportive as she envisaged it to be.

Figure 12.6: Student interview 3

1 **I:** Is there anything else surprising you about school life,
2 about being a teacher in Schools?
3 **P:** I think at the beginning I thought that teachers, I thought
4 the whole environment would be much more… it wouldn't
5 be as target driven and so egotistical as I thought the
6 Business environment was, and I'm starting to realise that
7 may not be the case.
8 **I:** In what way?
9 **P:** Teachers have very dominant points of view and
10 dominant characters and they're very quick to make
11 assessments of other people, which I didn't necessarily think
12 would happen in a school environment where you're all in
13 the same situation. You teach the same pupils and there's so
14 many similarities compared to if you're in a business
15 environment, I thought it would be completely different, but
16 no, I think I'm starting to learn now

Within a school student teachers enter the departmental "field", whole school "field", the staffroom "field" and even the classroom has a "field" that the student belongs to. Externally there are much larger "fields" that are controlled by external bodies, such as Ofsted and the Department for Education (DfE). All these "fields" have agents who dominate and control the field's power because they have the cultural and social capital needed to make decisions and rules. The student teacher has limited social and cultural capital and therefore less power or influence. Not having full ownership of a class impacted on all the student teachers in the case study. One student reflected on the class not being hers:

"At the moment, probably the fact that I'm taking on somebody else's class as a trainee and [not]… in the ways of their previous teacher. I am still a trainee so I don't know what works, what doesn't work and I suppose my own confidence in putting that into practice and not worrying about treading on anyone's toes or offending anyone."

As the student above articulated it is a difficult balance when teaching someone else's class. The student is constantly worrying about what the regular teacher is thinking. In addition the pupils have to become accustomed to someone else's style of teaching.

The subject mentor has a big role in the student teacher's development. When the participants were asked if there were any constraints on their teaching, a number were quite adamant that there were and the most frequent constraint was the mentor. The school's subject mentor had weekly meetings with the student teacher, observed them and graded them. This impacted on the students in a number of ways. Some students found their mentors had a certain way of teaching and wanted them to replicate it:

> "*I think within School A and within the business department there is only one way of doing things and <laughs> that's the head's way, the Head of Department's way.*"

Others referred to mentors imposing structures of lectures:

> "*I can't fault their idea of best practice and their grades prove that it works and you see the kids' books and you see… and it works, it's just… what I, I'm struggling to kind of… I'm not going against it but struggling to fully embrace it because I can see that it works, but it's just not my, my way… my idea, my ethos of teaching.*"

As the student above reflected, he could see why the school had prescribed a certain way of structuring the lessons, as it worked and the pupils did obtain the expected grades. The mentors themselves are accountable and some of the rules they enforce are because of the stakeholders they must answer to. The mentor is ultimately accountable for the student teacher and this is a major responsibility. The mentor is also responsible to the head teacher, governing body and the parents for the pupils' grades If a prescribed style of lesson achieves the desired grades then, due to the accountability of the senior management in the school, it is likely that style of lesson will be insisted on.

However the student felt himself constrained because the mentor was inhibiting him from trying new ideas "*I couldn't essentially be the teacher I wanted to be, I was just being on paper what you should be as a teacher*". Here the student was referring to the teaching standards set by the National College of Teaching and Learning (NCTL) and the criteria set by Ofsted (TDA, 2010). These criteria and targets, such as exam results, league tables and Ofsted criteria, must be met in order to be a "good" teacher (Mansell, 2007). The student teacher must also meet the criteria set by the university PGCE course thus they have two different accountability hierarchies to work within.

As argued earlier, reflexivity and critical reflection can occur simultaneously as the student teachers never seemed to question their own identity without also questioning either a dominant agent's actions or a social structure's power. This is illustrated in the extract below when there was a "clash" between the student's own beliefs and those of the school, but as he argues in lines 5-6 (Figure 12.7) *"there's no point swimming against the tide or swimming against the current in a river, you've got to swim with the current..."*

Figure 12.7: Student agency

1	**I:** Have you had to question your own identity as a teacher?
2	**P:** "Absolutely, and that's been quite difficult for me, and I
3	think as well it's quite difficult for the permanent teachers
4	who are there and … but it's like with all of these things you
5	have to, there's no point swimming against the tide or
6	swimming against the current in a river, you've got to swim
7	with the current and then work out ways of how you can
8	have your own, you can put your own flavour to your
9	teaching. But there's no way that you'll ever be able to have
10	as much room to manoeuvre within a secondary school,
11	with a tight management style within the department you're
12	in, than you would do at Sixth Form College.

The student wanted to comply and keep the mentor happy, even though he disagreed with the teaching style the management recommended. In the interview he commented on *"being forced into a hole"* and into a teaching style he was not comfortable with. He is convincing himself, with his narrative, that it is an expectation that he has to just "run with it" and is 'giving in' to this expectation, even though it is not his belief as to what a teacher is.

Discourse identity (D-identity) is the identity presented by the student teacher when discussing their role (Gee 2000). D-identity suggests that the identity of the student teacher is created through their discourse. It is the student's discourse that creates the teacher, rather than the teacher that creates the discourse. The discourse of the student teacher is also influenced by the social fields they belong to and the dominant agents within those fields. The discursive influences derive from the subject mentor (the dominant agent in the teacher's education field within the school); the university tutor (in the school and university), the head of subject department (in the school), head of teacher education (in the school) and the senior management (in the school). There are also the external "fields of play" the student teacher belongs to ranging from Ofsted to the NCTL. This study showed how the student teacher becomes a product of these agents.

The accountability hierarchy represents the dominant agents in the student teacher's "fields of play" (Fig 12.8). In the immediate field the student teacher's mentor is dominant, in the department the dominant agent is either the mentor or head of department, and within the school senior management are dominant agents.

In the outer "field" of education' there is Ofsted and the DfE which dominate policy. The latter's' powers are more distant but permeate the closer immediate domains which are the governing body, the head teacher, the departmental head, the mentor and the student teacher .

Figure 12.8. Accountability hierarchy

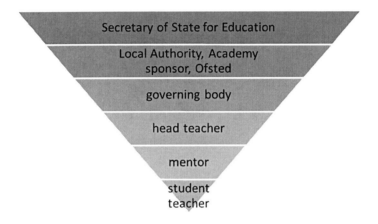

See centrefold for this image in colour

Although this study confirms that student teachers do engage in critical reflection and reflexivity it is not currently part of the teaching standards or the Ofsted criteria for assessing teacher education (Meierdirk,2016). It was however part of the PGCE curriculum and encouraged by the university. The student teachers did reflect on their environment and the way the social environment impacts on them. They also became aware of new environments and fields of play and by the end of the PGCE year it had become part of their discourse and professional identity i.e. what it means to be a teacher. There was clear evidence of this in the student teacher's reflective practice sheets, with the growing use of performance language over the three phases. There was also evidence from the interviews what the students thought about the impact of their mentors and the requirements of the ITE programme, Ofsted and individual school.

The research findings confirmed reflective practice is a key part of teacher education and training in all its forms. It is not, however, a simple linear process but is best presented as a spiral. It not only contains the practice of reflection as a means to develop skills and competencies in the technical aspects of teaching – lesson planning, pedagogy, behaviour management and performance, but also critical reflection and reflexivity which assist in the understanding of the power relationships within educational organisations and a consciousness of one's own identity both as a person, a teacher and a professional. All three forms of refection move in and out of the students lived experience and occur continuously and sometimes simultaneously as student teachers constantly examine their performances; work through the challenges from the power structures and seek identity equilibrium.

Conclusion

There is still controversy and different interpretations of what reflective practice includes here; reflection is not the same as critical reflection or reflexivity as discussed at the beginning of this chapter. Schon's (1987) "knowing in action", "reflection in action", "reflection on action" and Ghaye's (2010) "reflection for action" and "reflection with action" are all important for the development of the student teacher, but they involve a technical approach which is all about what and how rather than why and what for? They do not allow the student teacher to reflect on the broader workings of the school and the education system but focus on the task of teaching. Bourdieu (1989, p.4) believes that, unless individuals question the structures that limit and constrain them, they are more likely to be "the apparent subjects of actions". Reflexivity enables the individual to become aware of these structures that inhibit them. As Beck and Giddens (1994) state: "individualism is not based on the free decisions of individuals. It may be an illusion that people are free to pursue the life and goals they want but in reality, student teachers are subject to rules and regulations, some written, some unwritten, that influence what they do. Critical reflection makes the student teacher aware of these structures and their impact.

Dang (2013) wrote about the importance of student teachers reflecting on their preconceptions and what it means to be a teacher. The evidence here, from the case study, is that students do reflect on these preconceptions when engaging in reflexivity and critical reflection as they question their own teaching identity, but in the light of events caused by agents in their social fields. They also question the structures they find themselves part of, from the school's management to the NCTL's teaching standards. The reflective practice of the student also included their reflections on their lessons; the very reflective practice that Schon (1983) was first accredited with. Reflection has a very important role in the professionalization of the student teacher as they question their own teaching styles and try new ideas.

Recent changes in education policy and ITE has possible implications for the teaching profession and the role of reflective practice within it. Most teachers in recent decades have been graduates trained and educated in university Education Departments. Although that is still a route, the Government has introduced a new route - School Direct - where student teachers are recruited to one school, with perhaps a few weeks in a partner institution, instead of being based in a university department with practical training in two schools or colleges (DfE, 2013). The research conducted here suggests that having one mentor and being subject to one institutional identity could have a limiting effect on the development of the student teacher, resulting in less freedom to develop their own teaching style or become aware of different approaches and ethos.

Critical reflectivity may be inhibited outside of the university. It is not just thinking critically about education and education policies, critical thinking is an emancipator. It frees the mind from what one sees as the norm and allows one to question those social structures taken for granted. In the last few years there has been a shift in the ideology of teacher education, with a movement away from teacher education, run by universities, in favour of school-based training which looks likely to increase along with academisation.

All three types of reflective practice: reflection, critical reflection and reflexivity are important and almost equally so for the progression of the student teacher. The definition of reflective practice as the "process of learning through and from experience towards greater insights of self or practice" (Finlay, 2008, p.1) remains valid but there is so much more happening to the student teacher's reflective practice during their PGCE year. They are not just gaining "greater insights of self" they are redeveloping and questioning their identity and their social environment. They are recreating their own practice almost daily by changing and improving that practice. Finlay's definition of reflective practice is a belief that there is a greater insight into the 'self' but does not recognise that the student's teaching identity is constantly changing and has not fully developed yet. From this study a more accurate definition of reflective practice in ITE, is posited, as "the questioning of practice, purpose, identity and the social context due to an increase in knowledge and experience".

Bibliography

Archer, M.S. (2007). *Making our way through the world: human reflexivity and social mobility.* Cambridge: Cambridge University Press.

Beck, U. and Giddens, A. (1994). *Reflexive modernization: politics, tradition and aesthetics in the modern social order.* Cambridge: Polity Press.

Bourdieu, P. (1977). *Outline of a theory of practice.* R. Nice (trans.) Cambridge: Cambridge University Press.

—. (1989). *La Noblesse d'état. Grandes écoles et esprit de corps.* Paris: Minuit. (English: *The State Nobility: Elite Schools in the Field of Power.* Cambridge: Polity Press.

—. (1990). *The logic of practice.* Cambridge: Polity Press.

Dang, T.K.A. (2013). Identity in activity: Examining teacher professional identity formation in the paired-placement of student teachers. *Teaching and Teacher Education,* Vol. 30, pp.47-59.

DfE. (2012). *Teachers' Standards.* London. TSO.

—. (2013). *How schools direct works.* Retrieved from: http://www.education.gov.uk/schools/careers/traininganddevelopment/initial/b00205704/school-direct/schools.

Eraut, M. (1994). *Developing Professional Knowledge and Competence.* London: Falmer.

Fairclough, N. (1995). *Critical Discourse Analysis. The Critical Study of Language.* Harlow: Pearson.

Finlay, L. (2008). *Reflecting on reflective practice.* Milton Keynes: PBPL Open University.

Flemmen, M. (2013). Putting Bourdieu to Work for Class Analysis. *British Journal of Sociology,* Vol. 64, pp. 325-43.

Foucault, M.G. (1980). *Power/knowledge: selected interviews and other writings,* 1972/1977. Brighton: Harvester Press.

Freese, A. (1999). The role of reflection on preservice teachers' development in the context of a professional development school. *Teaching and Teacher Education,* Vol. 15, pp. 895-909.

Gee, J.P. (2000). Identity as an analytic lens for research in education. *Review of Research in Education,* Vol. 25 (1), pp. 99-125.

Ghaye, T. (2010). *Teaching and learning through reflective practice: a practical guide for positive action.* London: Routledge.

Harford, J.M. (2008). Engaging student teachers in meaningful reflective practice. *Teaching and Teacher Education,* Vol. 24(7), pp.1884-1892.

Horn, J., and Wilburn, D. (2005). The embodiment of learning. *Educational Philosophy and Theory,* Vol. 35(3), pp. 746-760.

Loughran, J. J. (2006). *Developing Pedagogy of Teacher Education: Understanding Teaching and Learning about Teaching.* London: Routledge.

Mansell, W. (2007). *Education by numbers: the tyranny of testing*. London: Politico's.

Meierdirk, C. (2016). Is reflective practice an essential component of becoming a professional teacher? *Reflective Practice: International and Multidisciplinary Perspectives,* Vol. 17(3), pp. 1-10.

Parkinson, P.T. (2009). Field-based preservice teacher research: Facilitating reflective professional practice. *Teaching and Teacher Education*, Vol.25, pp. 798-804.

Schon, D.A. (1987). *Educating the reflective practitioner*. San Francisco, CA: Jossey-Bass.

—. (1991). *The reflective practitioner: how professionals think in action*. Aldershot: Avebury.

—. (1995). *Reflective practitioner: how professionals think in action*. London: Arena.

Sweetman, P. (2003). Twenty-first century dis-ease? Habitual reflexivity or the reflexive habitus. *The Sociological Review*, Vol. 51(4), pp. 528-549.

Training Development Agency. (2010). *What are the professional standards?* Retrieved from:
http://www.tda.gov.uk/teachers/professionalstandards/standards.aspx.

Winkle-Wagner, R. (2010). Cultural capital: The promises and pitfalls in education research. *ASHE Higher Education Report*, Vol.36 (1). San Francisco: Wiley.

Zeichner, K. and Liston, D. (1996). *Reflective Teaching: an introduction*. Mahwah, New Jersey: Lawrence Erlbaum Associates.

Figure 12.4: The reflective cycle

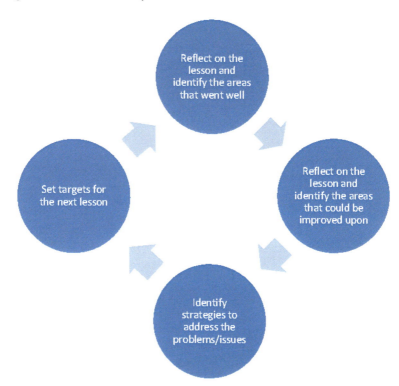

Figure 12.8. Accountability hierarchy

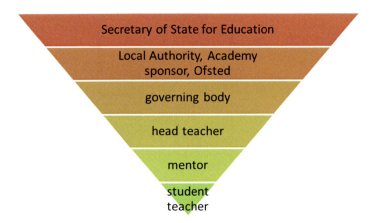